The Ministry of Transport
and Civil Aviation

THE NEW WHITEHALL SERIES

is prepared under the auspices of

THE ROYAL INSTITUTE OF PUBLIC ADMINISTRATION

and is edited on its behalf by Sir Robert Fraser, O.B.E.

*The purpose of the series is to provide
authoritative descriptions of the present work
of the major Departments of Central Government*

Already published

THE HOME OFFICE (*reprinted*)

THE FOREIGN OFFICE (*reprinted*)

THE COLONIAL OFFICE

THE MINISTRY OF WORKS

THE SCOTTISH OFFICE

THE MINISTRY OF PENSIONS AND
NATIONAL INSURANCE

In Preparation

THE MINISTRY OF LABOUR AND
NATIONAL SERVICE

THE MINISTRY OF SUPPLY

THE NEW WHITEHALL SERIES

The Ministry of Transport and Civil Aviation

SIR GILMOUR JENKINS

K.C.B., K.B.E., M.C.

LONDON · GEORGE ALLEN & UNWIN LTD
NEW YORK · OXFORD UNIVERSITY PRESS INC

FIRST PUBLISHED IN 1959

PRINTED IN GREAT BRITAIN
in 10 *point Times Roman type*
BY UNWIN BROTHERS LIMITED
WOKING AND LONDON

PREFACE

*

I MUST confess that when I undertook to write this book I had not fully realised the labour it would entail. The assembly of the text in its final form has in fact taken me five years. At one period—that of the Suez operations—the text had perforce to lie fallow and unattended for close on six months. I can only hope that any resulting unevenness in presentation has been ironed out and that no dating of the material is evident. Inevitably, of course, the material will date, but I have tried to write for the future as well as the immediate present. In particular I have tried to avoid spending too much time on issues which may be in the forefront of the news now but which may soon be forgotten.

Writing a book of this kind about a Government Department is not easy. In the first place it must be thorough and accurate. This means that the text must be worked over by many hands and differences of approach and style creep in. It also means that in the very effort to achieve thoroughness there is a danger of presenting a document that bears more relation than anyone would wish to an auctioneer's catalogue. Thirdly, the writer must put some check upon the expression of his own personal opinions and prejudices. I certainly do not imply that, in the memorable phrase of Lord Strang, 'the steamroller of official conformity' should be allowed to proceed steadily over the text flattening out all the high spots; indeed I have ventured to express a number of personal opinions in these pages and for them I take the sole responsibility.

I have concentrated upon our major tasks and must apologise in advance to those in the Department or outside who may feel that the particular work in which they are interested has not been given appropriate prominence. But the Ministry of Transport and Civil Aviation is now so large a Department that it is almost impossible to do justice to its full responsibilities within the scope of one slim volume. And if it were possible the result would be dangerously near to that auctioneer's catalogue which I have already mentioned. I hope, however, that what I have said about such important subjects as shipping and air policy, road and rail competition, the problems of accountability of the nationalised industries, the development of our roads and aerodromes and our efforts to improve safety on all forms of transport will be of interest not only to the specialist in transport but also to the general student of public administration both here and overseas.

As I have indicated, I have been helped by many willing hands throughout the office and I am deeply grateful for their aid and advice. Above all I am indebted to Mr. Patrick Shovelton who, in addition to the heavy burden of official work he has carried throughout, has played by far the greatest individual part in the production of this book. I can never be too grateful to him. Without his help and that of many others of my colleagues the book could not have been written.

G. J.

October 1958

CONTENTS

*

PART ONE

Functions and History

CHAPTER I

The Ministry in Perspective

Introduction — Protection of the Public Interest
— The State not directly responsible for operation — The relationship between the Minister and
the Nationalised Industries — The Formulation
of Policy.

*

A FORMER Minister of Transport and Civil Aviation used to say, perhaps with some trace of pardonable complacency, tinged more and more with regret as time went on, that he was never able to take up a daily newspaper without seeing some mention of an event or problem which concerned him and his Department. It might be the effect of competition between the different forms of transport, between road and rail, sea and air or air and rail; it might be a question of flag discrimination against our ships and aircraft abroad; or one of labour relations or of new techniques in manufacture or operation; it might very well be complaints about fares or demands for better facilities, such as new roads, matched by opposition from those through whose property or near whose houses they would pass, or proposals for pedestrian crossings or the imposition or removal of a speed limit; or it might be a situation demanding some emergency action to safeguard the movement of essential goods. Sometimes, unhappily, it might be a transport disaster for which he might have to order an inquiry. But these are the headlines. Behind the scenes are other less spectacular, but nonetheless useful, activities, some of them involving the Minister's major responsibilities, others the odd unexpected jobs such as maintaining certain lighthouses in the Indian Ocean and the Red Sea, providing for the comfort of monkeys at London Airport or the protection of whales in the Antarctic. Not everyone would readily associate these tasks with the Ministry of Transport and Civil Aviation.

These responsibilities—and many others which will be described in this book—have gradually been assumed, as often as not reluctantly and with misgivings, by Governments shrewdly aware of the fact that large industrial problems, though essentially non-political in themselves, may become national and political issues and so

involve Governments in the effort to solve them. This is certainly
true of the transport industries, which between them employ some
10 per cent of the working population, and contribute about 13 per
cent of the gross national product and where in the last dozen years
the effects of politics upon industry, particularly upon road
transport, have been most evident.

The full sum of these varied responsibilities has only recently
become the concern of one Minister. From the middle of the nineteenth century transport matters were dealt with by the Board of
Trade. At the end of the First World War inland transport was split
off and a new Ministry of Transport was set up, partly because of
the emergence of motor vehicles as a major factor in the movement
of passengers and goods, partly to supervise a large new road-
building programme (which did not in fact develop on anything like
the scale originally envisaged), and partly to deal with the amalgamation of the railway companies. Shipping remained with the Board
of Trade till the outbreak of the Second World War, when the vast
problem of war-time shipping control necessitated the setting up of
a separate Ministry, the Ministry of Shipping. Then in 1941 in order
to meet 'the need for combining the arrangement of all our ships
with all the movement of our supplies by rail and road from our
carrying ports'[1] the Ministry of War Transport was formed by amal-
gamating the two separate Ministries of Shipping and Transport.
These arrangements were continued after 1945 except that 'War'
was dropped from the Ministry's title. Until 1946 Civil Aviation had
been the responsibility of the Air Ministry. In that year a separate
Ministry was set up, and in 1953 the Ministry of Transport and the
Ministry of Civil Aviation were amalgamated to form the present
Ministry—after an uneasy couple of years in which one Minister had
the unhappy task of presiding over the two separate Departments.

This development in the system of government has some advantages to compensate for the disadvantages which must inevitably
flow from great diversity of interests and great size. It is, for example,
advantageous to be able to deal in one Department with questions
of competition between airway corporations and shipping companies
or between coastal shipping and road and rail; and to consider under
one roof the need for improved surface communications with a new
aerodrome; or, when dealing with port problems, to have easy contacts with shipping, railways and road transport. But, despite these
opportunities for co-ordination, it is inevitable that the Ministry
should, for the most part, wear the look of three separate Departments—or four, if the ownership and operation of the main civil
aerodromes is regarded as a separate responsibility, as in many ways

[1] Sir Winston Churchill: *The Second World War*, Vol. 3, p. 132.

it is. It would be pleasant if there were a convenient set of principles which could be applied equally to the administration of all forms of transport; if such subjects, for example, as safety, freight rates, international competition and the promotion of new services could all be handled in a similar fashion, irrespective of the mode of transport under discussion; if, to use the jargon of the efficiency experts, the Ministry could be organised on a functional basis. But in practice the problems of administration seldom lend themselves to so easy a solution. On the contrary, each form of transport, with its own history and its own operational peculiarities, poses its own separate problems.

Take safety in transport as an example. The State must be interested in the safety of passengers and crews of all vehicles, but the problem of ensuring that a ship is safely constructed is entirely different from the same problem in relation to aircraft and different again for railway trains or road vehicles. The word 'safety' is almost the only common factor. Moreover, safety of travel by sea depends not only on the staunchness of the ship but also on the competency of the crew, the accuracy of charts, the lighting of coasts, the buoying of channels and half a hundred other factors all more or less closely interlinked; and so it is with the analogous, yet very different, problems of other forms of transport. The Government machine is thus inevitably constructed—as are the numerous outside interests with which it is in constant contact—to deal with problems of the sea, problems of the land, and problems of the air and not with problems as they affect all three.

PROTECTION OF THE PUBLIC INTEREST

What then are the main interests of the State in transport, apart from any special and incidental interest it may have as owner of ships or railways or road vehicles or air lines? Surely they must all be covered by the broad answer, 'the protection of the public interest'. This has involved a diversity of functions: first, of regulation —of load-lines for ships and signalling systems for railways, for example; second, of protection—whether of one form of transport against another, or of British interests in the international field; and third, of encouragement and assistance—for instance in the provision of aerodromes and of navigational aids for aircraft and in the expenditure of large sums of money for maintaining and building roads. All these activities are dealt with in detail later. But right at the outset it is as well that two broad principles which dominate all this work should be clearly stated. First, successive Governments have taken the view that transport should, so far as possible, be financially self-supporting and should be a source of strength to the economy and not a burden upon it. Second, they have done their best to avoid becoming involved in the direct operation of transport— except in war-time when quite special needs arise.

The Department's responsibilities towards the public interest naturally involve it in a conflict of loyalties: for no development in transport takes place without upsetting someone. Aerodromes and roads eat into valuable agricultural land and the aircraft and vehicles for which they make room may be a source of serious discomfort from noise. Railways we have become accustomed to, but their coming was the occasion of the most strenuous opposition as the curious reader of mid-nineteenth century Parliamentary debates will readily find out. Indeed even now the railway modernisation scheme finds some critics—and outside the ranks of the economists at that. Ships perhaps least of all disturb the peace of the subject, but even they may pollute the seas and the beaches with oil. New services in any form of transport are seldom started without some criticism or without exciting envious glances, or written complaints, from those who do not benefit from them. And increases in fares are capable of becoming the most talked of subject of the day. In all these matters the Department may be involved and its object must be to try to steer a sensible course through the competing claims of traders, travellers, providers of, and workers in, transport and the wider public.

Equally the State has to try to settle difficulties that may arise between providers of different forms—or sometimes of the same form—of transport. So the Government have had to step in from time to time to regulate competition. Strongly as the doctrine of *laissez-faire* appeals to an overworked civil servant, there is nowadays general agreement that unrestricted competition in transport may react in the long run to the disadvantage of providers and users alike. This has been the general conclusion of many investigations—the Royal Commission on Transport of 1928–31 and the various Committees which examined the difficulties of civil aviation before the Second War. The Royal Commission, for example, found that unrestrained competition had resulted in uneven provision of services, in a lack of facilities for sparsely populated areas, in badly maintained and possibly unsafe transport and in the inability of the companies or individuals to set aside sufficient sums for depreciation and development. The remedy has been the licensing of road passenger and goods services, the object of which is to find a happy mean between a free for all on the one hand and out and out monopoly on the other. In the air the problem has been met by the 'chosen instrument' policy—that is to say, the selection of one or two particular corporations to run the main services, coupled with the licensing of a number of independent companies to run subsidiary services.

Even more important is the duty to protect the public. This involves, among other things, the Minister's responsibility for safety—a subject which is common to all forms of transport. This responsibility, as has already been indicated, has to be exercised very differently in each case; each different way of discharging it has assumed its particular form not only because of the peculiar individual characteristics of each kind of transport but also for reasons of history and of the impact of public opinion.

The difference in treatment of safety questions merits closer examination. In respect of ships, a staff of qualified Marine Surveyors, administering a series of Acts and detailed Regulations, control in detail the building of passenger ships and carry out an annual survey of each one. Certain duties, mainly concerning cargo ships, are delegated to the Classification Societies. Inquiries into casualties (other than minor ones) are carried out by independent judicial Tribunals. In the case of the railways the last hundred years has seen the development of a system of control which differs significantly from marine practice. The Railway Inspectorate of the Ministry approve new works but thereafter responsibility for maintenance and operation has rested, and still rests, with the railway operators. The Inspecting Officers themselves conduct inquiries into accidents, and their recommendations, although they are not enforced by law, are accepted and acted upon. In the air the Minister's responsibility for the safe construction of aircraft is delegated to the Air Registration Board. The control of air traffic, the provision of radio aids to navigation and the other arrangements for safety are directly the Department's concern. Inquiries into accidents are carried out by the Air Accident Investigation Branch of the Ministry, while major accidents usually become the subject of a public inquiry.

On the roads, where safety, it need hardly be said, is one of the most baffling of all problems, the subject is vastly complicated by the multiplicity of interests affected—individual car owners and road transport operators, cyclists and pedestrians, who use the roads, highway authorities who provide them, and the police. Here Governmental control cannot be nearly so effective as elsewhere. Something can be done in improving roads, in imposing speed limits, in testing the competence of would-be drivers and, above all, in policing adequately. But in the end the remedy does not lie with a highly skilled professional body but with the general public, driver and pedestrian alike. It calls for competence, care and courtesy by every one of us.

Thus the manner of discharging the responsibility for safety varies with each form of transport. Even the system of controlling those who drive cars or railway engines, or command ships or pilot aircraft differs. All motorists have to pass a test and, of course, air pilots and the masters of sea-going vessels have to undergo long and intensive training and to pass stringent examinations; but engine drivers need only satisfy their employers, yet they are competent enough in all conscience. It has all grown up empirically in a very English way, and it works—with some reservation perhaps about the road.

Under the same heading, the protection of the public interest, comes the international work which involves the Department in contacts with the Governments of other countries. In shipping and civil aviation this is not surprising, for they are the most fully international of all industries, and the work is of first importance. The negotiation of treaties affecting air traffic rights and Conventions covering the safety or operation of ships and aircraft is the Minister's responsibility in conjunction with the Foreign Office. So are such things as the efforts to protect shipping from discrimination abroad and the participation in international planning for defence purposes. But the extent of international work on railways and road transport is also large, and is growing. The Transport and Communications Commission of the United Nations has started off a number of international studies in this sphere. Also in 1956 the United Kingdom became a member of the Berne Convention on railways to try to simplify conditions for the passage of goods and travellers to and from the Continent. Similar work, designed to standardise the regulations for European road transport, is being done by the Economic Commission for Europe, by the Organisation for European Economic Co-operation and by other bodies. Over all these European activities the European Conference of Ministers of Transport holds a watching brief. There is, admittedly, important work to be done— the method of control, for example, of lorries and coaches entering other countries with goods and passengers and the attempt to get world-wide agreement on conditions of carriage of dangerous goods by all forms of transport. But in connection with land transport the world is suffering from a surfeit of international bodies with active secretariats pursuing studies and producing proposals, many of which seem to have little value except to call for larger and more frequent conferences and bigger and more powerful secretariats. These conferences make heavy demands upon officers in various sections of the Department.

THE STATE NOT DIRECTLY RESPONSIBLE
FOR OPERATION

Except in war-time, when the reverse is true, the State has always avoided assuming direct responsibility for transport operation, although the Ministry of Transport Act of 1919 seemed to envisage direct participation in certain inland transport services. Section 9(1) begins: 'It shall be lawful for the Minister to establish and, either by himself or through any other person, to work transport services by land or water. . . .' But there are formidable provisos and the definition of 'water' generally excludes shipping services. In fact, the section had its origin in the desire of the Government of the day, amid the aftermath of war, to be in a position to do something for the needs of agriculture and light industries in the remoter country districts. The power has not in fact been used.

Now all shades of political opinion seem to agree that the Minister should not be directly responsible for running services. In shipping, private enterprise is certainly the order of the day. Even when the Government have large numbers of troops to move they prefer to charter tonnage rather than to own it, and always to leave operation and management to the experienced shipping companies. In the other forms of transport the issues of public ownership have been in the forefront of the political arena since the war. The extent to which the State should interest itself financially in the railways and road transport has been the subject of prolonged contention, and the uncertainties that have resulted have not been to the benefit of the industries affected. But when nationalisation came, operation and management of the nationalised industries was given not to a Department of State, which is usually ill-equipped to operate commercial enterprises, but to public corporations with a wide measure of freedom to manage their own affairs.

THE RELATIONSHIP BETWEEN THE MINISTER AND THE NATIONALISED INDUSTRIES

However great the degree of freedom intended for these industries, it is obvious that there must be some Governmental control since the State is the sole shareholder in the undertakings; or, to look at it another way, if it were not so the Boards of the industries would have a degree of independence unknown, and inconceivable, elsewhere. The problem of reconciling the freedom to conduct the business of these great industries on commercial lines with the natural and proper desire of the fifty million shareholders to exercise some control is one of the most difficult problems posed by nationalisation. So far as the legal position is concerned, Parliament has reserved to the Minister a number of specific powers designed to secure a reasonable degree of public control. These Ministerial powers fall into five main groups and, although there are some important differences dictated by the circumstances of each industry, they are generally similar whether they relate to the British Transport Commission or to the Air Corporations. In the first place the Minister has the power of appointment: he appoints the Chairmen and members of the different Boards and of the various advisory bodies or Consultative Committees. Secondly, he has the power to obtain information: the Boards must make annual reports which he in turn presents to Parliament and which are almost always debated; the principal consultative and advisory committees also report to him. Thirdly, he has considerable power to control development; the Airways Corporations must submit their yearly programme of activities with estimates of revenue and expenditure and the British Transport Commission, in framing programmes of development involving substantial capital outlay—such as the recent railway modernisation plan—must act on lines settled from time to time with him. The Minister's consent is required before the Commission may acquire certain businesses and he may direct them to dispose of certain parts of their undertaking. In the case of all three Boards, borrowing may take place only with the Minister's agreement. Fourthly, he has the power, and sometimes the duty, to make regulations, amplifying and filling in the details of the Acts in many cases: those, for example, dealing with the pensions of employees or the bringing into being of the scheme of railway reorganisation including the establishment of Regional Boards. Lastly, he has the power of direction. Direction may, in the case of the British Transport Commission, be specific in two cases only, following a recommendation from the Central Transport Consultative Committee or from the Coastal Shipping Advisory Committee. In the case of the Airways Corporations, the Minister may, by order, limit the powers of the corporations. He may also issue 'directions of a general character . . . in relation to matters appearing to him to affect the national interest'. This is clearly not a power that can be easily or lightly exercised. Its use may indicate a fundamental disagreement between the Government of the day and the Board concerned—as it did in 1952 when, after much discussion, the Minister gave the British Transport Commission a direction as to the way they were to exercise the latitude which the Transport Tribunal had allowed them under the London Passenger Charges Scheme. Alternatively, it may be used as a matter of policy by agreement between the Government and the Board—as it was in 1947 when a direction was given to British European Airways in order to overcome certain legal difficulties overseas. It could be used, also, in a national emergency, to ensure that the transport system obeyed Government orders irrespective of its legal commitments to other parties.

So much for the formal relationships. In practice informal contacts have been built up which, in the daily interchange of business, become of much greater importance. Consultation, discussion and exchange of ideas between the Minister and the Chairmen of the Boards and between the senior officials on both sides are frequent. The Minister can thus be informed in advance of major proposals and of the general policy of the Boards. The Boards, for their part, can get his advice about the probable public reaction to their plans and how they may affect the general industrial, financial and commercial policy of the Government.

While the formal and informal relations between the Minister and the Boards of the nationalised industries are the most important factors in securing accountability to the public for the conduct of these great undertakings, they are not the whole story. The Minister is answerable to Parliament, and so to the nation, and he represents the Boards in all those matters which concern Parliament. Members can debate their Annual Reports and can address questions to the Minister on the policies pursued by the Boards. It was originally envisaged that their day-to-day adminstration should be entirely free from Parliamentary probing; as Mr Herbert Morrison said in the House of Commons in the early days of the nationalised industries, 'Undue intervention by the Minister would tend to impair the Boards' commercial freedom of action'.[1] But some dissatisfaction was felt at this position and when, in 1948, questions to the Minister of Fuel and Power on a 'large-scale' failure of the electricity grid system were not allowed, the Speaker offered to modify the Rule so as to admit 'questions on matters of public importance'.[2] His offer was accepted by the House and this criterion is still in force today. Even so Members have felt that Parliament does not obtain enough information on which to base a judgment of the efficiency of the undertaking and two Select Committees of the House of Commons have gone into this difficult question of Parliamentary accountability. As a result a Select Committee of the House has been set up to examine the annual reports and accounts of the nationalised industries.

But direct action by Parliament is not the only means which has been used to inquire into the efficiency of nationalised undertakings. Another is the appointment of *ad hoc* Committees to examine particular parts of an enterprise. One such Committee in the transport field has been appointed by the Minister: that presided over by Mr S. P. Chambers to inquire into the London Transport Executive. The Committee reported very favourably on the efficiency of the Executive.

[1] *Hansard*, H. of C., 4th December, 1947, Col. 566, *et seq.*
[2] *Ibid.*, 7th June, 1948, Col. 1635, *et seq.*

THE FORMULATION OF POLICY

The following chapters give a short account of the way the widely differing tasks of the Ministry are carried out. They will also show that the work of the Ministry has grown up, not as the result of anything remotely resembling a comprehensive and continuously evolving Government policy for transport, but mainly by the compulsion of events. The problems have posed themselves and the answers have had to be found in legislation and administration. The nationalisation of a great part of the inland transport industry in 1947 is an exception to the general rule; there the policy was dictated not by events but was pursued deliberately as part of the general scheme for nationalising the basic industries.

All this is not to say that the Ministry has no positive part to play. It has built up a living body of knowledge and experience of transport in all its forms and has developed principles of policy and administration of continuing application. Over broad issues of political controversy a Government Department has, of course, no influence. If a Government comes into power pledged to carry out a policy of nationalisation of certain types of transport, for example, the function of the Department concerned is to work out practical means of carrying out the policy of the Government in the way best calculated to produce an efficient pattern for the future with the least disturbance of the country's transport services during the difficult transition period. The Labour Government of 1945 posed exactly this problem, the size of which can be judged from the fact that the Transport Act, 1947, which put the policy into effect, contains no less than 128 Sections and 15 Schedules dealing with all kinds of inland transport, each in a different way.

The preparation of the Bill upon which the Act was based will serve as an example of the role which a Government Department plays in the formulation and execution of policy. The main outlines of the proposals have to be worked out in consultation with the Minister, who is often, in such cases, assisted by a small committee of his interested colleagues, and a rough preliminary draft is prepared of the contents of each separate part of the proposed Bill. Then follow consultations with the industries affected to obtain expert guidance so that the advantages and disadvantages of particular ways of tackling different problems can be compared and the best practical solution arrived at. At all stages the Minister and his colleagues must be brought in to consider and approve or reject or suggest modifications, and these must go backwards and forwards till practical schemes are worked out. At an early stage Parliamentary Counsel come in to start drafting the detailed provisions of the Bill, and their work, which must take into account the existing law on the matters under consideration, may often affect the content as well as the form of the resulting legislation. It is a continuous, and confusing, process, different parts of the proposed Bill being at different stages and all in a fluid state until quite late. The whole process is an example of team work, with the Department in the centre drawing advice and assistance from everyone who can assist, often including those who, while opposed in principle to what is being done, are willing to help to find the best—or, as they might say, the least damaging—way of doing it.

At the other end of the scale from this highly political process of changing policy is the case where the pressure of events and developments in the means or the instruments of transport cause the Department itself to initiate action. A particular case will be described in Chapter V where developments in naval architecture, marine engineering and electronics led to the calling in 1948 of another International Conference on Safety of Life at Sea. Here politics did not enter into the picture at all, nor was there any pressure from outside bodies. There was general agreement in the Ministry and the industry about what was required, and, when the International Convention had been agreed and accepted, the legislation to put its provisions into effect went through Parliament without controversy.

A case falling somewhere between these two extremes is that of oil pollution of our coasts. Here there was wide public dissatisfaction at the spoiling of beaches by oil and well-justified agitation by bird lovers at the maiming and destruction of sea birds from the same cause. As a result the Minister set up a Committee consisting of representatives of those with an interest in the problem, with a senior representative of the Department in the chair. This Committee made certain recommendations, notably for international action on the subject.[1] Meanwhile British shipowners voluntarily took steps to control the nuisance as far as their own vessels were concerned. The next step was the summoning of an International Conference in London at which all the leading maritime nations were represented and which agreed upon a Convention for the Prevention of Pollution of the Sea by Oil. The Convention has since come into force, providing, among other measures, that the participating Governments shall make it an offence for their ships to discharge persistent oils into the sea within certain very wide ocean areas. The United Kingdom and some other countries had in fact anticipated the coming into force of the Convention by passing their domestic legislation in advance. As a result, oil pollution of the coasts of the United Kingdom

[1] Report of the Committee on the Prevention of Pollution of the Sea bv Oil (H.M.S.O., 1953).

and other countries protected by the prohibited zones has been very much reduced. Thus from the complaints of bird lovers and holiday-makers and from the labours of civil servants and legislators, assisted by many representatives of the shipping and oil industries, has come international action which has materially improved the situation. The work is still going on, and, for its part, the Ministry will not be satisfied until the discharge of persistent oil into the sea anywhere in the world is prohibited and the prohibition enforced.

So much then for an introduction to the work of the Ministry as a whole. It remains now to show how the Government's interests in transport have grown up before proceeding to examine the different parts of the Ministry in detail.

CHAPTER II

The Ministry in History

Shipping — Inland Transport — Civil Aviation

*

SHIPPING

THE history of the State's relations with shipping stretches back through many centuries—at least as far as 1381 when the first Navigation Act was passed. But the modern pattern of marine administration came into being rather more than a hundred years ago in response to the special pressures resulting from the impact of the rapidly growing commerce of the nineteenth century on a merchant marine which in the early decades of the century had failed to maintain its efficiency against its foreign competitors and which, by the middle of the century, was facing the full tide of revolution in techniques brought by the advent of iron ships and steam engines and the full blast of competition through the repeal of the Navigation Acts. At this time such responsibilities as existed for the safety and manning of ships were scattered through a variety of public authorities, among them the Board of Trade, the Admiralty, the Customs, Trinity House and Lloyd's Register of Shipping. There was no machine with sufficiently comprehensive knowledge or powers to deal with the regulation of ships and their crews which the Reports of the Select Committee on Shipwrecks in 1836 and the Board of Trade Commission of 1847 showed to be so sorely needed.

A hundred years ago unseaworthy ships, undermanning, bad food, filthy conditions, crimping—that is the fleecing of the sailors on shore and tricking them on board, or making them incapable, by drink or drugs or other means, and forcibly delivering them to the master—were the men's daily misfortune. Nor did they help themselves; incompetence, indiscipline and drunkenness were widespread. The reports of Consular Officers from all over the world in response to a circular sent them in 1843 by James Murray, an official of the Foreign Office, left no doubt that reforms were overdue. In submitting the reports Murray brought out the evident decline of British shipping and the want of education in masters and men. He recommended 'that some new system is requisite, for the benefit of

British interests generally, in order to remedy the existing defects and to keep up the character which Great Britain has for years maintained of supremacy in commercial navigation and commercial enterprise. I venture to suggest this desirable result might best be served by the establishment of a Board or Department of Commercial Marine.'[1]

It was six years before Murray's recommendation was carried out —the delay being due to the debates about the repeal of the Navigation Acts, which were themselves the subject of a further Commission of Inquiry. After the repeal of these laws, the Mercantile Marine Act of 1850 was passed, making the Board of Trade responsible for the affairs of the Merchant Navy and establishing Local Marine Boards which set up shipping offices at the principal ports, each under a Shipping Master, before whom agreements between the master and the crew in foreign-going vessels had to be signed. The 1850 Act also made the examination of masters and mates compulsory and gave power to the Board of Trade to cancel certificates for incompetency or misconduct. All these duties are still carried out by the Ministry today, but, to begin with, the first attempts to better the seaman's lot were not welcomed by those whose lives they sought to benefit. Strikes occurred at the Shields and Sunderland within a month of the passing of the Act and then at Hull and Dundee, the register tickets recording the men's particulars being termed 'badges of slavery'. The local offices, moreover, had to wage a continual war against the crimps whose questionable inducements to the sailors to part with their wages were strictly illegal but whose activities were exceedingly difficult to suppress. As late as 1867 the Directors of the Dock Street Sailors' Home wrote to the Board about the London crimps to say they were 'constantly reminded that improper characters against whose malpractices these prohibitions are expressly levelled, do gain access on board the ships arriving at Gravesend and follow their illicit occupation until the vessels are finally secured in the docks; moreover these unlawful proceedings frequently terminate in disgraceful exhibitions of uproar and contention between the before-mentioned law-breakers and their confederates on the quay. Thus the seamen are exposed to those evil consequences from which a parental law was designed to protect them and are hurried into scenes of debauchery and licentiousness before they have time to consult either their own choice or better interests.'

Gradually things improved and, on the foundations laid by the 1850 Act, a whole edifice of nineteenth- and twentieth-century statutory provisions on merchant shipping has been built. Today, with

[1] Papers relating to the Commercial Marine of Great Britain (Foreign Office, 1844).

statutory standards of accommodation, food and medical supplies, with strong unions and independent organisations representative of both owners and men dealing with employment, wages, terms of service and training, the picture would scarcely be recognised by the seaman of 1850. Equally the same seaman would be amazed to find the prestige which his successors have built up for their calling since the riotous days of a century ago. In particular the heroic example of officers and men in two World Wars has given the profession a very high standing and regard in the public mind, a regard which found expression in the action of King George V in 1927 when he conferred upon the then Prince of Wales the title of 'Master of the Merchant Navy and Fishing Fleets', a title which the Prince retained on coming to the throne as King Edward VIII, and which has been successively assumed by the Late King George VI and by her present Majesty, Queen Elizabeth II.

As regards the ships themselves, the Steam Navigation Act of 1851 gave the Board of Trade power to appoint Surveyors of Steamships and thus brought into being the Marine Survey Service, with offices at the principal ports, responsible for the supervision and enforcement of the regulations for the safety of ships. One of the Surveyors' earliest preoccupations was the regulation of the conditions in which the growing number of emigrants were carried overseas, and, from this concern for a class of passenger who could do little to protect himself, arose many detailed provisions about inspection of the equipment of the ships and of the competence of the crew in using it as well as other matters of less interest today. At the same time there developed the very close control which the Ministry, among its varied and wide-reaching responsibilities for safety, exercises through its surveyors over the construction, maintenance and equipment of all passenger ships.

Thus there came into being a Department of Government, with its organisation at headquarters and at the ports which continues today; but the third bit of machinery, which was necessary in the early days of a relatively weak central administration and of less rapid means of communication, has proved less durable. This was the system of Local Marine Boards, set up at all the principal ports and composed of elected representatives of shipowners, of local dignitaries and of members nominated by the Board of Trade from among the port business community. These Boards were among other things charged with the examinations, then made compulsory, of masters and mates and they had powers to discipline certificated officers. Administration of the examinations finally passed from the Boards to the Marine Department itself, but the Boards' disciplinary powers remain. They have, however, gradually fallen into disuse and many of the Boards have disappeared, but Hull, Belfast, Cardiff and Newcastle still hold their elections and keep their Boards in being.

The first business of the new Marine Department was to codify existing marine law and in 1854 the first comprehensive Merchant Shipping Act was placed on the Statute Book dealing with safety of ships, the qualifications of masters and officers and the control and protection of crews and many other matters. But in spite of its good intentions the Department did not have an easy life in its earlier years; shipowners, and to some extent the crews themselves, suborned by interested parties, showed open hostility to the efforts of the Board and its local offices to achieve better safety and working conditions. Meanwhile sinkings of ships continued to be all too common and by 1870 the average loss of life at sea from British ships had reached the appalling figure of 3,100 each year. The Department was then brought into the very centre of controversy by Samuel Plimsoll, the energetic, if somewhat eccentric, Member for Derby, who spent a large part of his life impressing upon the Government the urgent need for legislation making it compulsory for ships to have a load line. Plimsoll's methods were often questionable and he was frequently carried away by the force of his own rhetoric which led him into violent accusations, including some directed against the Marine Department, for which a Royal Commission later found no justification. The climax came in 1875 after a violent scene in the House of Commons in which Plimsoll advanced across the floor, shook his fist at Disraeli and referred to certain Members as 'villains' and 'shipowners of murderous tendencies'. Nevertheless, he gained his point and an Act was passed by which a load line became compulsory for the first time: but no rules were laid down to determine the position of the line, each shipowner being left to decide its position for himself. There was no immediate reduction in sinkings; indeed such casualty returns as then existed indicated that losses were caused much more frequently by faulty navigation than by overloading. Thomas Gray, who was the Assistant Secretary in charge of the Marine Department, summed up in a Departmental minute the agitation of these years as follows:

It is to Mr Plimsoll, no doubt, that is due the credit of calling special attention to this evil and of creating a popular force which was capable of grappling with it. It has failed in its intended object, if that object was the prevention of wrecks with their attendant loss of life.

Little by little, however, these improvements—and the more positive attitude towards safety they brought with them—began to have some effect. The sinkings gradually became fewer. The loss of life from casualties to ships registered in the United Kingdom fell from an average of 2,650 in the years 1879 to 1882 to less than 1,000 at the turn of the century. Safer ships were being built and the science of navigation improved. In 1890 a more detailed Act on the load line was passed laying down rules for calculating the position of the mark and entrusting the supervision of the Act to the Department, which was empowered to fix load lines itself or to delegate authority to do so to the Classification Societies, such as Lloyd's Register. Then in 1894 the many Merchant Shipping Acts of the previous half-century were consolidated and the Act of that year still remains the 'principal Act' and, incidentally, almost the longest on the statute book.

The present century, while witnessing no diminution in the State's concern for the safety of ships and the well-being of seamen, has seen a shift of emphasis, first in the application, by an Act of 1906, of British safety standards to foreign ships in British ports and thence to the world-wide adoption of international standards through the successive International Safety Conferences, the Load Line Conference of 1930 and the maritime sessions of the International Labour Organisation. In the labour relations field the representatives of the Merchant Navy officers and seamen play their part along with the representatives of the shipowners and shipbuilders and other marine interests. Their rise to strength is part of the general history of trade unionism, but the shipping industry's negotiating machine for wages and conditions and service, the National Maritime Board, had its origins in a board set up by the Ministry of Shipping in the First World War to deal with urgent war-time manning problems. The Government withdrew from the Board after the war, but the representatives of the shipowners and of the officers and seamen continued together and have fashioned the Board into the robust and efficient machine it is today.

To turn from safety and labour relations to the field of commercial activity, the State has from the very earliest times sought to further its trading interests and to protect its shipping and commerce through a system of commercial treaties. The objects which interest shipping were, and, as will be seen in the next chapter, still are broadly threefold: to secure for British ships the same treatment in ports of a foreign country as that country affords its own ships; to secure for cargoes the best treatment afforded by a foreign state to those of any other foreign state; and to preserve the full competitive freedom of shipping by securing undertakings not to discriminate against persons or cargoes on the ground of the flag of the ship in which they are carried.

The immense importance of merchant shipping in time of war was responsible for the setting up in 1917 of a separate Ministry of

Shipping to control the use of ships in support of the war effort, while the normal peace-time duties of the Marine Department remained with the Board of Trade. The Transport Department of the Admiralty, which dealt with the transport by sea of all military forces and their supplies, was transferred to the new Ministry and was not returned to the Admiralty after the war but became part of the Mercantile Marine Department of the Board of Trade, the old Marine Department being renamed to mark this extension of its scope. Shortly afterwards, the Mercantile Marine Department took over from the Admiralty the control of the Coastguard Service, whose main duty is watching the coasts to warn ships running into danger and to rescue those on board wrecked ships. In 1939 a Ministry of Shipping was again formed to deal with the immense tasks of controlling merchant shipping in furtherance of the war effort, but this time the new Ministry took over the whole work of the Marine Department of the Board of Trade. The subsequent amalgamations which have produced the present Ministry have already been described.

Relations between the shipping industry and the Government Department responsible for its affairs have grown from the antagonism and suspicion of a hundred years ago to the friendliness and trust and mutual co-operation which is, happily, the rule today. Indeed, it is true to say that in no industry are relations more close and friendly. Progress toward this state of affairs has been specially rapid over the last half-century, accelerated by the intimate relationship which necessarily existed between Government and the industry during the course of the two wars, when the Department, largely staffed from the industry, controlled the movement of all British ships and the majority of allied ships. Provision for the manning of our ships and the welfare of crews—often in places where no facilities were needed in peace-time—for repairs and bunkers and supplies and mails and for a thousand other needs could be met only by the combined efforts of all parties, Government, owners and masters, officers and seamen. Fortunately the close relations of war have continued in peace and the formal machinery set up by the Merchant Shipping Act, 1906, for consultation with the industry on the drafting of regulations concerning ships has been replaced by an informal day-to-day contact on all matters of mutual concern. For many years no legislation on shipping matters has been placed before Parliament, and no rules or regulations have been made which have not carried the support of all parts of the industry. There is general agreement on broad policy and on matters concerning ships and seamen, and where differences arise, as they often do, they are hammered out in an atmosphere of understanding and goodwill. That such relations could exist would have seemed incredible to the forebears of all parties a hundred years ago.

INLAND TRANSPORT

In the latter part of the eighteenth and the early part of the nineteenth centuries such interest as the State took in inland transport was manifested in the Select and Private Bill Committees of Parliament. Canal and river navigation and turnpike companies came to Parliament with Private Bills seeking authority to develop their undertakings and to levy charges. As a general rule scrutiny of these Bills was prompted only by the opposition they were likely to evoke from competitors and landowners; there was no examination from the standpoint of public policy. But the coming of the railways soon altered that. Here was something on an infinitely bigger scale than the piecemeal efforts of the inland waterway and turnpike companies to construct or improve selected stretches of road, canal or river. The industrial implications of the railways for the country as a whole, and not only for particular localities, considerations of public safety, and the tremendous increase in the weight of Parliamentary business all showed the need for a system of administration and control that could both provide advice for Ministers and put the decisions of Parliament into effect. Eleven Select Committees, Gladstone and Cardwell among their Chairmen, reported on railways between 1838 and 1853, and in 1846 alone 64 Private Bill Committees sat for 867 Parliamentary days discussing railway Bills.[1] But since 1840 there has been a permanent Department—the Railway Department of the Board of Trade and its successors—to advise the Government and the Committees on the many railway issues of the day—the boom of 1844–46 and the collapse of 1847, the associated problems of amalgamation and monopoly, the control of charges and of dividends, competition with the canals and, particularly, on safety. Many important public Acts resulted—for example, Gladstone's Regulation of Railways Act of 1844 which included enabling powers for State revision of railway rates and, a century before its time, for State purchase of railways. But others of its provisions were of more immediate practical import—those, for instance, for the 'Parliamentary train' whereby railway companies had to run at least one train each way over every passenger-carrying line each lawful day, stopping at all stations, and conveying third-class passengers at 1d. a mile at an average speed of not less than 12 miles per hour. Other significant measures followed—for example,

[1] E. Cleveland-Stevens: *English Railways: Their Development and Their Relation to the State*, pp. 62–5.

C

the Railway Clauses Consolidation Act of 1845 which provided for equality of charges in like circumstances and the Railway and Canal Traffic Act of 1844 which forbad 'undue preferences'. It is interesting to note that these two Acts set the pattern of railway charges for close on a hundred years by provisions which, as will be seen in Chapter IX, were only repealed by the Transport Act of 1953.

While the great railway arguments went on, the administration began to interest itself in other parts of the transport industries. Railways remained, of course, the dominating factor in inland transport until the invention of the internal combustion engine, and indeed for some time after. At first this invention created problems for the Local Government Board, which since 1872 had been concerned with the few highway problems in which the central Government then took an interest. But there was a growing demand for roads with good surfaces and good drainage, which could be used by motor cars without covering the inhabitants and the country with layers of dust, and at length in 1909 Lloyd George, then Chancellor of the Exchequer, set up the Road Board. This Board had power to make grants to local authorities for road improvement and construction out of the funds collected from vehicle licensing and petrol taxation.

Ten years later the fortunes of inland transport had changed beyond recognition. The 1914–18 War left a legacy of problems and there was much concern about the lack of progress in the development of transport. In many ways the situation bore a striking resemblance to that with which we are familiar after the Second World War, and the arguments then used sound remarkably like those of 30 years later. The railways had been heavily worked and had not been adequately maintained during the war and were already beginning to suffer from road competition. The Government, in whose hands control of the railways temporarily lay, had artificially maintained rail rates at the 1913 level, with the result that the tax-payer was faced with a bill for some £60,000,000 for 1919 alone.[1] Motorists and road transport interests were pressing for more funds to build better roads. Other aspects of inland transport and services closely allied with it were causing anxiety too; for example, there was uneasiness about wasteful practices and lack of development in docks and harbours, and about the fact that coastal shipping services had been virtually killed by the maintenance of pre-war rail rates. Above all, the Government were concerned that there was no single agency which could look at inland transport as a whole and undertake such measures of co-ordination as might be necessary. As Sir Eric Geddes, formerly Lord Haig's Director-General of

[1] *Hansard*, H. of C., 10th July, 1919, Col. 1282, *et seq.*

Transportation in France, put it, 'There is no policy and no one is responsible'.[1]

These were the reasons that led the Government to introduce a Bill setting up a separate Ministry of Transport. Even so there was considerable opposition. Some regarded it as a gross extension of bureaucracy. Sir William Joynson-Hicks, for example, envisaged the proposal as one for 'the most powerful Ministry that it has ever been suggested to set up in this country'.[2] Others saw it as the first step on the road to nationalisation. There were those who sensed a sinister encroachment by the railways upon all other forms of transport: they decried 'this Railway Bill'. Others again protested bitterly about the lead it gave to control docks. Amendments were secured which went some way towards mollifying the Opposition and the Bill received the Royal Assent on 15th August, 1919, Sir Eric Geddes becoming the first Minister of Transport three days later. The Ministry then took over from the Board of Trade responsibility for docks, canals and railways, together with the duties of the Road Board. For the next 20 years the problem of the railways, the various attempts to regulate road and rail competition, and the development of the roads themselves were the main preoccupations of the Ministry.

The 1919 Act continued the Government's control of the railways for a further two years. During that time preparations went strenuously ahead for the amalgamation of 119 companies into four, which was brought about by the Railways Act, 1921; but it did not for long ease the railways' difficulties. The story of road and rail competition is told in greater detail in Chapter VIII and only passing reference is needed here to the major legislative measures, the Road Traffic Act, 1930, and the Road and Rail Traffic Act, 1933, which were the outcome of the work of the Royal Commission on Transport of 1928–31 and of the Salter Conference of 1932. As well as promoting greater safety on the roads, these Acts introduced licensing systems which sought to prevent uncontrolled competition among road operators themselves and to relieve the railways of some of their competitive handicaps. But the problem had by no means been solved when the Second World War broke out and when the Government once more took financial control of the railways, as they had done 25 years earlier.

A determined attack upon road accidents was made in the Road Traffic Act of 1934, which brought in driving tests and the 30 m.p.h. speed limit in built-up areas. The effect was immediate and appreciable, though not spectacular, the number of killed and injured falling from the peak figure of 240,000 in 1934 to 228,228 in 1935.

[1] *Hansard*, H. of C., 17th March, 1919, Col. 1759.
[2] *Ibid.*, 26th February, 1919, Col. 1816.

As for the roads themselves, many new roads were built and standards of improvement and maintenance were achieved which were admitted, by some Britons as well as by foreign visitors, to be high. A system was developed for classifying roads according to their importance, on which grants to local authorities for building and maintaining them were based, and in 1936, by virtue of the Trunk Roads Act of that year, the Government first took over full responsibility for the major trunk routes. Now, as is described in Chapter X, a start has been made, under powers given by the Special Roads Act, 1949, on the construction of roads exclusively for motor traffic, with no crossings and with access at a limited number of points, on the lines of the highways of the United States of America and similar roads on the Continent.

CIVIL AVIATION

The earliest years of the State's concern with civil aviation, and the Paris Conference of 1910, have been graphically described[1] by one who took part in them from the Home Office, which was at first the Department responsible. The Paris Conference was the first attempt to reach international agreement on the problems of air navigation and in particular on the vexed questions of sovereignty of the air and rights of passage, which have exercised the minds of international jurists and negotiators for most of this century. It was in fact on this vital subject that the Conference broke down, though not before agreement had been reached on many lesser matters—a fact which proved of great advantage at the next Paris Conference nine years later. After the Paris Conference, the small aviation section in the Home Office turned its attention to more mundane aspects of the subject and piloted the Aerial Navigation Act of 1911 'to provide for the protection of the public against dangers arising from the navigation of aircraft'. It was a very short and simple Act, merely making it an offence to navigate aircraft over areas prohibited by order of the Secretary of State and being passed in something of a rush to guard against the dangers of reckless flying at King George V's Coronation. But the House of Commons did not fail to recognise the wider significance of the arrival of transport in a third dimension. Mr Winston Churchill, as he then was, introduced the Bill as Home Secretary in the following words: 'Let me say that the Government would greatly regret to do anything in any way to hamper the development of this vast industry which, we believe, is fraught with immense consequences—I will not say whether good or bad—but immense consequences to the strength and fortunes of

[1] Sir Harold Butler: *Confident Morning.*

the peoples of these islands, quite apart from its general effect on civilisation.' And later he added, 'Aeronauts are a small and adventurous class, and I think we all owe a great deal to these men who risk their lives and give a fine exhibition of human power'.[1]

Two years later a further Aerial Navigation Act was passed, introduced this time by the Secretary of State for War, Colonel Seely. Power was taken in the interests of defence to fire at or into any aircraft flying over prohibited areas. Both Acts were administered by the Home Office. It was not, however, until after the war that civil aviation entered the field of public transport. Its new importance was then recognised by the establishment in 1919, in the newly created Air Ministry, of a Department of Civil Aviation under a Controller-General, Major-General Sir Frederick Sykes. This arrangement continued for the next 20 years, although there was constant pressure in Parliament and elsewhere to separate responsibility for civil flying from that for military flying.

The first United Kingdom commercial air service—from London to Paris—was inaugurated in 1919, and the next few years in civil aviation can be compared to 'the early railway age' of a century earlier. There was the same spirit of enterprise and adventure among the first merchant airmen as had animated George Stephenson and his associates: there was the same feeling of being pioneers, similar wrestlings with the practical problems set by a great new mechanical invention and the same mistrust of its safety on the part of the general public. But the essential difference was that, from the beginning, civil aviation was competing in an international market. Thus the first praiseworthy but optimistic policy of making civil aviation 'fly by itself' soon had to give way, in the face of the subsidised competition of foreign airlines, to Government grants for selected British companies and, following the Hambling Committee of 1923, to the policy of assistance for the 'chosen instrument'—Imperial Airways. Although it was created primarily to establish air services in Europe, Imperial Airways started a service in the Middle East in 1927 and then gradually directed its principal effort to the development of the Empire routes. The Company's resources and subsidy were not equal to the task of developing both the Empire and the European routes and in 1935 the Government filled the gap left in Europe by nominating British Airways as a second chosen instrument to develop the European services. British Airways had only a short life, for in 1938 the Government decided to merge Imperial Airways and British Airways into one public Corporation—the British Overseas Airways Corporation. These frequent changes reflect a not unnatural uncertainty in the minds of the Government about the best way to

[1] Hansard, H. of C., 29th May, 1911, Col. 837-8.

develop air transport, but in trying to find the best pattern for the industry they showed themselves very willing to seek, and to profit from, external advice. The Hambling Committee of 1923 had recommended that it would be more economical to have a single operating company to develop Empire routes, rather than several competing concerns, and that it should be made the sole recipient of financial help from the Exchequer. On the recommendation of the Maybury Committee, which followed in 1935–36, the Government established an Air Transport Licensing Board to regulate and control internal services, and undertook to provide radio, air traffic control and meteorological services of which more is said below; from the two Gorell Committees came the Air Registration Board and a number of measures to improve air safety; while the setting up of the British Overseas Airways Corporation already mentioned followed the advice of the Cadman Committee. But in spite of the difficulties—and perhaps, thanks to the wise suggestions of the Committees—our civil air communications progressed, in particular those with the Far East and Australia, helped by the success of the Empire Air Mail Scheme introduced in 1937. But with the coming of the Second World War the entire resources of civil aviation were placed at the disposal of the Government.

After the war, the Government lost no time in getting commercial air services re-established, but, in doing so, they again moved away from the idea of a single 'chosen instrument' by setting up two new public Corporations—British European Airways and British South American Airways—to share with BOAC the responsibility of providing the country's air services. The Government explained in their White Paper 'British Air Services' of December 1945[1] that the two considerations which influenced them in reaching their decision were the need for flexibility in meeting international competition and the necessity for encouraging different methods of approach to the techniques of airline operation. BOAC were left with routes between the United Kingdom and other Commonwealth countries, the United States and the Far East; BEA took over routes between the United Kingdom and the Continent and the internal routes of the United Kingdom; and BSAA routes between the United Kingdom and South America. The British South American Airways Corporation was merged with the British Overseas Airways Corporation in 1949.

During the inter-war period the ground services were steadily improved. From the early days of civil aviation the Government provided some of the ground services, including aids to aerial navigation and the meteorological services. Most of the civil aerodromes were

[1] Cmd. 6712.

provided by the local authorities, but the Government owned and operated three airports—two near London (Croydon and Heston) and one, Lympne, on the south coast. As for air traffic control, movements were at first too few to create much risk of collision, navigation was generally by map reading, and completion of flight in anything but reasonable weather depended mainly on the skill and determination of the pilot. Moreover, the comparative slowness of the aircraft gave the ground communications system ample time in which to handle messages. In 1918 an extremely far-sighted report was received from the Civil Aerial Transport Committee which emphasised the need for aerodromes, the planning of main routes, the provision of directional wireless and other aids to assist navigation in fog and a considerable extension of the meteorological service. Among its distinguished members was H. G. Wells who was able to give practical, if indirect, expression to his pre-1914 forecasts of the growth of air power. Following the report of this Committee good progress was made in providing the minimum navigational facilities by the time the first commercial air service started, and in 1920 the Advisory Committee on Civil Aviation was able to report that a telecommunications service to the Continent had been provided, directional wireless was being installed at Croydon and radio-telephony equipment at five other aerodromes in the United Kingdom, that visual beacons had been installed for night flying, and that the meteorological service had been expanded. These services were further developed during succeeding years as the volume of air transport itself gradually expanded. Eventually the stage was reached when so many aircraft were operating in weather conditions where pilots could no longer see each other in time to avoid a collision that an Air Traffic Control Organisation was instituted, beginning with the London/Continental routes. In 1936 one of the first effective instrument approach aids was installed at Croydon to provide a beam along which a pilot could, by the use of instruments, approach the landing strip in bad weather. This was the German Lorenze apparatus, subsequently developed into the Standard Beam Approach system that was used extensively during the war and has only recently been superseded by the Instrument Landing System ('ILS').

The need for ground services was not confined to these islands. As a great trading nation, and the centre of a Commonwealth of Nations, the United Kingdom had naturally to provide for its long-distance overseas routes, which also required ground services, and, by 1926, radio and meteorological facilities had been installed on the Cairo–Karachi route. In the following years aerodromes and other ground facilities were gradually provided on the routes to South

Africa and to Singapore. The success of the Empire Air Mail Scheme led to much greater use of the Empire routes and to additional facilities for the Short 'C' Class flying boats which became well-known as the Empire Flying Boats. One more great route remained to be established, and by 1936 work was well under way on land and water aerodromes, together with radio and meteorological facilities, for the North Atlantic service. To increase the sources of weather information, a meteorological observer was stationed for a year in ships crossing the North Atlantic in order to collect more observations.

Towards the end of the war much thought was given to the future administrative arrangements. It was realised that, with the enormous progress made in the air during the war, civil aviation was bound to occupy a place in transport of far greater importance than in 1939 and that much concentration of effort and material resources would be needed to make good the ground lost by our exclusive war-time concentration upon the manufacture of military aircraft. It was with these factors in mind that the decision was taken to set up a separate Department and Lord Swinton was appointed as the first Minister of Civil Aviation in October, 1944, an Act being passed the following year to establish the new Ministry. Much of the work of the succeeding years is told in Part IV of this book. It remains only to record here that, on being returned to power in 1951, Sir Winston Churchill decided that civil aviation no longer warranted the undivided attention of one Minister. A single Minister was appointed to be Minister of Transport and Minister of Civil Aviation and two years later, as the logical sequence of that single appointment, the two Departments were amalgamated.

Thus it has come about that the State's interests in transport are now centred in one Ministry. In a period of 12 years three Departments were rolled into one and the British public became accustomed to the spectacle of this particular Ministry changing its name with practically every change of Government. Who knows whether the last change has yet been made?

PART TWO

Shipping

CHAPTER III

Shipping Policy

British Policy — Statistical Background — The importance of shipping to the United Kingdom — Relations with other Governments — Domestic problems and the outlook for British Shipping.

*

BRITISH POLICY

IT has already been made plain in the previous chapter that there has been complete continuity in the United Kingdom's shipping policy for over a hundred years. In 1849, the repeal of the Navigation Laws introduced a period during which the British merchant marine gradually attained pre-eminence in carrying the world's trade by sea without protection or financial assistance from the Government. The new policy of free trade, as applied to shipping, rested on the principle that Governments should treat ships coming to their ports, and the goods carried in them, without differentiation whatever the flag of the vessel might be. When the coasting trade of the United Kingdom was thrown open to foreign ships in 1854 the last vestige of protection for British shipping vanished. The United Kingdom treats foreign vessels as favourably as its own in British ports and waters and tries to secure the same freedom and rights for British shipping abroad. An up-to-date expression of British shipping policy exists in a Convention ratified by the United Kingdom in 1949— the Convention for the establishment of a United Nations body known as the Inter-Governmental Maritime Consultative Organisation. Its purposes include the following:

(*a*) 'to encourage the general adoption of the highest practicable standards in matters concerning maritime safety and efficiency of navigation';

(*b*) 'to encourage the removal of discriminatory action and unnecessary restrictions by Governments affecting shipping engaged in international trade so as to promote the availability of shipping services to the commerce of the world without discrimination'.

There are no provisions about the welfare of crews or labour relations generally since these matters are the province of the International Labour Organisation.

If a country heavily dependent for its livelihood on imports and exports is to prosper, its merchants must be able to count on reliable and efficient shipping services, and the charges for carrying goods by sea, while they must be sufficiently remunerative to enable shipowners to provide such services with up-to-date and competitive vessels, should not be so high as to add unduly to the cost of imports or to handicap trade by adding too much to the price of exports. The most effective way of securing the necessary adjustments in the supply of world tonnage to the demands of trade, and of enabling freight rates to find their appropriate level, is the hard competitive struggle under which the penalty of not providing as attractive a service as the other man is to be run out of business and off the seas. Interference by Governments increases costs of transport and tends to damage the smooth working of the complex commercial processes built up by the shipowners and shippers of the world to secure tonnage to meet the day-to-day requirements of trade. The truth of these assertions has been proved by experience and accepted by British Governments of all parties for over a century. Their particular importance for the United Kingdom is obvious, but it is, in fact, in the best interests of all countries that those best fitted to supply efficient shipping services at the lowest charges should have the opportunity to do so. Any other course raises costs all round and checks and distorts the flow of trade.

This being the basis of a sound commercial policy, the Ministry's activities in support of British shipping are directed towards maintaining throughout the world the conditions in which our ships can compete fairly with the ships of other flags without interference by other Governments. At home also the Ministry is concerned to see that the world-wide interests of our shipping are fully taken into account in working out domestic policies affecting the economy of the United Kingdom. Internal policy should always have regard to its effects upon British ships operating in a world market in competition with the ships of all other nations. While, therefore, it is our policy to give no privileges to British ships in international competition, it is also our business to see that they are not unnecessarily handicapped by the impact of other aspects of United Kingdom policy.

STATISTICAL BACKGROUND

A few figures will throw light on our shipping policy. The most important point is that the British merchant marine is the largest block of tonnage operating under a single flag in international trade. At the end of June 1958 there was a total of about 18·9 million gross tons of vessels of 500 gross tons and over on the United Kingdom register, including about 439,000 tons of tramp shipping belonging to Canadian owners transferred under a special arrangement which provides for their return to Canadian register in certain circumstances. This compares with some 25·1 million tons of ocean shipping on the United States register at the same date, but of this only 10·9 million tons need to be taken into account as 14·2 million tons of shipping are laid up in reserve. The next largest merchant marine is that of Liberia, one of the 'registers of convenience', with some 10·3 million tons in the middle of 1958, followed by Norway with 9·0 million tons. The total figure for world tonnage of all flags at this date (vessels of 500 gross tons and over) is approximately 97·6 million gross tons, excluding the United States tonnage in reserve and United States and Canadian ships on the Great Lakes.

Since the British merchant fleet is so large compared with others, it is peculiarly vulnerable to restrictions and discriminatory measures imposed by foreign Governments, the more so because a very important part of its earnings comes from voyages between one overseas country and another (the 'cross-trades'—which include voyages from one overseas port to another by ships whose complete voyage starts from or terminates in the United Kingdom). The British shipowners' organisations, who made a special investigation for the purpose, found that the proportion of the total gross freight earnings of our shipping that was derived from these trades outside the United Kingdom amounted to 46 per cent in 1952.

THE IMPORTANCE OF SHIPPING TO THE UNITED KINGDOM

It is more important now than ever before to maintain conditions in which our shipping can make the maximum contribution to the national economy. As a result of the liquidation during the Second World War of our investments abroad and the accumulation of vast external liabilities, the foreign currency which we earn by our shipping services to customers abroad is of crucial importance in balancing the nation's accounts and in building up reserves to create a margin for overseas investment. The importance of these contributions to the national income is indicated by the fact that the investigation by the shipowners' organisations already referred to showed that in 1952 vessels owned or operated by United Kingdom shipowners earned £221 million net from other countries, after deducting the expenses incurred by our ships abroad. In addition, a sum of £218 million is estimated to have been earned from freights on imports carried in United Kingdom vessels, which, as a saving of expenditure on foreign shipping, may be regarded as representing an indirect contribution to the balance of payments.

The fortunes and interests of the shipping and shipbuilding industries are inevitably interlocked. The stability of our shipyards depends upon the prosperity of the merchant marine. Equally, the ability of our shipyards to build ships of the finest quality at a competitive price is an essential factor in the competitive resources of our shipping: the Ministry is therefore closely interested in Government policy towards the shipbuilding industry and maintains constant liaison with the Admiralty, the Department responsible for that industry.

A policy which has made it possible for the British merchant fleet to render an immense contribution to our peace-time economy has also justified itself in enabling the country to emerge successfully from two world wars. But the Second World War drove home the lessons of the First—that, however large and efficient a nation's own shipping may be, it is no more adequate than its other resources to carry it through a war alone, and that any attempt to use each nation's shipping for its own purposes only would bring disaster. In war, demands on shipping are so far in excess of supply that the shipping of all allied nations must be pooled and used as one unit for the good of all. How this was done in the last war and how planning is being carried on in case of a future emergency are described shortly in the next chapter.

RELATIONS WITH OTHER GOVERNMENTS

Success excites envy and emulation. The sight of the valuable asset which has been built up over the years by the traditional shipping nations has influenced other nations, particularly those which are developing their industrial potential and wish to assert their political independence, to try to follow their example, not by the slow and laborious process of acquiring and exercising the skills of the sea and establishing traditions of reliability and efficiency, but by the short-cut methods of Government subsidy and Government preferences and discriminations. Political and social pressures, the desire for prestige, the urge to build up a measure of self-sufficiency against a future war, the wish to conserve foreign exchange, are all factors inducing Governments to create merchant fleets under their flags. They overlook the fact that in the long run, if policies of protection and financial assistance are used to achieve these aims, they are likely to defeat their own object by introducing rigidity and unnecessary cost into the exchange of goods and services between nations and to lead to unfortunate results for the country adopting them as well as for the maritime nations that provide world-wide shipping services in fair competition. Unhappily, the tendency of Governments to adopt such policies has been particularly marked since the end of the Second War. The apparatus of exchange control and of the licensing of imports and exports, developed to deal with the post-war balance of payments problems of so many countries, has provided a subtle method of giving preference to ships of the national flag. The old-fashioned ways of giving preferential treatment in respect of port charges, consular fees, berthing arrangements, and so on, have on occasion also been used. But the most notable and pernicious discriminatory device is to provide compulsorily for a proportion (usually a minimum of 50 per cent) of a country's trade to be carried in ships of the national flag. This practice has been adopted by a number of countries in recent years and has distorted the economic operation of shipping; if applied universally it would lead to the absurdity of ships regularly carrying cargoes in one direction only, with the result that twice as many ships would be used as were necessary. The world's trade would pay dearly for such lunacy, as it pays now for its more limited application.

It is one of the Ministry's main responsibilities to concert action with the Departments directly responsible for handling the country's commercial and external policies to ensure that everything possible is done to check such practices. Her Majesty's Representatives overseas have standing instructions to report to London any developments which may be of significance, and diplomatic action is initiated whenever the need arises. In Washington, owing to the number of maritime subjects in which this country and the United States have a mutual interest, an officer of the Department serves on the staff of the Ambassador as Shipping Attaché. His life is a busy one, not merely because of the great importance of the shipping policy adopted by a country of such enormous commercial importance as the United States, but also because United States policies in many fields of administration—defence, commerce, foreign policy and so on—are bound to affect the interests of British shipping, directly or indirectly, in ways that may not always be obvious and that require constant vigilance. The Department also provides a Shipping Adviser at Singapore on the staff of the Commisioner-General for the United Kingdom in South East Asia, in view of the many problems of shipping policy which, for geographical, political and economic reasons, continually arise in the Far East.

Safeguards for the fair treatment of our shipping have been secured in commercial treaties negotiated with many countries in the past, but they are not always adequate and there are no treaty safeguards in some of the countries most prone to flag discrimination.

Few bilateral arrangements containing satisfactory shipping clauses have been made since the Second War, as post-war trade conditions have been generally unfavourable for negotiations. The Inter-Governmental Maritime Consultative Organisation has at last been set up as the specialised shipping agency of the United Nations, and it is to be hoped that by providing a forum where Governments' different points of view can be ventilated in common council it will contribute to the general adoption of sensible shipping policies. Useful but limited discussions on questions of shipping policy also take place in the Organisation for European Economic Co-operation, whose Maritime Transport Committee is attended by representatives of the Ministry. These consultations have had some effect in promoting the development of trade by reducing restrictions on the carriage of goods and have helped to secure some support for combating discriminatory practices throughout the world.

Obstacles to the free movement of shipping in international trade may give rise to the widest issues of foreign policy. The Ministry was naturally very closely concerned with the situation created by the Egyptian Government's seizure of the Suez Canal on 26th July, 1956. Quite apart from the practical work of organising, as a precautionary measure, the armada of troop-ships, cargo ships and landing craft which subsequently took part in the Anglo-French intervention at the end of October that year, the Department had an important part to play in the interdepartmental work of formulating the issues of policy for consideration by Ministers and in dealing, in close contact with the shipping industry, with all the day-to-day problems that emerged. The Suez crisis has left behind it continuing problems of which the implications for shipping will emerge over many years. At all times, and throughout the world, it must remain an essential policy objective for the United Kingdom, as the greatest maritime country, to maintain freedom of navigation through international waterways and to preserve the freedom of the seas against the increasing claims of States to enlarge their domestic jurisdiction over the oceans—claims which are a serious danger not only to the shipping nations but also to those who possess deep-sea fishing fleets. These great principles indeed involve issues affecting the relations between Governments in many fields. The attitudes of other Governments will be as varied as their interests, while the ability of the United Kingdom to secure acceptance of its views on shipping policy depends largely on its ability to make its influence felt generally in world affairs.

DOMESTIC PROBLEMS AND THE OUTLOOK
FOR BRITISH SHIPPING

If our policy in relation to other Governments consists in attempting to secure a fair field for competition by our shipping on equal terms, it is just as important that our own domestic policies should place no impediments in the way. It has been common ground to successive post-war Governments, as to their predecessors, that the national interest is best served by the minimum of restriction on the freedom of the shipping industry to manage its own business. Although the Government still retain certain of the powers affecting shipping which they had to take for war purposes and have not yet been able to relinquish because of defence needs, the powers are used so as to cause the least possible interference with the freedom of the industry. For example, the Ships and Aircraft (Transfer Restriction) Act, 1939, under which the Minister's sanction is required before a shipowner can transfer a ship to another owner, is still in force, and limited restrictions have had to be imposed, in consultation with other Departments, particularly as a means of keeping the sale of ships abroad in line with general policy on exports to countries behind the 'Iron Curtain'. But these restrictions have progressively been reduced, since the ability to sell old vessels in order to acquire vessels better suited for their purposes has long been one of the means by which British shipowners have kept up the quality of their fleets to meet foreign competition, and it is essential that no unnecessary obstacles should be placed in their way in finding funds for this purpose. Since the war, the combined effects of heavy taxation and the rise in the cost of shipbuilding, coming on top of the crippling war losses of the British merchant marine (which amounted to nearly $11\frac{1}{2}$ million gross tons, out of a pre-war fleet of 17 million tons) have presented owners with a most difficult problem in replacing their fleets. Nevertheless the industry has done a great deal. Over $5\frac{1}{2}$ million gross tons of new ships are under construction or on order at home and overseas for British shipowners. And the increased investment allowance when new ships are acquired, given to the industry by the Chancellor of the Exchequer in his 1957 Budget, should prove over the years to be of real assistance to those owners who wish to modernise and develop their fleets.

The constantly shifting factors in world affairs and in political, social and economic developments at home raise fresh problems for shipping all the time and make the administration of shipping policy a task of perpetual novelty and diversity. Among the problems of the future, the development of air transport may be expected to give rise to important questions of policy. It might easily have been assumed, before experience proved the contrary to be true, that air and sea would be competitors to such an extent that gains made by the one would be entirely at the expense of the other. This is certainly not so; the air seems to have generated a new traffic, and the spectacular increase in the numbers of passengers carried across the oceans by air has been accompanied, not by a decrease, but by an increase in the numbers carried by sea. The decline in the number of British passenger ships since 1939 has sometimes been regarded as the consequence of air competition; the fact is, however, that the present fleet is carrying more passengers than the pre-war passenger fleet. On the freight side there is as yet little direct competition, although air transport is becoming the recognised carrier in some rather special fields.

An interesting illustration of the different approach which the Department must make to apparently similar problems is provided by the contrast between maritime policy and air policy. Whereas at sea the generally accepted practice for more than a century has been free competition, trades being developed and built up by private enterprise and policy being directed to preserving this pattern as effectively as possible from interference by Governments, the picture in the air has been almost the direct opposite. Spectacular advances in technical progress for war purposes, particularly in the Second War, placed at the disposal of air lines technical resources which required for their exploitation financial means far beyond the capacity of private enterprise in most countries. At the same time, for commercial and prestige reasons, most countries regarded it as essential to possess an air transport industry. So, in the place of slow growth of sea transport in the cold hard world of competition, there was in the air the hothouse atmosphere of protection against chill winds and biting frosts, and policy was inevitably protectionist. As a result, as will be seen in Chapter XII, individual bargains with other countries for the reciprocal exchange of traffic rights must be made for air services. The tendency in the future may be towards freer conditions but in the meanwhile policy on these two sides of the house must remain very different.

So far as cargo carrying is concerned, another great change in the country's economy is the reduction in exports of coal from the United Kingdom. Traditionally, the economics of British tramp shipping rested on the carriage of coal outwards from the United Kingdom and of grain and raw materials homewards by the same vessels. Now the tendency is for cargo liners, which are better fitted to carry outwards the manufactured goods making up the post-war pattern of exports, to bring homewards increasing quantities of grain and other bulk cargoes. To meet this need the cargo liner fleets have been increasing. But the most spectacular growth in the world's fleets, as well as in our own, has been in tankers. The United Kingdom tanker fleet has almost doubled since 1939; and, although many of the new ships have been built by the oil companies themselves, an appreciable part of the expansion has been made by dry cargo shipowners who have entered the tanker field. Over half the tonnage on order for British shipowners now consists of tankers, a healthy state of affairs when considerations of national well-being and security both dictate that there should be increased tanker tonnage under the British flag. At the same time this growth of the tanker element, with its close connection with the oil industry, raises special problems of shipping policy which are likely to become increasingly important—quite apart from the physical problems in shipbuilding, and in dry docking and discharge facilities which the rapidly increasing numbers and size of the tankers are creating. One of the most notable features of the post-war structure of international shipping—the huge increase in tonnage flying the flags of convenience—is closely associated with the growth of tanker fleets. Besides the Panamanian merchant fleet, which existed before the war and which is now the sixth largest in the world, an even larger fleet, well over half of it tankers, has sprung into being since the war on the register of Liberia. These ships do not serve the trade of the countries whose flag they fly, and their effective control lies elsewhere. As their earnings are virtually free from the taxation necessarily imposed by the established maritime powers, they represent a formidable new factor in competitive shipping. One partial answer, within the power of the maritime nations, is to ease the burden of taxation on their own shipowners, who are engaged in direct competition with ships of these flags. No other answer has yet been found but the maritime nations will certainly go on seeking one.

Coastal shipping also has its own special problems, while sharing many of those of deep-sea shipping. For, although in some areas geography makes it the principal supplier of essential transport needs, it is immediately affected by developments in rail and road transport, with which it both competes and co-operates in the public service. The rates charged by rail and road transport and the policies of successive Governments in relation to inland transport are of vital interest to the coasting industry. This fact was recognised in the Transport Act of 1947 which set up the Coastal Shipping Advisory Committee for the purpose of 'considering, and from time to time reporting to the Minister on all matters which may jointly affect the interests of the British Transport Commission and coastal shipping'. Altogether the dry cargo coastal fleet, of some 870,000 d.wt., provides, besides passenger services and liner services for general cargo, tramp tonnage in which some 34 million tons of bulk commodities, mainly coal, were carried between United Kingdom ports in 1957. Moreover, besides its value as part of the internal transport system of the country in peace this section of the industry has great strategic importance. In time of war the special value of the coasting fleet lies in its ability to use shallow ports and anchorages both for carrying cargoes from port to port and for ferrying cargoes discharged at anchorages by deep-sea ships. It can also give great assistance to other forms of inland transport.

To return to the wider picture, there is no reason to doubt that, in spite of the many changes of conditions that have taken place and are likely to come about in the future, the basic principles of shipping policy which have stood for over a hundred years are still sound. Undoubtedly, neither domestic nor world conditions are as favourable for our merchant shipping as they were earlier in the century. In face of the ambitions of other nations and the prevalent determination to pursue narrow nationalistic policies at whatever cost, there are obvious limits to what Her Majesty's Government can achieve towards keeping the field open for fair competition on equal terms. The prosperity of British shipping will therefore still depend in the future as it has in the past on the qualities of the men in the shipping industry itself. Nevertheless it is possible that the problems of the future may call for the development of new methods and for even closer co-ordination of policy both within the industry itself and between the industry and the Government. It must be remembered too that, apart from the retention of our traditional maritime skills, prosperity in shipping depends upon an ample flow of world trade, and that the United Kingdom's position in international trade in turn depends on the strength of the economy as a whole, on the development of the resources of the Commonwealth and on the strength of sterling as an international currency. The future prosperity of British shipping calls for not only a sound shipping policy, applied with skill and determination, but also an expanding world economy which it is the aim of our commercial policy as a whole to foster. The promotion of the principles of free trade in shipping is, in itself, a valuable contribution to the maintenance and the expansion of world trade.

CHAPTER IV

Shipping Operations

Trooping and Service Cargo Movements —
Planning for Military Movement in War —
General War Planning — War Risks Insurance
— Emigration — The Western Highlands and
Islands of Scotland — The Adequacy of Shipping
Services

*

THE extent to which the Ministry engages in the actual business of
shipping, though very great in war-time, is not large in times of peace.
But even then, despite the desire to give the industry as much freedom
as possible, the Ministry finds itself involved in some shipping operations; first, through the Government's obligation to see that adequate and satisfactory arrangements are made for the movement of
the Armed Forces and their families all over the world, as well as
of their equipment and stores; second, because there are certain
planning responsibilities to be discharged against a future emergency;
and third, because there is an important role for the Government to
play—though seldom a direct operational one—in seeing that suitable shipping services, both passenger and cargo, are available to
support the trade of the Commonwealth, especially the import and
export trades of the United Kingdom, and for accommodating the
constant flow of passengers to and from all British territories.

TROOPING AND SERVICE CARGO MOVEMENTS

The need for an organisation to arrange the movement by sea of
the men and supplies of the Armed Forces has been felt since the
days of Cromwell and has become more and more important as
British responsibilities overseas have grown with the years. The duty
of providing shipping for these movements was undertaken at first
by Special Commissions or Boards and later by the Admiralty. The
transfer of this work to the Ministry of Shipping in the First World
War, then to the Board of Trade and so to the present Ministry has
already been described in Chapter II. The present arrangement has
its advantages; in peace-time it concentrates the task in a Ministry
in daily contact with the shipping industry and with the constantly

changing phases of the freight market. In war-time it ensures that Service movement by sea in merchant ships is controlled by a Department which has control of all shipping and so can secure its most efficient and economical use in meeting the various demands made upon it, whether civil or military. Further, the Department is not itself a bidder for shipping space and has no interest except to secure the utmost service from the ships at its disposal.

One of the most difficult problems of the Ministry and the Service Departments in peace-time is to estimate the volume of movements of personnel for periods ahead and to divide them between sea and air and so to decide on the size of the troopship and aircraft fleets to be provided. Arrangements have to be made for formed units, for drafts of various sizes or for individuals: in peace-time the units are normally of battalion strength, but at times of international crisis much larger units may have to be moved. Service cargo includes goods of every kind, provisions, clothing, medical supplies, engineer's stores, ammunition, tanks, guns, lorries, bulldozers, mobile cranes and many other types of vehicle as well as tugs, lighters and launches. Following the principles of shipping policy outlined in the previous chapter, commercial shipping is used as much as possible, and passages for individuals can usually be booked in ships on commercial voyages. But it is not possible, even in peace-time, for most of the servicemen and their families to be moved by commercial passenger ships on their normal voyages. This is partly because there are so many people to be moved on the main trooping routes and partly because some of the troops have to be moved as complete units. The Department therefore controls a fleet of specially fitted troopships, all of them having cabin accommodation for the officers, warrant officers and families, and dormitories, fitted with standee bunks[1] for other ranks. But the Department does not attempt to manage or operate ships itself. The normal practice for very many years has been to charter troopships from passenger shipping lines specially skilled in this trade and to leave the owners to run the ships. Even when the ships are Government-owned—which has happened for special reasons caused by the Second War—they are handed over to experienced shipowners to manage and operate. And when a new troopship is required it is the practice of the Department to enter into a long-term charter with a shipping company selected by tendering. The company arranges for a ship to be built to comply with the Department's trooping requirements as agreed with the Services.

Despite this established practice of delegation, the task of con-

---

[1] Tubular hinged steel bedframes with spring bottoms, fitted on either side of central pillars and supported by chains. They can be folded away. Usually they are three berths high.

trolling the trooping fleet is still a heavy one. The present fleet, though reduced since the war in step with the Services' contracting requirements, still totals 110,000 gross tons and includes *Dilwara*, *Dunera* and other ships whose names will be familiar to servicemen and their families who have served overseas during and since the war, as well as three short-sea troopships operating between this country and the Continent. The latest additions to the fleet are *Nevasa* and *Oxfordshire*, which are particularly fine vessels. Altogether the outgoings for maintaining and operating this fleet are something like £6 million a year. Much of the work can be done only at the ports and the Ministry has offices at the main trooping ports in this country and abroad, staffed by men appointed as Sea Transport Officers who have had sea-going experience, usually in the Merchant Navy, and who are the link at the ports between the Department at Headquarters, the Service Departments and the shipping companies operating the troopships. Abroad, these Sea Transport Officers, besides looking after the interests of troopships and any cargo ships and tankers taken up for military requirements, have to book passages for Government-sponsored passengers and arrange for the movement of service cargo from their area. In the United Kingdom the Ministry's staff of surveyors supervises the initial fitting or the modification of troopships and checks their upkeep. There are Stores depots at home and abroad, in or near the principal trooping ports, to hold and issue stores and equipment required for trooping and for the handling of service cargo. Some of these things are specialised, such as trays for ammunition and slings for very heavy and awkward cargo, but some are very ordinary, such as bedding and blankets, which together comprise one of the largest of the requirements.

Service cargo can usually be moved in peace-time by commercial shipping. In booking space, which involves detailed negotiations with shipping companies, and in calling forward cargo from Service depots, the Department is helped in the United Kingdom by specially appointed freight agents. But often the movement of service cargo presents the Department with difficulties—particularly in the case of large and awkward vehicles and of ammunition and other dangerous goods. For some vehicles, like tanks, special handling gear is designed by the Ministry, bought and stored in the depots and issued to the shipping company when the vehicles are shipped. In the Mediterranean and Far East, it is difficult to obtain tonnage commercially for many of the local movement tasks and seven landing ships (L.S.T.s) and two other vessels are therefore run by the Ministry to ferry vehicles between military stations in those areas.

PLANNING FOR MILITARY MOVEMENT IN WAR

These are some of the peace-time tasks of the Division of the Ministry whose most important function is to be the nucleus of the very large organisation needed in war to deal with the transport overseas of the Armed Forces and their equipment and supplies. Equally, the troopships, which in peace transport men and their families all over the world, are in war or other emergency the ideal ships in which to mount an operation. They are designed to carry large numbers of troops and can rapidly be converted to carry still larger numbers in the more austere conditions of war-time. In addition, they can carry, or can be readily fitted to carry, landing craft to get the troops ashore at their operational destination. In extensive operations they must be supplemented by passenger ships taken from their regular employment, as they were in the two World Wars when many ships—including the two 'Queens' in the Second War—were converted into troopships. In the more recent Suez crisis, by a fortunate chance there were seven troopships in near waters at the critical time and it was possible to mount the operation without taking up any commercial passenger ships.

The Suez operation can be used to illustrate in miniature the functions of the Department in war-time in relation to the Armed Forces. (The part played by the air, which has added a new factor of mobility in the movement of troops—but not of their equipment or supplies—is not examined here. The major burden of transporting both troops and supplies fell on ships.) In very simplified terms the problem was to transport to the scene of action complete units of men with their light equipment and, at the same time, to carry for them their heavy equipment—tanks, tank transporters, guns, vehicles and the like—their food, their stores and the fuel for their vehicles. All these, men, stores and equipment, had to be shipped in such a way as to be available at the proper place, at the right time, in the right order and with the necessary facilities to get them all ashore. For the transport of the troops the troopships were used, but for the equipment and stores it was necessary to requisition cargo ships —that is, to take them on time-charter compulsorily for the use of the Government. Altogether, 76 ships—ranging from large ocean-going cargo ships to coasting ships and small tankers for petrol and also for water—were taken up for this small operation.

So far as the Department is concerned a military operation falls into two parts, carried out by different people. The first is the planning and mounting of the operation itself, in which members of the Department are intimately concerned with the Military authorities. No military plan involving transport overseas is of any practical value unless it has been worked out in conjunction with the authorities who know the shipping possibilities and limitations, the way to prepare the ships for their operational tasks and, finally, how to plan and supervise the proper loading and operation of the ships. This lesson was fully learned only by experience in the last war, and it is of vital importance not to forget it. The second problem is to choose and to prepare a register of available shipping and then to take under control the ships needed for the operation, a task needing wide knowledge and great tact and discretion. For this, as for help in the work of planning and mounting the operation, the Ministry is able to call on friends in the shipping industry, many of whom worked in the Department throughout the war.

GENERAL WAR PLANNING

Planning for the movement by sea of military forces and their equipment is not the only responsibility of the Department in war planning. It has also to make plans for its main task, which would be to exercise control in war over all British shipping. During the Second War the whole of the ocean-going shipping of the free world was controlled by the United Kingdom and the United States of America and was regarded as a single pool of ships directed from two centres, London and Washington, to be used for the common purposes of the war effort as a whole—and this included supplying the needs of neutrals also. The world had to be fed and supplied with raw materials and finished goods for civilian consumption and for warlike purposes. Towards the end of the war when Western and Northern Europe was freed from occupation, each country took its own ships under its own control usually by taking over the time-charters from the United Kingdom Government, but left them in the common pool for allocation to employment by an international organisation.[1] That is the pattern envisaged for any further conflict and worked out by an organ of the North Atlantic Treaty Organization, the Planning Board for Ocean Shipping, of which the Permanent Secretary of the Ministry and the Federal Maritime Administrator of the United States of America are joint chairmen.

The threat of nuclear warfare has posed new problems to the Planning Board, as to the rest of the NATO organisation, and has called for elaborate plans for devolution of authority in the early stages. But it has not altered the basic conception that all ships should be used, irrespective of flag, to the best advantage for the

[1] For a full account of these war-time problems, see Miss C. B. A. Behrens: *Merchant Shipping and the Demands of War, History of the Second World War* (Civil Series) (H.M.S.O.).

common good of the free world as a whole. The Department has taken, and is taking, a leading part in the planning of broad policy and of detailed operations to this end.

WAR RISKS INSURANCE

The subject of war risks insurance will serve as an example of the sort of detailed planning that has to be undertaken. British ships are insured by their owners against war risks by entering them in a shipowners' Mutual War Risks Association. The Associations, usually known as Clubs, are, in effect, mutual insurance organisations. There are 13 such Associations, which between them cover almost the whole of the British mercantile marine. Nine deal with deep-sea liners, tankers and tramps, two with coasting vessels and the other two with fishing vessels. Each Association, among other things, holds its members indemnified against war risks, and in peace-time funds to meet claims are collected from members in proportion to the tonnage of the ships entered in the Association. In peace the war risks covered by the Associations are, of course, small—virtually only the risk of a British ship becoming involved in a conflict between two foreign powers, or of loss or damage from mines laid during previous wars. When this country is at war, however, it is quite different. The losses to be faced are such that the Mutual Associations could not bear them without charging very heavy and fluctuating premiums, which might well hamper the owners in operating their ships even to the extent of making them reluctant to send them to sea at all. To meet this situation and to ensure that ships remain at sea and not in port, the Government, under the Marine and Aviation Insurance (War Risks) Act, 1952, as under previous similar Acts, undertake to provide the Associations with reinsurance. No elaborate machinery for issuing policies and handling claims is needed because the reinsurance arrangements enable the Government to make full use of the machinery of the Mutual Associations, and the full co-operation of the Associations in examining claims is secured by leaving them with a financial interest in the insurance. Under the Ministry's agreements with the Associations a 95 per cent reinsurance is provided if the United Kingdom is at war, in return for which the Ministry takes 95 per cent of the premiums chargeable for the original insurance, the rates of premium being determined by the Ministry. The values at which ships may be insured are controlled by the Ministry and the reinsurance Agreements provide a convenient additional means for ensuring that ships comply with Government orders in war-time in that the original policies of the Associations, which are reinsured by the Ministry, embody warranties that all Government orders on such matters, for example, as routeing and ports of call, must be complied with. Another important stipulation of the reinsurance arrangements is that owners recover in cash only 80 per cent of the insured value of a vessel lost, the remaining 20 per cent being credited to the owners' account in what is known as a Government Tonnage Replacement Account, which is released only against evidence of expenditure on replacement of lost tonnage.

War risks insurance cover must also be available in war for foreign ships operating in the allied cause where complete cover cannot be provided by their own Governments. In the last war, this was done through the Government War Risks Insurance Office which was set up at the outbreak of war primarily for the purpose of insuring cargoes. The whole of the allied tonnage which was operating in the interests of this country was insured or reinsured by the Ministry, and, in addition, quite a lot of neutral tonnage was induced to operate in the allied cause by the offer, among other considerations, of war risks insurance.

Cargoes are, of course, insured by the owners of the cargo and not by shipowners. In peace-time cargoes are covered against war risks (unless the owner elects to carry his own risk) at Lloyd's or with Insurance Companies. In war-time, market premium rates are liable to fluctuate violently with the risk at a particular time and to rise to a level which hampers trade. This is why in the First World War and again in the Second the situation had to be met by the establishment of the Government War Risks Insurance Office. This office, as is mentioned above, also insured foreign ships and was able, because of the immense spread of its risks, to insure cargoes and ships at a reasonable premium.

Just as it was necessary in the last war to reinsure foreign ships against war risks, so it might happen again. Accordingly, as a precautionary measure, an agreement was made in May, 1954, with the Norwegian Government under the powers given by the Marine and Aviation Insurance (War Risks) Act, 1952, by virtue of which Norwegian ships would be reinsured by the United Kingdom Government against war risks arising in any war or other hostilities (for example collective United Nations action) in which the United Kingdom and Norway were both engaged. Reinsurance, which in any event is given only to the extent of 80 per cent of the original insurance, is conditional upon all the ships obeying instructions issued under the authority of the United Kingdom or Allied Governments and upon no voyage being made to enemy territory. The agreement also provides that the values of the ships for insurance purposes shall be calculated in sterling and shall not be higher than the values of comparable British ships. An agreement on similar lines was made in March, 1957, with the Danish Government. In certain circumstances the reinsurance provided in the agreements can be replaced by direct insurance.

EMIGRATION

Turning now to the third aspect of the Ministry's operational responsibilities in the field of shipping—that is the general oversight of the facilities available—the subject of emigration may be mentioned first. Since the war the Ministry has been actively concerned in assisting the movement of emigrants to Australia and New Zealand under the schemes for assisted passages introduced by the Governments of these countries. For some years after the war there was a shortage of passenger ships, mainly because of war losses, and the Ministry adapted some ships, which were not at the time needed for trooping, as emigrant ships. By the end of 1949, 13 passenger ships were employed in this way. Although they were owned by, or were on charter to, the Ministry, the ships were managed and operated, in accordance with the Department's policy, by specially appointed shipping companies. Between 1948 and 1953 some 150,000 emigrants were carried to Australia and New Zealand in these ships. On their homeward voyages the ships were sometimes used for other purposes, one of the most interesting being the repatriation of Dutch subjects from Indonesia after the grant of self-government there. The net costs of the emigrant voyages were met by the Australian and New Zealand Governments, who were given credit for all subsidiary earnings. When the number of emigrants fell, the size of this passenger fleet was reduced, and at the time of writing only two ships remain in the service.

THE WESTERN HIGHLANDS AND ISLANDS OF SCOTLAND

Another special example of the Ministry's close interest in particular routes is provided in the case of the services between the Western Highlands and Islands of Scotland run for over a hundred years by Messrs David MacBrayne Ltd. After his journey to the Western Islands in 1773 Doctor Johnson wrote 'The great business of insular policy is now to keep the people in their own country'. This is still true. Paradoxically, one of the measures most likely to keep people where they are is to give them good transport, and successive Governments have recognised that if the outlying communities are to survive they must have their shipping links maintained. The services are uneconomic because of the small amount of traffic moving compared with the distances involved and the large number of calls to be made. The Government therefore subsidise Messrs MacBrayne to help them to maintain a network of specified services at fares and freight rates which the economy of the area can bear. Two Departments come into the arrangements, apart from the General Post Office who pay for the carriage of mails. The Scottish Home Department bears the cost of the subsidy and is chiefly responsible for determining the nature of the services to be provided and the level of fares and freights to be charged; the Ministry of Transport and Civil Aviation acts as the agent and negotiates the agreements with the Company. This arrangement has the advantage of bringing experience of transport finance and economics to bear on the financial terms of the contract; but, from the selfish Departmental point of view, it has the disadvantage of laying open two lines of attack to Highlanders and Islanders who wish for cheaper and more frequent services—a desire not unknown elsewhere—or who may be otherwise dissatisfied with the services provided. It is of the essence of the relationship created by the contracts with the Ministry that the Company shall be able to act as independently as possible and the contracts themselves are drawn in such a way as to provide financial incentives to efficient and economical working.

THE ADEQUACY OF SHIPPING SERVICES

Apart from its interest in these special services the Ministry keeps in close touch with exporters and importers on the one hand and shipowners on the other. Most Government Departments which do a good deal of business abroad, for example, the Ministry of Supply, and the Crown Agents for Oversea Governments and Administrations, make their own shipping arrangements, but from time to time, especially when ships are scarce and freight rates high, as they were during the Korean war, the Ministry is asked to help in obtaining the right sort of ships—whether liner, tramp or tanker—and to advise on the freight or charter rates to be paid. Even in times when shipping space is easier to get, it sometimes happens that shippers are not satisfied that the services between certain ports are good enough or that the freight rates charged for certain commodities are reasonable. On occasion the Ministry is told that if only there were better shipping opportunities, or if lower freights could be quoted, additional business, especially export business, could be gained. It is always difficult to test the validity of these assertions. And there is of course no way of influencing tramp or tanker charter rates, which follow the world market alone. Liners are in a different position since they provide a continuous and regular service between fixed points. Liner companies usually work together in Conference and shippers have organisations which can negotiate with them on these matters. Conferences are organisations, usually international, of the shipping companies serving ports in the same areas who have agreed to even out sailings so as to make adequate and regular provision for the needs of the traffic and to stabilise freight rates and passenger fares in the form of tariff rates, which apply to all the ships in the Conference. Experience has shown that the Conference system is beneficial to shipper and shipowner alike; to the former it provides regular services on which he can rely at reasonable rates which he knows are the same as those quoted by the Conference to his competitors, and to the shipowner an economic basis for his operations. A number of inquiries, including the Royal Commission on Shipping Rings of 1909, have in general reported favourably on the system and it has the general support of the Government. But not all inquirers are satisfied customers and in many situations the Ministry finds itself acting as 'honest broker' between the competing claims.

CHAPTER V

Marine Safety

The Merchant Shipping Acts — The International
Aspect of Safety at Sea — The Marine Survey
Service — Passenger Ships — Cargo Ships —
Tonnage Measurement and Registration —
Approved Appliances — Dangerous Cargoes —
Radio and Aids to Navigation — Courts of
Inquiry — Safety off the Shore — The Coast-
guard Service — Lighthouses and Pilotage —
— Wreck and Foreshores — Oil Pollution —
Some Developments in the Years to Come

*

SINCE 1850 the safety of British ships and all who sail in them has
been increasingly the concern of the Government and such disasters
of recent years as those in which *Princess Victoria* and the troopship
Empire Windrush were lost are sufficient reminders that the task remains unending. Yet the achievement of the last hundred years is
no mean one. The number of lives lost at sea from casualties to
British ships in the 1850's was nearly 2,000 every year. Apart from
1953, when the loss of the *Princess Victoria* brought the casualty roll
for the year up to 233, the number of lives lost from casualties to
United Kingdom ships averaged no more than 71 over six years
1952–57, with five times as much shipping on the Register.

THE MERCHANT SHIPPING ACTS

The legal foundations of marine safety are contained in the Merchant Shipping Acts, 'except for the Finance Acts, probably the
most complicated body of legislation devoted to a single subject
matter'.[1] These began effectively with the Mercantile Marine Act of
1850, were consolidated in the Merchant Shipping Act of 1894, and
have been frequently extended and amended since. They cover,
besides safety matters, standards of competence and certain conditions of employment for the masters, officers and crews—the subject of the next chapter—as well as other more picturesque details,
such as the powers of Receivers of Wreck to commandeer waggons,
carts and horses, and the extent of a shipowner's liability for the

[1] Preface to Temperley's *Merchant Shipping Acts* (5th edition, 1954).

loss of a cargo of 'jewels or precious stones'. The greater part of the Acts is concerned with the safety of life at sea and involves the fundamental principles that the owner of every British ship sent to sea is responsible for keeping her seaworthy and that a ship is not to be considered seaworthy by a surveyor unless she is sound in hull, equipment and machinery, is adequately manned and is not over-loaded or improperly loaded. The Acts permit the Minister to make Rules on nearly every aspect of marine safety, on construction, load line and loading, life-saving and fire appliances and radio. They also contain provisions on the rule of the road at sea, lighthouses, sea-marks, pilotage, wreck and salvage.

The factors which have influenced the growth of this legislation are three: first, the pressure of public opinion, which reached its peak in the Plimsoll agitation of 1870–80, that the Government should assume more responsibility for the safety of ships; second, the use of new materials and of new methods in shipbuilding and the continuous development of marine engineering, all of which present their own problems of safety; and third, the trend, which has been so marked in the present century, towards establishing international standards of safety for the ships of all nations. The first two factors are largely self-evident, though the details of the second are absorbing in themselves and some recent developments, particularly those affecting the work of the navigator, will be touched upon later. The third factor—the international aspect of safety at sea—is more complex.

THE INTERNATIONAL ASPECT OF SAFETY AT SEA

The Merchant Shipping Act, 1894, is the most comprehensive piece of marine legislation in the world. But clearly it was unreasonable that British ships should be subject to such comprehensive requirements while less was expected of ships of other nations. So the Merchant Shipping Act of 1906 applied our own safety regulations to foreign ships when in our ports, but it was realised that international agreement to apply safety measures to ships of all nations at sea and in ports all over the world ought to take the place of such limited unilateral action. The trend towards international agreement is first visible in the United Kingdom Collision Regulations of 1910. Before these came into force the United Kingdom had secured the separate agreement of 30 countries that each would regard its ships as subject to them when meeting British ships at sea. The 1910 Regulations—which were our own domestic code—thereafter became recognised by all countries as the standard international code and remained so in this rather informal way until quite recently. Two years later, in 1912, the tragic loss of *Titanic* after collision with an iceberg led to the first International Conference on the Safety of Life at Sea. The Conference was held in London in 1913 and most maritime nations sent representatives to it. War broke out in the following year, and the resulting Convention was not ratified, but the North Atlantic Ice Patrol, which came into being in 1920 as a result of the Conference, has ever since helped to protect ships from the danger to which *Titanic* succumbed. This disaster also resulted in the acceptance of the principle of 'lifeboats for all' for passenger ships on long international voyages and—what was even more important—in the institution of a continuous wireless watch either by operator or by auto-alarm to make sure that no call for help would go unheeded.

In 1929 the second International Conference was held in London and drew up the first effective International Convention for the Safety of Life at Sea laying down standards for such vital matters as watertight subdivision below the strength deck, fire-resisting bulkheads in the superstructure, life-saving appliances and fire-fighting equipment of passenger ships, and radio requirements for cargo ships of 1,600 gross tons and over and all passenger ships. Much of this embodied the statutory requirements already in force in this country. This Convention and the International Convention respecting Load Lines of 1930, which laid down rules for the calculation of freeboard and allied matters, was given effect here by the Merchant Shipping (Safety and Load Line Conventions) Act, 1932.

By the end of the last war, it had become clear that the 1929 Convention needed revision. Much that was new in shipbuilding and marine engineering, as well as the experience gained in the working of the 1929 Convention itself, required careful study, and in 1948 the third International Conference met, once more in London, to produce a new Convention.

The preparatory work for the 1948 Conference affords a good illustration of one of the ways in which policy is formulated as well as of the close co-operation which exists between the Ministry and all those in this country who are concerned with ships and shipping. The first steps were taken in the Department collating all the provisions and requirements of the 1929 Convention which ought to be considered to see whether they required revision. Proposals were formulated, drafts of new provisions and amendments to old ones were prepared and then the industry were asked for help. They gave it in full measure. Shipowners and their staffs, the Classification Societies, shipbuilders, representatives of seagoing officers and men, other Government Departments and the rest worked for months,

E

each in the sphere in which he had special knowledge, to produce the British idea of what the new Convention should be. The result was that the United Kingdom delegation went into the Conference with a fully agreed and carefully worked out policy on all the matters coming up for discussion. The Conference, though the subjects were dealt with concurrently by six Committees, lasted for seven weeks of concentrated work—a clear enough indication of the calls which had been made upon the time and the goodwill of those who had helped the Department in laying the foundations for its deliberations, and the Convention that emerged conformed very closely with the proposals made by the British delegation. Co-operation of this kind is of inestimable value in producing sound, workable and far-reaching agreements on matters of international, as well as of national, concern, and the Department have every reason to be grateful for the unstinting help they receive from their friends in the industry.

The resulting Convention includes new standards for passenger ships, notably in structural fire protection, and extends many of its requirements to cargo ships. For example, cargo ships engaged in international trading must now undergo a survey of their life-saving and fire appliances at least every two years. The radio requirements are also extended to cargo ships down to 500 gross tons and agreement was reached on the first truly international Collision Regulations modifying those which were introduced by this country in 1910 and which had for nearly 40 years been generally accepted as law throughout the world. The Convention has been made effective for United Kingdom ships by the Merchant Shipping (Safety Convention) Act, 1949, and its subordinate Rules.

The work arising from the Convention has not ended with the application of its measures to United Kingdom ships or to ships in United Kingdom ports. The initiative in calling the International Safety and Load Line Conferences from 1913 onwards has always lain with this country, and the successive Conventions largely reflect British marine practice. One result is that the United Kingdom has been entrusted with the administration of the International Conventions, though this particular task will end when the Intergovernmental Maritime Consultative Organisation, referred to in Chapter III, takes over. Until then the Ministry remains responsible for the bureau work of the Conventions, for accepting and promulgating ratifications, reports, suggestions and other communications from member countries. Forty-seven countries are members of the Safety Convention and 60 of the Load Line Convention and there are very few maritime nations, on either side of the Iron Curtain, that are not included.

THE MARINE SURVEY SERVICE

The making of the law is one thing, its application another; and the success of the Ministry's work in administering the numerous provisions of the Merchant Shipping Acts and the International Conventions depends to a very great extent on the competence and energy of its 250 Marine Surveyors, who, among other powers and duties, may inspect any ship, British or foreign, in United Kingdom ports and detain any unseaworthy vessel. Some Surveyors serve as advisers at Headquarters; foremost among them are the heads of the three branches into which the Survey Service is divided, the Professional Officer (Chief Nautical Surveyor), the Engineer Surveyor-in-Chief and the Chief Ship Surveyor (a naval architect). The main body of Surveyors is stationed in the ports of the United Kingdom; it is they who carry out the practical day-to-day survey work. For administrative purposes they are organised in nine districts—London, Southampton, Cardiff, Liverpool, Glasgow, Hull, Newcastle, Leith and Belfast—each district under a Principal Officer who is himself responsible to Headquarters. To a considerable degree the duties of Surveyors are common to all three branches of the service but specialised knowledge is also necessary. For example the Nautical Surveyors, each of whom has held command of a foreign-going merchant ship and holds an Extra Master's certificate, have the duty of inspecting ships' navigational aids, manning, life-saving appliances, navigation lights and sound signals, and stowage of cargo. The special responsibility of the Engineer Surveyors, who have all been at sea, and all of whom hold the Extra First Class Engineer's Certificate or equivalent qualifications, is the soundness of a passenger ship's engines, winches, steering gear, anchors and cables and electrical and fire-fighting equipment. The Ship Surveyors, who are naval architects with experience of designing and building ships, see that the hulls and superstructure are sound, stable and seaworthy, that load lines are assigned and tonnage measured, that passenger ships are subdivided against flooding and fire and that life-saving appliances are constructed properly.

PASSENGER SHIPS

For reasons of public safety, the law on the survey of passenger ships (defined as ships carrying more than twelve passengers) is much more stringent than the law for cargo ships. Not only must passenger ships, like other ships, comply with the rules for life-saving appliances, fire appliances, radio and load line but precise requirements are also laid down for their construction. The ship has to be divided into a number of watertight compartments which will retain their buoyancy even if others are holed. She must also, if engaged on international or cross-channel voyages, have main fireproof bulkheads at intervals of not more than 131 feet (40 metres) together with an automatic fire detection and alarm system and must either be fitted with sprinklers or must have additional fireproof bulkheads and accept restrictions in the use of combustible fittings and furnishings.

The Ministry's survey of the passenger ship begins with the plans, even before the keel plates are laid on the slipway, and goes on until almost the day on which she starts out on her maiden voyage. Thereafter, a survey is carried out each year of her life, apart from any other inspections which a Surveyor may consider to be necessary, and it is only after each survey that the Certificates which allow the ship to sail can be issued by the Department. These are the Passenger Certificate, stating the greatest number of passengers that may be carried and the limits within which the ship may ply, and, if she is engaged on international voyages, a Safety Certificate testifying that the requirements of the 1948 Convention are complied with. This Certificate is accepted by other Governments which are parties to the Convention as evidence of compliance with Convention requirements on the safety of ships.

The problems which crop up in dealing with passenger ships are refreshingly various. There are always instances where a passenger liner may not exactly comply with every detail of one or other of the Rules on construction and the case for exemption by the Minister must be argued. Again, a Company may wish to carry local stevedoring labour on board between, say, some of the ports on the West African coast. Does this infringe the terms of the passenger certificate? A nautical school charters a ship in which to send cadets on a training cruise. The boys may be paying a fee and yet at the same time be helping to man the vessel. Are they passengers or crew? A trawler is seen taking more than 12 persons on a day trip: is she a passenger ship and should proceedings therefore be instituted? Many such problems of great diversity arise and must be settled from day to day.

CARGO SHIPS

The survey which matters most to a cargo ship is the annual survey for load line, the requirements for which are laid down by statute. Unlike the passenger survey, which in the United Kingdom is always carried out by the Ministry, the load line survey of most cargo ships is carried out under delegated powers by one of the classification societies, Lloyd's Register, the British Committee of Bureau Veritas and the British Technical Committee of the American Bureau of Shipping, whose main function is to class ships for insurance. The load line, sometimes popularly known as the 'Plimsoll Mark', consists of a series of lines, cut into the ship's sides and painted, to indicate the depth to which she may be loaded according to the season, the geographical zone and the density of the water. The load line certificate, besides recording the measurements of freeboard, testifies that the vessel's hull is soundly constructed. A more extensive survey takes place every five years. There is also an annual radio survey for cargo ships and, following the 1948 Safety Convention, the two-yearly survey of safety equipment, that is of lifeboats, liferafts and fire appliances. These surveys are both made by Government Surveyors.

TONNAGE MEASUREMENT AND REGISTRATION

The Ministry's Surveyors also measure ships for tonnage. Tonnage figures are calculated according to rules laid down in the Merchant Shipping Acts; first for gross tonnage, which may be described as the total cubic capacity of the vessel in units of 100 cubic feet, and second for net tonnage, which is broadly the gross figure less the figure for all the spaces which do not earn revenue. Many ships are also measured according to the different rules for the Suez Canal and for the Panama Canal. The figures for gross and net tonnage according to British rules are then registered along with the dimensions and other particulars of the ship at the office of the Registrar-General of Shipping and Seamen, of which more will be said in the next chapter. This formal act of registration has two important effects, first it provides proof of the vessel's title to be a British ship, and therefore to the enjoyment of all the privileges which attach to that title, and, second, it constitutes legal evidence of ownership and of the size of the ship, from which the dues and charges borne by the ship for the upkeep of lighthouses and the use of docks are calculated. Lastly, registration is of value to the Government in that it contributes to a precise record of the nation's shipping.

APPROVED APPLIANCES

Much work is devoted to testing and formally approving the numerous products of manufacturers which have to satisfy the requirements of the Merchant Shipping Acts—engineering components, fire-resisting bulkheads, hatchways, lifeboats and their equipment, and so on. When an item is submitted for approval for the first time it usually has to be subjected to tests witnessed by the Ministry's survey staff or on behalf of the Ministry by the National Physical Laboratory or some other part of the Department of Scientific and Industrial Research. If it is found to be satisfactory the Ministry issues a certificate or a formal letter of approval. Surveyors and shipowners are then advised.

DANGEROUS CARGOES

The safety of a ship may depend not only on the correct stowage of her cargo to maintain stability but also on the handling and stowage of particular kinds of cargo which may be dangerous either in themselves or by reason of their proximity to other kinds of cargo. For this reason the Department regulates the carriage of certain cargoes which need to be treated with special care. The statutory rules for packing and stowing dangerous goods are supplemented by the detailed advice given in the Report of the Minister's Advisory Committee on the Carriage of Dangerous Goods and Explosives in Ships—known throughout the shipping industry of most maritime countries as the 'Blue Book'. This document is continually being revised and expanded to cover more and more substances. The most dangerous types of cargo, such as certain explosives and phosphorus and sulphuric acid, are normally not permitted at all in ships with more than 25 passengers. But even a cargo innocuous in itself can be a serious source of danger; for example, a ship may be capsized in a heavy sea by timber shifting on her decks or loose grain or coal in her holds. Special Regulations and recommendations are therefore issued for stowing safely cargoes of this kind.

RADIO AND AIDS TO NAVIGATION

The importance of radio to safe navigation needs no emphasis. The International Conferences since 1913 have paid much attention to the subject and, since it first became compulsory for British ships in 1920, radio has probably been responsible for saving more lives at sea than any other single device. It is by radio that distress calls and messages are sent and received, it is by the auto-alarm that ships not keeping continuous watch are alerted to receive distress calls, and it is by the direction-finder that a ship is able to plot her position by means of radio waves received from radio beacons at fixed points on the coast or to find a ship in distress by homing upon her radio signals. The installation and maintenance of all this equipment is subject to survey by officers of the General Post Office who are appointed as Radio Surveyors under the Merchant Shipping Acts.

It is of interest to remember that the requirements for the efficiency of the apparatus and for watch-keeping and the use of the auto-alarm are imposed primarily so that a ship shall be in a position to help other ships and only secondarily for the benefit of the ship herself.

An increasing amount of other navigational equipment, such as echo-sounding machines, radar equipment and devices to fix a ship's position, is being carried in ships voluntarily, and the Department took a leading part in adapting these new inventions for the use of the Merchant Navy. The Ministry's Scientific Research Group at the Admiralty Signal and Radar Establishment developed an all-purpose radar equipment suitable for merchant ships and on this prototype was based a specification and a set of performance standards which the Department recommended that all Merchant Navy radar equipment should meet. This specification and its successors have been accepted as a yard-stick, and manufacturers now voluntarily submit specimen models of their new radar sets to the Ministry's scientists to be tested against the current standards; if a set meets the specification, a Certificate of Type-Testing is issued. The scientists have also developed radar reflectors, which greatly improve the radar response from buoys and other marks which define shipping channels, and radar beacons which are radar's equivalent of a lighthouse.

Apart from radar, a number of radio systems were developed during the war to help navigators to establish their position. One of these is the Decca Navigator, one of the early exploits of which was to play a vital part on D-Day by giving the ships which were to make the artificial harbour their exact positions so that they could sink themselves just where they were required. The device was at the same time being used to assist in controlling the invasion fleet in the English Channel. It was this system which the Ministry decided could best be adapted for peace-time Merchant Navy needs. In its present form, it enables a navigator to plot his ship's position on a special chart with a high degree of accuracy at distances of up to 240 miles from the transmitting stations. The effectiveness of the cover depends upon the correct siting of the radio 'chains', as they are called, and the Ministry, besides advising the operating company on the siting, has carried out trials to determine the accuracy and reliability of the system. Supervision of its working is a continuing task if the navigator is at all times to be able to rely implicitly on the accuracy of the information with which his Decca Navigator receiver provides him.

Despite these new aids collisions at sea still happen, sometimes between two ships both of which are fitted with radar. It is very true that, great as are the benefits which modern devices can confer on the navigator, they have not replaced good seamanship as the most important factor in safe navigation at sea. However efficient his radar and however well trained he may be in its use—a Certificate of Proficiency as Radar Observer, obtained after attendance at an officially approved course, is now a compulsory qualification for a Certificate of Competency as Second Mate (foreign-going) or Mate (home trade)—the prudent seaman navigates his ship in strict conformity with the International Regulations for Preventing Collisions at Sea using his new devices as aids in doing so.

COURTS OF INQUIRY

Notwithstanding all the precautions which are described in this chapter, ships still fall victims to the hazards of violent weather, of faulty navigation or loading, or of fire. When a ship is lost or damaged from any cause it is the responsibility of the Ministry to decide whether the casualty warrants an inquiry and, if so, to see that it is carried out. Preliminary Inquiries into all casualties and accidents of any significance are made either by a surveyor of the Ministry or by a chief officer of customs. The officer holding the inquiry examines all the evidence available to him, takes depositions from those whose information may throw light upon the cause of the casualty, and reports to the Minister. The Minister then decides whether the public interest requires that a Formal Investigation shall be held. Formal Investigations in England and Wales are usually held by courts presided over by a Wreck Commissioner, who is selected in rotation from three Queen's Counsel at the Admiralty Bar appointed by the Lord Chancellor. The Commissioners are assisted by Assessors with nautical, engineering or other technical qualifications appointed from a panel maintained by the Home Secretary. Formal Investigations can also be held in magistrates' courts in England, Wales and Northern Ireland and are in fact held in Sheriffs' courts in Scotland, again with the assistance of Assessors. The court holds its hearings in public and all individuals and parties interested in the court's findings may be legally represented. Courts of Formal Investigation are empowered to cancel or suspend Certificates of Competency of Masters and Ships' Officers and their reports are published. Appeals from their decisions in England and in Northern Ireland lie to the High Court and in Scotland to the Court of Session.

For the investigation of boiler explosions the procedure is rather different. In the first place the Minister's jurisdiction extends not only to explosions on board British ships but also, under the Boiler

Explosions Act of 1882, to those occurring in factories and other establishments on land. Reports from Preliminary Inquiries have to be published and, if a Formal Investigation is ordered, the Court must consist of at least two Commissioners, one a lawyer and one a practical engineer 'specially conversant with the manufacture and working of steam boilers', but there are no assessors.

The findings of all these courts are studied with great care and, as necessary, the Ministry issues advice in the form of notices and memoranda, and makes Regulations or promotes legislation aimed at preventing similar casualties in future.

SAFETY OFF THE SHORE—
THE COASTGUARD SERVICE

In securing the safety of ships a vital part is played by H.M. Coastguard, a body with great traditions and a fine record of service for which the Ministry is now responsible. Originally the force was part of the Board of Customs and Excise, being the Board's chief weapon against smugglers. Gradually the emphasis changed to coast defence, under the control of the Admiralty, and then to life-saving, which by 1923, when control was transferred to the Board of Trade, had become the Coastguard's main responsibility. It remains so today, though the tradition of recruitment from the Royal Navy is maintained. There are now 158 regular Coastguard stations, covering the whole coast of Great Britain and Northern Ireland, manned by some 537 regular Coastguards. In addition there are some 6,400 volunteer civilian auxiliaries forming the Coast Life-Saving Corps, who man another 152 auxiliary stations and assist the regular force in emergency. The Coastguard are concerned with marine casualties in the widest sense and, besides warning ships which are running into danger and starting rescue operations when they are reported in distress, may be called on to help bathers in difficulties, aircraft that come down in the sea or foolhardy climbers who become stranded on cliffs. On occasion they may even be called on for rescue work inland, as they were during the disastrous floods in the Border counties in 1948. During rescue operations at sea they are the focal point in touch with the efforts of all those bringing assistance to the ship and, when the casualty is near to land, the Coastguard become active rescue workers using rocket line throwers and other life-saving apparatus. The Coastguard work closely with the Royal Navy and the Royal Air Force and may ask them to provide assistance in the form of search and rescue aircraft, including helicopters. There is the closest collaboration also between the Coastguard and the officers of the Royal National Lifeboat Institution, a voluntary and independent organisation, which performs a great public service in maintaining lifeboats at strategic points around the coasts of the British Isles.

LIGHTHOUSES AND PILOTAGE

In 1836 the administration of the lighthouses and other navigational warnings around the coasts of the British Isles was placed in the hands of three general lighthouse authorities—the Corporation of Trinity House (for England and Wales), the Commissioners of Northern Lighthouses (for Scotland) and the Commissioners of Irish Lights. Between them these authorities look after 341 lighthouses, 45 manned lightships and 1,041 beacons and buoys around the coasts. The Ministry approves the annual budgets of the authorities as well as their expenditure on works and, with the advice of a committee of shipowners and underwriters, fixes the scale of light dues which must be paid by British and foreign ships when they enter port in the British Isles. These light dues go into the General Lighthouse Fund, which the Department administers and out of which comes the revenue of the lighthouse authorities. The Permanent Secretary is the Accounting Officer for the Fund. In their day-to-day operations the authorities have complete freedom.

There is, in addition, a number of overseas lighthouses, which, by a series of historical accidents, the Department looks after directly. Ten of these are in the West Indies, four on the coast of Ceylon, one in the Falklands Islands, and two in the Red Sea.

The pilotage service is not directly controlled by the Government, but by various pilotage authorities throughout the British Isles. Most of the authorities cover a single port or estuary but the Corporation of Trinity House is an exception covering not only the very extensive London pilotage district (which stretches from London Bridge downstream, northwards to Felixstowe and southwards to Dungeness) but some 40 others in England and Wales as well. The whole system, being based on ancient custom, is complicated and diverse. Pilots are not employed by the authorities but are licensed by them, and are usually paid according to their services from the pool of pilotage charges. Their conditions of service are governed by bye-laws which are made by each authority on its own account but which need the confirmation of the Minister. In cases of dispute the Department must, therefore, undertake the responsibility, particularly where pilotage charges are concerned, of taking the final decision after hearing the interested parties—the pilotage authorities, pilots, and shipowners. It must also examine the annual accounts of the authorities before they are presented to Parliament.

WRECK AND FORESHORES

The general concern of the Ministry with the coasts extends by tradition and usage to a particular concern with wreck. Wreck includes all vessels, their equipment and cargo washed up on the shores of the United Kingdom. The local official here is the Receiver of Wreck—usually a customs officer, but appointed to that office by the Ministry. It is his duty to safeguard the respective rights of the Crown, the owners of ship and cargo, the underwriters and the salvors. When wreck is sold by the Receiver, the owners, if they can be traced, receive the proceeds after payment of an award to the salvor and the Receiver's expenses and fees. If the owners cannot be found, the balance is paid into the Exchequer or to the local Lord of the Manor if he has proved that he possesses wreck rights. The provisions of the Merchant Shipping Acts dealing with this subject have an archaic ring, but they work well and they became of great practical importance during the two wars when many wrecks were washed up on the coasts. Receivers of Wreck also have the curious duty of maintaining the Crown's right to 'Fishes Royal', a duty which may involve the irksome task of cutting up and burying the unwanted carcass of a stranded whale. The Ministry's records include a vivid telegram sent many years back when a large whale was steadily decomposing on a Scottish beach and threatening to asphyxiate the inhabitants. Dispute was going on as to the place and the cost of burial. The telegram, which might serve as a model for the settlement of urgent problems, meant, translated into more polite language than the original, 'Bury the whale; we will argue who pays later'. Even the Public Accounts Committee might approve in the special circumstances.

One of the few duties of the Department mentioned in this chapter which is not based on the Merchant Shipping Acts is the preservation of certain rights on the seashore. These are primarily the common law rights of navigation and fishing which cannot be altered except by Act of Parliament. Any proposals affecting the seashore, such as the building of piers or jetties or the laying of cables below high-water mark, and any harbour authorities' or local authorities' bye-laws which may affect navigation must be scrutinised to ensure that these rights are safeguarded. For important works, such as big harbour schemes, Parliamentary sanction is usually obtained. Problems of this kind arise also from the establishment of bombing and artillery ranges by the Service Departments and the Ministry of Supply.

OIL POLLUTION

The Department's responsibility for safeguarding our coasts today includes the prevention of pollution of the sea by oil. The Oil in Navigable Waters Act, 1922, prohibited the discharge of oil or oily water into United Kingdom territorial waters from ships or shore installations, and in 1926 the shipowners of the United Kingdom and of a number of other leading maritime countries agreed to refrain voluntarily from discharging oil within 50 miles of land. Thanks to such measures, the nuisance was not particularly serious in the years before the Second World War. But since then nearly every part of our coasts has at one time or other been polluted by oil; many seaside resorts have suffered seriously and thousands of sea birds have perished every year. The increase in the nuisance since the War is partly due to the big change to oil fuel but even more to the import of vast quantities of crude oil for refining in this country and neighbouring European countries. The washings from the cargo tanks of tankers which have carried crude oil and the oily ballast water discharged from dry-cargo ships which use tanks alternately for fuel and ballast water are the main sources of pollution. Most oils, including crude and fuel oil, persist indefinitely in the sea and may eventually drift to land even though they may have been discharged hundreds of miles out in the ocean.

In 1952 the Minister of Transport set up a Committee to recommend practical measures for preventing pollution by oil of the waters around the coasts of the United Kingdom. The Committee reported that the only entirely effective remedy would be to prohibit the discharge of persistent oils anywhere at sea by ships of any flag. This meant providing facilities ashore to take the oily residues and installing separating apparatus in many dry-cargo ships. The Committee recommended that an International Conference should be summoned to try to reach agreement on such action. Meanwhile, they recommended that United Kingdom ships should be required to refrain as far as possible from discharging persistent oils into a wide zone of the sea around the coasts of the United Kingdom. Immediately the Committee's Report was published the United Kingdom shipowners' organisations recommended that United Kingdom ships should voluntarily comply, so far as they could, with the restrictions proposed, and towards the end of 1953 H.M. Government invited maritime countries to send representatives to an International Conference: this was held in London in 1954 and was attended by 42 countries.

In one of its Resolutions the Conference endorsed the view already expressed by the United Kingdom Committee that the only entirely effective known remedy lay in the complete avoidance of the discharge of persistent oil into the sea. Such a total prohibition was not thought to be immediately practicable, but a Convention was drawn up creating specific zones within which the discharge of persistent oils was to be prohibited. Among other Resolutions adopted was one that Governments should create national committees to keep the problem under review, to carry out any necessary research and to recommend preventive measures. The Minister of Transport and Civil Aviation set up a Committee in accordance with the terms of this Resolution in July, 1954. The new legislation to enable effect to be given to the Convention took the form of the Oil in Navigable Waters Act, passed in 1955. The Convention itself came into force on 26th July, 1958.

In preparing for this Conference, and during its course, the Department had invaluable assistance and support from industry—shipowners, the oil companies, seafarers and others—as they had had in connection with the Safety Conference and other ventures, small and large, domestic and international.

As a result of these efforts, the oil pollution situation around our coasts has steadily improved, but much still remains to be done. Many maritime countries have not yet ratified the Convention and the ultimate objective of total prohibition of the discharge of persistent oil anywhere at sea has still to be achieved.

SOME DEVELOPMENTS IN THE YEARS TO COME

The extent of the Ministry's work for safety at sea and off our shores has been briefly described. But what of the future? Casualty returns show clearly that, while the standard of safety in large British ships is extremely high, the little ship in particular remains vulnerable. The Merchant Shipping Rules prescribe minimum standards of strength and stability and scales of life-saving and fire fighting equipment for ships but no law can guarantee safety against the forces of wind and sea or errors of navigation, and, when disaster comes to a small ship, it usually comes quickly. Deep-sea fishing vessels are in a class by themselves, small sturdy ships going regularly into some of the most inhospitable and stormy seas of the world. The average number of fishing vessels lost each year between 1948 and 1956 was 24 while the similar figure for all other power-driven vessels was only 28. It is with these facts in mind, and with the object of giving crews a greater chance of safety, that the Ministry has encouraged and prescribed the use of the modern inflatable life-raft developed from the war-time rubber dinghy used in aircraft. These rafts differ from conventional lifeboats in that they are not manœuvrable and that the problem of embarking passengers into them from the high decks of big passenger ships has yet to be solved. But they have other great advantages; they can be easily launched and are quickly inflated by gas on the simple pulling of a line; they withstand buffeting against the ships' sides and even against rocks; and, a most important point, they provide considerable protection from exposure with their canopied roofs and double sides and floors which effectively insulate the occupants from the elements. Those advantages are of special importance to fishing vessels and it was a notable result of the Ministry's policy that in 1956, the first year which saw the widespread use of the new equipment in the British fishing fleet, 57 lives were saved by these rafts and although 11 fishing boats were totally wrecked no lives were lost in them. Now merchant ships are being steadily fitted out with the new apparatus and the aim is to secure by international agreement their full and appropriate place in the life-saving equipment of all ships.

Three other modern technical developments occupy the Department's attention in particular. These are, first, the all-welded ship which, though cheaper and quicker to build than the riveted ship, yet has structural problems of its own and, secondly, the increasing use of aluminium. Aluminium alloys are freely used in the construction of lifeboats and more and more in the structure of ships themselves. The lightness of these alloys is a great advantage, but their melting-point is well below that of steel and they thus create special problems in connection with a ship's system of fire precautions. Thirdly, fibreglass has made a most promising début as a material for lifeboats. It is extremely strong and, a great advantage to the shipowner, needs little maintenance. The Department's surveyors are watching closely to see how in practice these new boats stand up to prolonged exposure in all marine weathers and temperatures.

Looking further ahead, the Department is embarking on a detailed study of the safety problems thrown up by the proposed application of nuclear propulsion to merchant ships. These problems will affect not only the ships and their crews but also all ports to which the ships may go. Much work and much consultation will be needed before this latest newcomer takes its place, side by side with the older problems, in the day-to-day work of the Department.

CHAPTER VI

Marine Crews

Well-being — Efficiency — Records — International Work

*

WELL-BEING

THERE are few groups of workers in this country in which the State
takes as much direct interest as it does in the officers and seamen of
the Merchant Navy. The reasons go back a century and more and
have been set out in Chapter II,[1] since some knowledge of them is
essential to an understanding of the Department's current work.
The term well-being is used in the widest sense and not merely to
denote hostels, canteens and the like. In fact a most important
duty is still that first adopted by the State in 1850 of witnessing the
engagement of crews of British sea-going vessels (with the exception
of small coasters) and their signing-on, man by man, under the
proper form of agreement. This agreement, approved by the State
and witnessed by a public servant, is the seamen's first defence
against the old evils of forced labour and unfair conditions of employment. Moreover, while he is away the State sees to it that any
allotments he has made out of his wages are paid on his behalf, to
the person he nominates to receive them. Equally, at the end of the
voyage the wages due to each man are checked and the particulars
of the voyage entered in his Discharge Book in the presence of an
official. At this point disputes which may have arisen between the
master and any member of the crew may have to be settled and fines
checked to see that they have been legally imposed. The wages and
effects of any man who has been left behind or who has died in the
course of a voyage are held for him or his dependants. Special
Savings Banks are open to give the seaman the means of depositing
any sums he may have accumulated during a voyage before he has a
chance of falling prey to dockside temptations.

For these executive duties Mercantile Marine Offices exist around
the coast, each under a Superintendent, frequently still known to
seamen by the old-fashioned 1850 title of Shipping Master. Indeed
the Superintendent may be known by other names. One of these

[1] Pages 27–8

officers had the duty shortly after V.E. day in 1945 of superintending the return of Merchant Navy men from a Prisoner of War Camp in Germany. On arrival there, dressed in naval uniform, as was then necessary, his right to give orders, or even advice, to merchant seamen was warmly challenged until one of those present recognised him and said 'He ain't the Navy; he's the —— who stopped my pay'. Thereafter, the story tells, all was peace and friendliness and repatriation progressed satisfactorily. In fact relations between the staffs of the Mercantile Marine Offices and the officers and men of the Merchant Navy are good, the officials being appreciated as independent umpires who can adjudicate fairly when disputes arise and whose advice and guidance is sought when necessary.

Doubt is sometimes cast on the need for such elaborate safeguards for the merchant seaman in these days of strong Trade Unions and greatly improved conditions in the ports of the world. This much can be said with fair certainty, that if a fresh start were being made today the safeguards would be less elaborate. But it is equally the fact that the industry—owners and seafarers alike—set store by the maintenance of the present system and do not seek any change in it. It is, indeed, significant that, after the requirement to sign on men before a Superintendent had been extended to certain smaller home-trade ships for special reasons connected with the Second World War, strong pressure from the industry secured the passage of legislation to continue that requirement permanently.

It should not, however, be thought that the Mercantile Marine Offices cut across the more orthodox methods of industrial negotiation. The National Maritime Board, which is the Joint Industrial Council of the shipping industry and originated in the First World War as a form of Whitley Council under the auspices of the then Ministry of Shipping, controls—now without any Governmental assistance or interference—the conditions of service and the pay of the Merchant Navy. It is this body that introduced the Merchant Navy Established Service Scheme, which applies to all British ships of 200 gross tons and over. The scheme has almost entirely done away with the old system of casual employment by virtually guaranteeing to an established seaman at the end of a voyage a new job in the same ship or in another covered by the Scheme. The Scheme has in fact revolutionised conditions of employment for the seaman who, once he is accepted on the Establishment, and so long as he carries out his obligations, can be sure of regular employment in the industry. In times of full employment its true significance is not so easily evident, but those with long memories have not been slow to realise its benefits. Although the Ministry is not directly concerned in these matters, it is consulted by both sides in times of difficulty—which are happily rare. Indeed industrial relations in British shipping are remarkable for their continued harmony and for the confidence existing between the organisations representing the owners, officers and men.

Other matters touching the well-being of seafarers, such as accommodation, scales of food and medical supplies on board ship and the arrangements for the treatment and repatriation of sick or injured seamen and of those left behind for any reason in ports abroad, are more directly the Department's concern. The Merchant Shipping Acts, and the Regulations made under them, cover all these subjects in considerable detail. For example, at the principal ports in the United Kingdom are stationed Inspectors of Ships' Provisions, who have power to inspect, and reject if need be, either at the ship or at the place of manufacture, food intended for the crew's use on board.

In ports overseas, duties similar to those undertaken at the Mercantile Marine Offices are carried out, in foreign countries by H.M. Consular Officers, and in Commonwealth countries and the Colonies by officers appointed by the Government of the country or territory. The most general of these duties is to care for, and to send home, the seaman who has for some reason been left behind abroad. The distressed British seamen, or D.B.S. as he is commonly called, may be the victim of shipwreck or a man who has missed his ship or finds himself stranded for some other reason. The special vulnerability of the seaman abroad was early recognised and the handling of these men is governed by detailed regulations. The Consul or Shipping Master must provide for the D.B.S.; he will try to get him a new ship, but if he fails he will arrange to send him home, and for this purpose he can require the master of any British ship to take him and to provide for him during the voyage home. A seaman who is left behind abroad because he is sick or injured is normally the responsibility of the shipowner, who is required by statute to pay for medical attention and medicine and for the seaman's maintenance until he has returned home. Very often, for practical reasons, Consuls and Shipping Masters act for the shipowner in taking a sick seaman in charge and maintaining him as though he was a D.B.S. Whether sick or distressed, the man's safe return to a 'proper' port is ensured.

Finally, there are the splendid services of the voluntary welfare societies which the Ministry is glad to help whenever possible. All over the world these societies have done invaluable work providing Clubs, recreational facilities and general guidance to improve the seamen's lot. Since 1948 the efforts of the voluntary societies have been co-ordinated and supplemented by the Merchant Navy Welfare

F

Board, which, besides being a forum for considering seafarers' welfare problems and projects, also provides welfare facilities directly or by way of financial grants to welfare societies and committees in many parts of the world. The Ministry is represented on the Board, as also are the shipowners, the seafarers' unions, the voluntary societies and the other Government Departments concerned.

EFFICIENCY

Ever since the replies to Murray's circular of 1843[1] shed so painful a light upon the lack of navigational skill and the prevalence of indiscipline in many British ships of those days, the State has paid great attention to conduct and technical competence at sea. This interest begins early in a man's career. For though training is primarily the responsibility of the industry, the statutory requirements for technical competency clearly shape the courses that are offered and the Department has necessarily concerned itself with the arrangements that are made. For all grades of seafarers some pre-sea training is now necessary or desirable. Novelists should therefore note that their modern heroes will find it very difficult to run away to sea. This pre-sea training is conducted in a wide variety of establishments, including H.M.S. *Conway* and H.M.S. *Worcester*, Pangbourne, the National Sea Training Schools for deck and catering ratings and many others, some operated by private initiative, some by local education authorities, some by the industry, and others by a combination of these interests. The Ministry, in conjunction with the Ministry of Education, inspects these establishments and encourages their use by granting to the graduates of efficient schools remissions of the sea service required for Certificates of Competency as Second Mate or Able Seaman as the case may be.

Administration of the statutory requirements for Certificates of Competency also falls to the Ministry. For very many years all foreign-going ships have been required to carry a certificated Master and certificated Mates and Engineers: more recently Parliament has required persons engaged as Able Seaman or as ship's cook to hold a certificate which proves them competent in that capacity. Examination centres exist at all the main ports in the country, and there practical and oral tests are conducted by the Marine Survey staff, mentioned in the previous chapter. Deck and Engineer Officers, and Skippers and Second Hands of fishing boats, must also pass written examinations before being awarded a Certificate of Competency: to ensure uniformity of standards this work is supervised by the two Principal Examiners, one of Masters and Mates and one

[1] Pages 27–8.

of Engineers, at Headquarters. The Principal Examiners must always ensure that the syllabuses of the examinations and the practical experience required of candidates, whether on deck or in an engineering apprenticeship, remain abreast of the needs of the time. Another important duty of those who examine Deck Officers is to ensure that their sight, especially their colour vision, is thoroughly sound, for an officer on watch who mistook the colour of a light could cause untold havoc. In addition to the statutory examinations there are examinations for the award of the highly prized Extra Master's and Extra First Class Engineer's Certificates—indications, as their titles imply, of the highest professional standards.

The Merchant Shipping Acts, besides requiring that a certain number of certificated officers must be carried, provide that a vessel may be detained if she is unsafe by reason of under-manning. The manning is therefore checked, when necessary, by the Marine Survey staff at the ports.

Statutory authority for the enforcement of discipline at sea resides also in the Merchant Shipping Acts. These give the Master of a ship his authority on board and also impose or sanction penalties for desertion and other offences. Perhaps the most serious penalty for a certificated officer, though fortunately one which seldom has to be imposed by the Minister, or by the Court at a Formal Investigation into a shipping casualty, is the withdrawal of his Certificate of Competency.

RECORDS

No Government could feel satisfied that the nation's maritime manpower was being adequately used unless it had proper records of all its seamen. This is no modern fad for bureaucratic thoroughness. As long ago as 1803 Lord Nelson in a memorandum to the Admiralty wrote: 'I think a plan could be brought forward to register the certificates given to seamen. . . . The greatest good would result and the benefit to the seamen producing good characters, etc., never been concerned in mutinies or deserted etc., would much benefit them in getting good berths in the Merchant Service'.[1] Even so it was not until 1835 that the General Register Office of Seamen (now the General Register and Record Office of Shipping and Seamen, at Cardiff) was set up. The functions of the office now go far beyond Nelson's original conception. Here are deposited, as public records, the Agreements and Official Log Books of all United Kingdom registered ships and the records and qualifications of seamen. In time of war, and also at times of manpower shortage in the different ranks and ratings, the records of seamen's engagements and dis-

[1] *Letters from Lord Nelson* (Ed. G. Rawson), p. 361.

charges provide a unique source of information for all the organisations connected with shipping and the needs of seafarers. By arrangement with the Admiralty, the Office also maintains the records of, and calls up for training, officers of the Merchant Navy and officers and men of the Fishing Fleets who have joined the Royal Naval Reserve.

INTERNATIONAL WORK

Very few shipping problems are restricted to the domestic scene and the administration of crews is no exception. The increasing tendency towards international agreement, which a former Permanent Secretary to the Board of Trade noted 30 years ago,[1] has become much more marked since the Second World War.

The body responsible for organising the discussion of international problems in the field of labour relations is the International Labour Organisation set up at the end of the First War. Seafarers' questions, however, are dealt with separately from those of other workers and are considered at special Maritime Sessions, the first of which was held at Genoa in 1920. Here representatives of Governments, shipowners and seafarers meet to consider the adoption of Conventions, Recommendations or Resolutions on the various aspects of labour relations at sea. At these sessions the Government delegation comes from the Ministry and not from the Ministry of Labour as in all other I.L.O. meetings. Useful Instruments have been produced on such subjects as crew accommodation, articles of agreement, the certification of able seamen and ships' cooks (a matter of the greatest importance to maritime health and contentment of crews). But undoubtedly the most important of the matters under consideration have been wages, hours and manning on which the attempt to produce a universally acceptable international instrument has presented the most formidable difficulties and has given rise to the fiercest controversy.

In this country agreements on wages, hours and industrial—as distinct from safety—manning are negotiated within the industry through the medium of the National Maritime Board and are arrived at harmoniously and without fuss. But the day has not yet come upon which a Convention, the most binding form of international instrument, can be drawn up in terms which will have the general support of shipowners and seafarers. Attempts have been made on several occasions to reach international agreement but the Conventions adopted to date have never had the approval of both shipowners and seafarers and have obtained few ratifications. At the most recent Maritime Session of the International Labour Conference held in Geneva in May, 1958, a further attempt was made to

[1] Sir Hubert Llewellyn Smith: *The Board of Trade*, p. 111.

find common ground. It is as yet too early to say whether the Convention drawn up by the Conference will obtain more ratifications than those previously adopted, but the lack of agreement between shipowners and seafarers on its text continues. Happily the Conference also adopted a Recommendation on the subject. The greater flexibility inherent in a Recommendation permitted shipowners and seafarers to vote together in support of its adoption and to recommend standards higher than those in the Convention. This is the first occasion since the International Labour Organisation was set up that there has been such a general agreement on these subjects. It represents solid progress in the field of international agreement and augurs well for the future.

The Ministry has special contact with Indian, Pakistani, Malay, Chinese and Arab seamen, large numbers of whom have traditionally served in British ships and have made a notable contribution to the efficiency of the Merchant Navy. In war the part that these men played was invaluable, often in most dangerous waters and in most trying climates. The services of the Mercantile Marine Offices are available to them, as to all others who sail as crews of our ships, and the Superintendent and his staff frequently find themselves helping these Asiatic and African seamen, who may have little or no English, in any difficulties they may run into in this country. In particular Indian and Pakistani seamen, of whom there are some 35,000 serving in British ships, are specially protected by the signing of so-called 'Lascar agreements', generally in ports in India and Pakistan, which provide for their return to their country of origin for signing-off. One of the functions of the Mercantile Marine Offices is to supervise their transfer as necessary from one ship to another and to see that the men are not marooned in this country. In the same way the men can look for help in ports in the Commonwealth to the Shipping Master, and in foreign ports to the British Consul. Almost equally important—though cases are infrequent— is the protection which can be given through diplomatic and consular channels to British seamen who may appear to suffer hardship or injustice in foreign countries.

All this work brings the Ministry into daily contact and discussion with the representative bodies of the industry and it is rare for proposals to be put forward by the British Government for legislation here, or for consideration by international bodies, which do not carry the concurrence and the support of the industry as a whole— owners, officers and men. The system is a close partnership depending for its acceptance and its continuance upon a high sense of responsibility in all parties and a marked degree of confidence and trust between them. Long may it continue.

CHAPTER VII

Ports and Inland Waterways

The Ministry's Role — Special Inquiries — Ports
Abroad — Port Defence — Dock Labour —
Inland Waterways — Conclusion

*

THE MINISTRY'S ROLE

THE geographical situation of this country and its dependence upon overseas trade makes the rapid and easy interchange of goods between ship, train, barge or lorry no less essential to our prosperity than their economical carriage by those vehicles. Altogether over 100 million tons of imports and some 35 million tons of exports passed through the United Kingdom's seaports in 1957. And every day that an ocean-going liner of 10,000 tons spends in port costs about £750. It will therefore be readily appreciated that the efficiency of the ports is a matter of outstanding importance.

In war-time the Department undertook directly the responsibility for operating the ports so as to ensure that the practices and priorities which suited the peace-time pattern of trade were not allowed to stand in the way of the most efficient handling of the new problems presented by the entirely different pattern of war-time shipping. Control was vested in the Minister by Defence Regulations and in each main port a Port Committee was set up with wide powers to ensure that cargoes were handled expeditiously. All the interests concerned with the shipment of goods through the ports and with their distribution in the country were represented on these Committees. As a further measure, the Minister subsequently appointed a number of Regional Port Directors to co-ordinate and direct activities of the various individual Port Committees in their regions. Nor was the control at the ports in itself sufficient; if shipping was not to be delayed, it was also necessary to see that each incoming ship was sent to the port which, in all the circumstances, could best handle her. Special machinery, including a Shipping Diversion Room, was therefore set up at the headquarters of the Ministry to decide the destination of each incoming ship, taking into account where her cargo was needed, the ability of the nearby ports to receive her, the inland transport situation—coastal shipping, rail and road—and other relevant factors. So far as possible, destinations were determined before convoys sailed, but ships could be diverted at sea to meet changes in the situation. It was a fascinating sight to see the members of the Room at work. They sat at a very large table, representatives of the consuming Ministries knowing where each cargo was needed, representatives of the ports able to obtain the exact position at their ports at any moment by direct telephone, the coastal shipping, railway and road operators knowing the possibilities of movement from the ports, the Admiralty to advise on routeing and other defence problems, and the Customs and other authorities with important but less direct interests at stake. Many ships, even in a big convoy, could be dealt with quickly, but some would present special problems. It might be a mixed cargo for a number of destinations. The first consideration would be to avoid more than one port of discharge if possible. If what looked like the most convenient port was on the East coast, the Admiralty would have a view on safety, and possible alternative ports would be discussed in the light of their ability to deal with the ship, the availability of coasters and the capacity of rail and road transport on the proposed routes. Alternative destinations for parts of the cargo might be discussed, and in the end the Chairman, from the Ministry, gave his decision— never questioned in that assembly of men who had long worked together, understood one another's difficulties and trusted one another. The Room was one of the more colourful illustrations of the fact that wide policy decisions were not enough: an immense amount of detail was also involved in controlling shipping and inland transport resources in war-time. It was, indeed, the close link between all forms of transport, shown most clearly in the task of discharging and distributing cargo through the ports, that resulted in the merger of the Ministries of Shipping and Transport to form the Ministry of War Transport.

In peace-time things are very different. The Ministry has no direct responsibility for the working of the ports. This is the concern of a multitude of different authorities—the port undertakings, wharfingers, employers of port labour, stevedoring firms, barge and other harbour craft operators and road and rail interests. Even among the port authorities themselves there is a wide variety of different types of organisation. Some are public corporations or trusts such as the Port of London Authority, the Mersey Docks and Harbour Board and the Clyde Navigation Trust; some are municipal authorities as at Bristol and Preston; others are companies such as the Manchester Ship Canal Company which operates the Port of Manchester; while one-third of the country's total port capacity, originally the property of the railway and canal companies, is owned by the British Transport Commission and managed by their Docks Division (formerly the Docks and Inland Waterways Executive).

The Ministry remains in the background as the central authority to which major problems of port development and efficiency can be referred, and in the Minister are vested most of the statutory powers that the State possesses in this field. The bulk of these powers are of local application only, designed in the nineteenth century principally to protect the interests of port users. In addition, under the Transport Charges, etc. (Miscellaneous Provisions) Act, 1954, the Minister has power, exercised only on application by either the port authorities or the port users, to revise the statutory maximum harbour dues or port charges of the non-nationalised ports.[1] He also has powers which affect port development, quite apart from the operation of the Town and Country Planning Acts. For example, in the case of the nationalised ports, the Minister has to approve plans involving substantial capital outlay, and, as regards other ports, he is the channel for Government advice on capital expenditure policy. He may also be able positively to help in speeding up the construction of new works by making on behalf of any particular port a Provisional Order, later to be embodied in a Private Bill, under the General Pier and Harbour Act, 1861, or by supporting Private Bills seeking authority, for example, to raise loans on the security of the harbour revenue to cover the cost of new works and equipment such as cranes and mechanical handling gear.

In very exceptional circumstances the Ministry may have to promote legislation to establish a harbour or conservancy authority where there is no existing body with jurisdiction in the harbour or waters concerned which could appropriately promote private legislation for the purpose. The only modern example is Milford Haven for which a special Act was passed in 1958, to establish a conservancy authority.

The nature and extent of the Ministry's relations with any particular port authority varies according to the statutory links in each case, the importance of the undertaking and its activities and the needs of the moment. For the general reasons described in Chapter I, where the Minister's relationship with the nationalised Boards has been discussed, contact with the British Transport Commission over the previously railway-owned ports such as Southampton Docks, Dover, Folkestone, Hull and the South Wales ports and those such as Goole and Sharpness previously owned by canal companies is necessarily close, the Minister being answerable in Parlia-

---

[1] The maximum charges at ports owned by the British Transport Commission are determined by the Transport Tribunal.

ment for the general effects of the Commission's port policy. Under the Transport Act, 1947, the Commission had powers to prepare schemes for the development of particular ports or harbours or groups of ports and for creating new management structures either by vesting them in the British Transport Commission or otherwise. A number of such schemes were in fact prepared by the Commission but none of them materialised and the Transport Act, 1953, repealed the powers.

The Ministry is also in frequent touch with the other harbour authorities, particularly the two largest among them, the Port of London Authority and the Mersey Docks and Harbour Board, since London and Liverpool between them handle nearly 60 per cent of the nation's seaborne trade. The Minister appoints certain members to the Boards of both these authorities—as he does in the case of a number of other port undertakings. From the port users the Minister will receive representations about the facilities provided and, although unable to help in investigating allegations about particular consignments, he is always ready to consider with the authorities any practical suggestions for improving efficiency and the speed of turnround of ships.

SPECIAL INQUIRIES

Turnround time has indeed been a major question since the war. There has been much criticism that ships spend longer in port now than they should and far longer than they did before the war. There are a number of answers to this criticism. First, the ports suffered very severe war damage and repair and reconstruction have been slow owing to the shortages of labour, material and finance that have beset the country in the years since the war. Second, there has been a major change in the pattern of the country's foreign trade. Before the war coal exports, which are easily and quickly loaded by special appliances, amounted to 38 million tons a year. Now they are less than 10 million tons. Instead the vast bulk of our export trade is in manufactured goods, of great variety, which take much longer to load. Third, ships are larger and are more fully loaded, so that more work is involved in loading and discharging. These facts have not been universally accepted as the full explanation and the Minister has, since the war, ordered two investigations into efficient working at the ports, apart from other inquiries into the problems of dock labour. A standing advisory Committee has also been set up. The two investigations were the Working Party on the Turnround of Shipping which reported in 1948 and a more specialised inquiry into Increased Mechanisation in 1950; both these

Working Parties contained representatives of the ports themselves, shipowners and labour, and they sat in each case under a Ministry Chairman. The continuing Committee is the small Ports Efficiency Committee set up in 1952 to make recommendations in serious instances of port congestion or delay. The Ministry has the responsibility of following up the recommendations made by these Committees and seeking the co-operation of the interests concerned with port operation in putting them into effect.

PORTS ABROAD

Congestion in many of the major ports of the world in the post-war years has had a serious effect on the movement of ships and the Ministry has been invited to investigate the working of many of the ports abroad as well as those at home. Generally, Sir Eric Millbourn, the Minister's Honorary Adviser on Shipping in Port, has been the principal investigator. For example, both in 1948–49 and in 1953–54 the facilities of the Central and East African ports and the inland transport serving them proved quite unequal to the load of cargo required to be handled to and from the interior of the Continent. As a temporary expedient the volume of cargo moving was limited by organising a control over the number of ships destined for these ports and over the cargoes carried to and from them. The control was a voluntary one exercised by committees comprising port and railway authorities, shipowners, importers and representatives of the Government affected, while the Ministry took a leading part in formulating the arrangements. Further special reports have been made at the request of the Colonial Administrations concerned on the ports of Gibraltar, Malta, Cyprus, Jamaica, Trinidad, Barbados, as well as inquiries into the organisation of the ports of Singapore and Port Swettenham and also the ports of India.

PORT DEFENCE

Defence is the one aspect of port working which, even in peace-time, directly concerns the Ministry. The Government could certainly be charged with irresponsibility and lack of foresight if they did not pay great attention to what might happen to our own ports, and to overseas ports on our essential lines of communications, in another war. Detailed studies have therefore been made of the alternative arrangements that might be made in the event of major ports being attacked and put out of action. The whole of the United Kingdom coastline has been surveyed and certain emergency work has been put in hand. Thought has also been given to the needs of a number of small ports whose importance in purely commercial terms may be waning but whose value in war-time might be considerable.

DOCK LABOUR

In the public mind the restlessness of dock labour since the war is probably the one aspect of port working which stands out over all the rest. It overshadows the expenditure on new works and repairs which has covered up the trail of war damage and tends to obscure the many steps which have successfully been taken towards mechanisation. This unrest seems all the more surprising to the outside observer when he is aware of the revolutionary change which has replaced the casual employment that was the feature of the industry before the war by the present system of regular employment and payment for unavoidable idle time. The requirement for dock labour must necessarily fluctuate from tide to tide, week to week and season to season depending on the movements of shipping and the types of cargoes carried. During the war schemes were introduced in the major ports to provide greater regularity of employment; then in 1947 the National Dock Labour Board was set up to administer a single scheme under which dock work in all the main ports was, in the fashionable and horrible jargon of our time, 'decasualised'. Now regular dock workers are registered, and men who are on the register, and who present themselves for work, receive a guaranteed minimum payment whether or not there is work for them. The Dock Labour scheme is administered by the Minister of Labour but the Minister of Transport is necessarily interested in its efficient working as in the efficient working of all other port activities. It is to him that shipowners and other employers make representations about delays due to labour difficulties, and if port troubles result in a strike he bears the main responsibility for taking such steps as may be possible to keep essential services in operation and essential cargoes moving.

INLAND WATERWAYS

From the ports there extends a network of inland waterways ranging in size and importance from the principal navigable rivers and the Manchester Ship Canal to the many miles of narrow canals. It includes 2,000 miles of waterways owned by the British Transport Commission and a number of others (many of them river navigations) operated by independent statutory authorities. The Thames above Teddington is, for example, in the care of the Thames Conservancy and the Rivers Humber and Nene and long sections of the Trent, the Yorkshire Ouse and other rivers are administered independently. The Department is concerned with national questions affecting the navigational interests of all these undertakings and in particular with private legislation promoted by them, being called upon from time to time to give advice by making reports when their Private Bills are being dealt with in Committee by either House. The Minister also approves or confirms bye-laws and regulations made by the undertakings under their private Acts or under such Acts as the Explosives Act, 1875, and the Petroleum (Consolidation) Act, 1928. For the Commission's canals there are the additional functions, such as the examination of programmes for capital expenditure, that arise on all aspects of the Commission's activities. The Minister may also authorise under the Railway and Canal Traffic Act, 1888, the abandonment of any canal which has become derelict or unnecessary or after consultation with his colleagues agree to the transfer of the functions of a navigation authority to a River Board under the Land Drainage Act, 1930, or the River Boards Act, 1948. These powers are, however, little used and in recent years the Department's main preoccupation in relation to inland waterways has been with their economic situation and with the problems of law and organisation which their future presents. These problems, like so many transport problems, have their roots in history and to understand them it is necessary to trace some of the features of the history of the inland waterways in the last two hundred years.

Although the navigation of the country's rivers and streams goes back to the earliest times, the great development of the inland waterway system occurred in the middle of the eighteenth century, when the enterprise of the Duke of Bridgewater and the engineering skill of James Brindley marked the beginning of the 'Canal Era'. Within some 70 years about 4,000 miles of waterways were constructed, usually under powers granted by special Private Act of Parliament. For a time they enjoyed great prosperity; with coastal shipping, they formed the main highway for industrial traffic and had a profound influence on the social and economic developments of the time. An inherent weakness, however, in any comprehensive canal system covering the United Kingdom is the predominantly hilly nature of the country which severely restricts the number of economic routes. But apart from this inescapable handicap the system was developed in a somewhat piecemeal and haphazard manner and with a somewhat parochial outlook. It was designed for individual streams of traffic—ferrying agricultural produce and raw materials to consuming centres and manufactures to local markets or linking ports with their immediate hinterland. Few entrepreneurs visualised possibilities of through traffic, and consequently gauges were never standardised, through tolls never developed, and canal companies tried to kill rather than exchange each other's traffic. The railways were quicker to learn the lesson of developing inter-company traffic with through rates. And in the face of railway competition, the canals' livelihood and very existence began to be threatened. It was then for the first time that the Government began seriously to interest itself in the canal system and to endeavour to take steps to secure its well-being.

Many of the important legislative measures which resulted were aimed at preserving the system in competition with the railways and at ensuring that those railways which had purchased canals had a continuing obligation to maintain them. This statutory obligation imposed a procedure (known as the Warrant and Order of Abandonment Procedure), which made it difficult and often costly for a canal undertaker to close a navigation. But, despite these measures, the water transport industry never regained its earlier prosperity and by the end of the nineteenth century many of the canals had either passed into railway ownership or been abandoned.

In this century a number of inquiries, including the Royal Commission on Canals and Inland Navigations which sat from 1906 to 1911, have been initiated by the Government into the condition of the country's waterways and their financial position. These inquiries led ultimately to the general recognition that the waterway system would be considerably strengthened if it was brought under one management. Consequently the opportunity of the Transport Act, 1947, was taken to unify the system under the British Transport Commission. Under this Act the ownership of some 2,000 miles of waterway and about one-third of the craft passed to the Commission. But the placing of most of the waterways under the Commission, major step though it was, did not solve the waterways' problems. It was not long before the Commission reviewed the condition of the individual waterways vested in them and came to the conclusion that of the 2,000 miles which they owned only about 300 miles had an assured future for transport purposes and that there was not, and was never likely to be, any transport interest in another 700 miles. The remaining 1,000 miles—by far the greater part of which consists of narrow canals—carry commercial traffic, but not enough to cover the cost of maintaining and working them, and judgment on their prospects as part of the transport system was suspended until it could be seen whether efforts to encourage their greater use could succeed in reversing the declining traffic trend.

These views of the British Transport Commission have posed new problems for the Department. Would public opinion accept that the transport uses of our waterways were as limited as the Commission clearly thought? Were the old arrangements for dealing with waterways that had ceased to be required as navigations suited to present-day needs? In the old days when a waterway was no longer wanted for navigation, the proper course was for the owner to get rid of all responsibility for it under the Warrant and Order procedure of abandonment already mentioned. Since this procedure was devised in 1888, however, the whole character of the waterways of this country has undergone a change. They can no longer be thought of simply as parts of the system of inland commercial transport; they may form an integral part of the land drainage system; often the water supply is used for industrial purposes or for the discharge of effluent; many of the more pleasant stretches have become popular for boating and fishing and are regarded with affection by those who know them well. In a different category are those interests —usually in urban areas—who regard canals as a nuisance and a danger to public health, but who are at the same time opposed to total abandonment of a canal and would like to saddle the navigation authority, even after the waterway has ceased to have value as a navigation, with a continuing liability for works required to maintain the canal as a non-transport concern or for filling in the site so that it can be developed for other purposes.

The strength of opposition to any proposal to close a navigation, whether by Warrant and Order procedure or by Private Bill, is often intense and canal undertakers have in the past preferred to let canals become derelict rather than risk the costly procedure involved in a formal closure. That the present position is unsatisfactory was recognised by the Minister when he set up the Committee under Mr Leslie Bowes in 1956. The terms of reference of the Committee required that it should look at all aspects of the problem, both transport and non-transport. The Committee reported in 1958 and made a number of novel proposals. They included recommendations for the development of the transport use of the waterways and for changes in the law and practice for dealing with those waterways whose transport days have clearly gone for ever. As this book goes to press these proposals are being considered by the Government.

CONCLUSION

The reader will appreciate that the administrative system governing the United Kingdom ports and waterways is very varied. The different forms of management and their relations with the central Government have not evolved at all uniformly. They have been shaped by local circumstance and the historical accident of ownership as well as by political doctrine. So far as ports are concerned the result may be untidy, but the existence of a large number of independent authorities, each with a sense of pride in the entity which it has helped to build up and intimately aware of its local problems, has proved efficient and healthy. An incentive exists to attract trade and to vie with other ports in offering and giving the best service. The critics of the system will say that it is wasteful and uneconomic and that the small ports, possibly those that may be much needed in time of war, are handicapped for lack of funds. On the other hand, the idea behind the ports sections of the Transport Act, 1947, that there might be room for co-ordination between ports in the same area aroused fierce opposition in practice and, as has been said, these sections were repealed by the 1953 Act. Nor has it ever been suggested that the Department should assume, except in war-time, any direct operational responsibility. It is more likely to remain as now the central point to which questions of port, river and canal working and development can be referred and from which the statutory powers and persuasive influence that the State as central authority possesses can be exercised.

PART THREE

Inland Transport

CHAPTER VIII

Road/Rail Competition and the Road Transport Licensing System

Competition for the carriage of passengers —
The control of road passenger transport —
Competition for the carriage of goods — The
control of road haulage — Regional Transport
Commissioners

*

THERE are two fundamental differences which distinguish the administrative problems of inland transport from those of the sea and the air. First, competition between ships on the one hand and aircraft on the other is less intense than that between rail and road, though it may grow, particularly in the passenger field. Secondly, ships and aircraft operate mainly in the international field, and the control which individual Governments can exercise over competition between them is limited. It is obvious, for example, that attempts by a Government to handicap one form of its transport for the benefit of the other would result merely in the transfer of traffic to foreign competitors and not to the other form of transport. The customer in the international field has a wide choice of competing flags both at sea and in the air. That is not so in inland transport.

The outstanding feature of inland transport since the First World War has been the enormous growth of facilities for the movement of passengers and goods due to the development of the motor vehicle and its use on the roads in large and ever-increasing numbers for public transport purposes. Up to 1914 the railways were the predominant carriers for distances too great for horse transport, the only others being coastal shipping and canals, both limited by geography as regards the areas they could serve. But, after the war, road vehicles rapidly altered the picture. Much of the traffic they carried was new, but much was taken from the railways, which were hard hit by the abstraction of some of their most lucrative business, passenger and goods. On the one hand were the railways with vast capital assets in track, signalling equipment, passenger stations and goods depots, as well as expensive rolling stock, and on the other small undertakings requiring, at least in the early stages, practically no capital beyond the price of their vehicles, with complete flexibility as to routes and with access by road to even the smallest villages throughout the country. And whereas the newcomers were free to operate more or less at will and without any control over their charges, the railways were subject to the close statutory control which originated in the Victorian era of their monopoly and prosperity.

COMPETITION FOR THE CARRIAGE OF PASSENGERS

To begin with the competition between road and rail for the carriage of passengers was not severe. Many road passenger services did not compete with rail at all. Town services, for instance, had been running for many years, often through local authorities' undertakings and, apart from the suburbs of larger towns, did not serve areas which the railways could cater for. Again, most railways were built to link up main towns and were not particularly good on cross-country routes, whereas motor transport soon proved the ideal way of serving villages and isolated areas. But before very long these cross-country bus routes were cutting into what had hitherto been regarded as the railways' preserves, because they inevitably joined up and provided a network of good connecting services. There were other points of attack too. Coach excursion traffic grew quickly, and, with advances in design and performance of motor transport, the railways were challenged on their firmest ground by the use of long-distance coaches for journeys on trunk routes between large towns.

Side by side with road/rail competition there arose fierce competition within the road transport industry itself. Innumerable small operators were fighting for an expanding but not limitless market. Cut-throat competition—pirate buses and the like—led operators to lower their standards to save costs and there was little or no control over the extent of their operations, their maintenance or the quality of service they gave to the public. Often they had little idea of the financial problems of running a business and many found themselves bankrupt before long. Though some people were the gainers through lower fares as a result of the fierce competition, the public as a whole suffered because they had no guarantee that services would run to schedule or with safety or even at all. There was little encouragement for the responsible operator who ran unprofitable services in the off-season and on poor routes hoping to make up in good times and on his more paying routes; in the 1920s an operator with a sense of public duty to provide a regular and reliable service might well find that someone less scrupulous had come along to cream his traffic just at the time he was expecting to make a profit. This unbridled competition was of special public concern in passenger transport. Regularity and reliability of goods services (and the charges made for them) are very much a matter between trader and haulier; on buses every individual passenger is concerned. Safety is also more important where many people are being carried in a single vehicle.

This was the state of affairs that led to the appointment of the Royal Commission on Transport in 1928. The Royal Commission sat for three years and issued three reports. The first, entitled 'The Control of Traffic on the Roads' is not relevant to this chapter: the second, 'The Licensing and Regulation of Public Service Vehicles', and the third, 'The Co-ordination and Development of Transport', were to have a great influence on inland transport and on the work of the Ministry.

THE CONTROL OF ROAD PASSENGER TRANSPORT

The control of bus services stems from the Road Traffic Act, 1930, which put into force, *inter alia*, most of the recommendations contained in the second of the Royal Commission's reports. The Act divides the country into 'Traffic Areas'—11 at present, though the number has changed from time to time. Each Area outside London is run by three Traffic Commissioners—a full-time chairman appointed by the Minister but statutorily independent, and two part-time members appointed by the Minister from people suggested by local authorities. The Commissioners are supported by a staff which is part of the Ministry. This organisation fills the main need which the chaos of the 1920s showed to be essential if a workable and orderly system of passenger road transport was to be built up. Such licensing as there was before 1930 was done by local authorities exercising power they had—or hoped they had—under various ancient statutes. The Royal Commission had been outspoken on the subject '... [the law] in regard to the licensing of public service vehicles is archaic. ... The existing system of licensing, based upon Acts passed at a time when the internal combustion engine was unknown, is from every point of view totally unsuited to present-day requirements.' Obviously when each local authority could apply its own method of issuing licences, applicable only to its own area, the complications confronting the prospective operator were formidable. The 1930 Act makes the Areas big enough to avoid this sort of difficulty, though small enough for local conditions and local feeling to be known and understood. Moreover, some kind of co-ordination of transport services over an Area can be achieved since the Traffic Commissioners see things in perspective. They also have their independent statutory standing and should be free from any suspicion of bias. When local authorities were responsible for licensing it was difficult for them, especially those who ran their own transport undertakings, to appear impartial, however impartial they might really be. Their nomination of the persons from whom the Minister chooses the Traffic Commissioners, other than the Chairman, is intended, apart from its advantages on merits, as a recompense for the loss of the powers they previously exercised. In London there is only one Traffic Commisioner, since licensing was originally done by the Commissioner of Police of the Metropolis and not by the local authorities. But London is an exception to a good many of the licensing laws, as will be evident later.

The formal and fundamental work of the Traffic Commissioners is to consider applications for road service licences for stage or express services (the dividing line is that express services have a minimum fare of not less that 1s.) and for excursions and tours. First, each vehicle must have a Certificate of Fitness[1] attesting its safety and a public service vehicle licence which indicates that the operator is a proper and qualified person to run the service. The driver and conductor must also hold special licences. But the really significant control—and the really valuable licence—is the licence for the road service, which lays down what services may be run and under what conditions. The formalities for getting this licence are intended to make sure that both the applicant and the objectors get a fair hearing and that the Commissioners, with the public interest in mind, have enough evidence to assess the merits of the case. Every application is circulated and thus competing operators, including the railways, and the local authorities (who have a statutory right to be heard) can let the Commissioners know what they think about it at the public sitting which follows. Other people also often make representations and it would be unusual for them to be refused a hearing. The public sittings have many of the advantages of the formal proceedings of courts of law, but evidence is not taken on oath and the Commissioners are not unduly inhibited by protocol or precedent. They make their decisions on the evidence in front of them, taking account of the broad guidance given by the Act. They consider, for instance, whether the route is suitable and whether it is already adequately served; whether the service is 'necessary or desirable in the public interest'; what are the wider traffic needs for good and efficient services in the Area as a whole; and the co-ordination of all forms of transport, including rail. The Commissioners therefore have not only a narrow duty concerned with the needs of a particular route or the ambitions of an individual operator

[1] See page 149.

but also a wider duty, demanding considerable judgment and discretion, to hold the balance between transport needs and the supply available to meet them. The conditions which they attach to the licences enable them to ensure that fares 'shall not be unreasonable' and, by approving routes, schedules, stopping places and so forth, they try to secure—in the words of the Act—'the safety and convenience of the public'.

There are two other essentials for a fair licensing system. The first is the right of appeal; the second is that there must be some higher authority to guide policy and to give consistency—where consistency is desirable—in the decisions reached. These two essentials are in fact brought together in the 1930 Act, under which appeals lie to the Minister,[1] who usually appoints an Inspector to look into the facts of any case under appeal and to report. The considering and deciding of appeals is a formidable business and a good deal of time is spent on it. Careful study is well justified, for the interests of the many people who must use the buses in question are at stake, and perhaps the livelihood of an operator.

The system of appeals to the Minister has been criticised on the grounds that it is slow; that the Minister, as a politician, may be influenced by political considerations; that it is difficult for him to be or to appear to be impartial, since he appoints both the Commissioners and the Appeals Inspector; and lastly that a tribunal dealing with appeals would give authoritative decisions interpreting the Act and would guide future decisions in much the same way as the Courts do. The case for both sides is argued fully in Chapter IX of the Report of the Thesiger Committee[2] which reported on passenger transport licensing in the light of modern conditions in 1953. They came down (with one dissentient) in favour of the Minister's continuing to decide appeals. Briefly, their reasons stem from the fundamental difference between the work of the Traffic Commissioners and that of a court of law: the Commissioners do not generally have to decide on questions of fact or of law but on considerations of what is desirable in the public interest. Parliament intended the system to work flexibly and much that might have been laid down in the Act was left to the discretion of the Commissioners or the Minister. Appeals should not therefore be bound by precedent. The Minister, while his appeal decisions will help to give consistency, can nevertheless remain sensitive to changes which may be made

[1] Except in the case of drivers' and conductors' licences, where appeals lie to the magistrates' courts.
[2] Report of the Committee on the Licensing of Road Passenger Services (H.M.S.O., 1953). More recently the Committee on Administrative Tribunals and Inquiries (the Franks Committee) (Cmd. 218) has endorsed the Thesiger Committee's majority recommendation.

desirable by changing conditions. A tribunal might be more concerned with past decisions and rigid interpretations of the law; it could less easily interpret the intentions of Parliament. The whole system of bus and coach licensing in fact received a remarkably clean bill of health from the Thesiger Committee and it is a testimony to the legislators of a quarter of a century ago and to the operators and the Commissioners since then that the Committee were able to conclude, 'the licensing system viewed as a whole has worked well and continues to work well'.

Admittedly it may seem hard to the local traveller when he learns from the Traffic Commissioners—or the Ministry, as he might inexpertly say—that one company has not been allowed to supplement another on a particular stretch of road; or that a bus which is carrying workpeople on a contract basis is not allowed to take up other passengers en route; or that a new service directly between two points already served adequately by rail has not been licensed. But viewed in the general context of the road/rail problem and the need to establish the regularity of bus services in the long term it will perhaps be more understandable. And, although the bus companies are faced with rising costs and declining traffic—more and more people taking to their own transport—the English countryside is by no means badly served, taking into account the multitude of villages and hamlets dotted about and the tortuous lanes that join them.

Before leaving passenger transport something must be said about the special situation of London. London's problems in the 1920s were much the same as those elsewhere but greatly magnified by so many people living and travelling daily in a small area. After three public inquiries by the London and Home Counties Traffic Advisory Committee[1] into travelling facilities in different areas of London the conclusion was finally reached that a single transport system for the whole area was the proper solution. This was achieved in 1933 by the London Passenger Transport Act. Responsibility for all forms of passenger transport, except the suburban services of the main-line railways, was transferred to a single body, the London Passenger Transport Board, with the privileges—and the obligations —of a statutory monopoly. The Board could run services anywhere within their 'special area'[2] without road service licences while anyone else wanting to run road passenger services in the area had to get not only a road service licence but also the Board's consent. The only control the Traffic Commissioners have over the London Transport Executive (as successors of the L.P.T.B.) services is the normal

[1] Page 136.
[2] Roughly a radius of 25 miles from Charing Cross.

road service licence control outside the special area and, inside the area, control of certain minor matters such as the approval of routes and stopping places.

The licensing system does not affect trams and trolley buses outside London. These forms of transport, which operate in or near towns, have always been controlled by local Acts or Orders which limit their activities as strictly as the lines or overhead wires restrict their movements. They are often run by municipalities and usually have, for obvious reasons, a monopoly in their own sphere. They were therefore left outside the licensing system, though their right to the privilege has been challenged on the ground that it prevents co-ordination of all road passenger services. The point was considered by a Select Committee of the House of Commons in 1936 and again by the Thesiger Committee which reported that, in view of the opposition of the municipalities, the small number of trams and trolley buses compared with ordinary buses, and their declining importance, strong justification would be needed for bringing them under the Commissioners' control, except for fares which have since been made subject to their jurisdiction.[1]

COMPETITION FOR THE CARRIAGE OF GOODS

In the carriage of goods the rivalry between road and rail developed with remarkable speed. Up to 1914 the railways had had little to fear from the roads; the war then showed what road transport could do and at the same time provided admirable opportunities for its growth. It brought mechanical advances and taught mechanical skills to many who before the war would have had no chance of acquiring them. In the difficult years that followed many ex-servicemen with a little capital set up transport businesses and the effect on the railways proved far-reaching. Trade depression meant less traffic to be carried and made competition keener. Moreover, traders who formerly used the railways discovered the convenience of carrying their own goods in their own vehicles. Simultaneously, the railways were faced, as they have been in this second post-war period, with large rises in costs outside their control. Further, a substantial proportion of the railways' total costs were fixed and did not vary with the volume of traffic handled; whereas the fixed costs of road vehicle operators were low and their running costs bore a much closer relation to the traffic carried.

Competition was still more unbalanced because the railways were subject to strict statutory control whilst for road hauliers there were

[1] The Transport Charges, etc. (Miscellaneous Provisions) Act, 1954.

few controls of any kind and none at all on charges. The railways were subject to 'equality of charging'—and had been since 1845. Their charges had to be the same for goods of the same description passing over the same stretch of railway line in similar circumstances and no special bargains could be made with particular traders; all their charges had to be published. Secondly, under an Act of 1854 they were prohibited from giving 'undue preference', so that a trader in one area could not be given unreasonable advantages over a trader in another. Complaints of inequality or undue preference could be determined judicially. Thirdly, the statutory system of classification of goods meant that their charges were based primarily on the value of the goods carried and not on the cost of carrying. These restrictive principles could be justified for a form of transport when it had a near monopoly, but in the twentieth-century battle of competitive inland transport it meant that the railways were left with one hand tied behind their backs. Road hauliers could, and generally did, base their charges on the cost of carrying and not on value; thus they easily undercut the railways for the most paying traffics. The railways retaliated by quoting more and more 'exceptional' rates which the authors of the Railways Act of 1921 had hoped to see drastically reduced in number and range. The Railway Rates Tribunal, which had the task of fixing rail charges at a level designed to produce the 'standard net revenues', defined in the 1921 Act, were never able to overtake the snowball. The situation, though of obvious advantage to the road haulier and also of short-term advantage to the consumer (who was assured of competitive rates), was not in the public interest in the long run.

THE CONTROL OF ROAD HAULAGE

The Royal Commission on Transport, which has already been mentioned in connection with passenger traffic, and, later, the Salter Conference,[1] went into the problem fully and the result was the Road and Rail Traffic Act, 1933, which formed a pattern of control which, despite nationalisation and denationalisation, is not very different today.

The new Act did not treat the railways' problems very radically; indeed it could not be expected to do so, or to give them much new freedom, until the effects of control of road haulage were seen. They were, however, given power to arrange 'agreed charges' with individual traders, which meant they could make a contract for carrying all or part of a trader's goods at, for example, a flat rate per unit, thus binding the traffic to rail and saving administrative expenses

[1] Report of the Conference on Rail and Road Transport (H.M.S.O., 1932).

for both sides. This certainly helped, but it was far from complete commercial freedom. Agreed charges had to be approved by the Railway Rates Tribunal and published. Although the old provisions about equality and undue preference did not apply to these new charges, traders doing similar business who thought that the charges were against their interests could oppose their approval or apply to have similar charges fixed for their own traffic.

On the roads the strict control of goods transport which is still in operation today came into being. Superficially it is not unlike the passenger licensing system. The Traffic Areas are the same and the Licensing Authorities are the Chairmen of the Traffic Commissioners. There are precautions to protect public safety—to ensure for instance that vehicles are roadworthy and that records are kept of drivers' hours of work and of the loads carried. But the actual control over operations—the equivalent of the road service licence—is necessarily very different. There are basically three kinds of hauliers' licences: 'C' licences which confine traders to the carriage of goods 'for or in connection with' their own business (these are granted quite freely and are not limited in any way); 'B' licences for traders carrying partly their own goods and partly those of other traders for payment (usually with some limit of area or kind of goods carried); lastly 'A' licences for the professional road haulier who may carry other people's goods for hire or reward (but not his own). There were two ideas behind the institution of the 'A' licence: first, to ensure that anyone who was genuinely running a road haulage business before 1933 could continue to do so, and, secondly, to enable increased facilities to be provided if they were proved necessary. The Licensing Authorities' obligations were therefore expressed rather broadly; they had to 'have regard primarily to the interests of the public generally, including those of persons requiring as well as those of persons providing facilities for transport', bearing in mind the previous conduct of the applicant and the number and type of vehicles he intended to use; they also had to consider whether 'suitable transport facilities' were already available 'in excess of requirements'.

The Transport Act, 1953, which will be considered in greater detail in the next chapter, modified these criteria, particularly by changing the emphasis on the different considerations Licensing Authorities must bear in mind; apart from the interests of the public generally, the emphasis was placed primarily on the interests of persons requiring facilities for transport and only secondarily on those of persons providing facilities. For 'A' licences Licensing Authorities cannot impose conditions which might limit their scope, though they will naturally hear evidence from applicants and objectors about the traffic which applicants normally intend to carry. But, if an 'A', or for that matter a 'B', licence is granted and the holder then uses it for substantially different purposes, the Licensing Authority can suspend or revoke it. Further, when licences come to be renewed the Authority can consider whether the applicant has materially changed the nature of his operations since the original licence was granted.

Licensing Authorities cannot fix the charges which hauliers may make to their customers, but in considering applications for licences they now have the power under the Transport Act, 1953, to take into account, to the extent they think proper, the charges the applicant proposes to make and those made by competing road hauliers. The Road Traffic Act, 1956, gave them the additional power to suspend or revoke a licence if the holder had been persistently charging less than the cost of providing the service and so had placed other road hauliers at an unfair disadvantage.

Appeals against decisions of the Licensing Authorities are dealt with by a tribunal. Something has already been said in connection with passenger transport about the relative merits of the Minister and of a tribunal as a court of appeal. Each system has its advantages and there has never been any serious proposal to change the system for road haulage, where appeals lie now to the Transport Tribunal.[1]

The goods licensing system has its critics, but what licensing system has not? Those who have failed to obtain a licence or who find it difficult to enter the industry are naturally foremost among the critics. Some more dispassionate observers take the line that the vital words of the Road and Rail Traffic Act do not allow sufficient weight to be given by the Licensing Authorities to the future anticipated needs of traders and that the licensing control unnecessarily stultifies the natural growth of road transport for hire or reward. Others again say that the restrictions on plying for hire have encouraged the increase in the number of vehicles used for carrying the owners' own goods—the C licensed vehicles. But looking at the movement of goods as a whole throughout the country, by rail as well as by road, the need for licensing is still there. And though there are pressures for modifications in the system—and many changes have been made from time to time—there is at present no pressure amongst those most intimately affected for any fundamental alteration. More is said of the ever-present problem of road/rail competition towards the end of the next chapter.

[1] Page 112.

REGIONAL TRANSPORT COMMISSIONERS

Each Chairman of Traffic Commissioners has, in addition to his second post as the Licensing Authority for goods vehicles, yet a third, and a most important one, as Regional Transport Commissioner.[1] Whilst in the other two capacities the holder of the office has his independent position under statute, in the third he reports directly to the Ministry. As Regional Transport Commissioner he is responsible for the oversight of transport needs and requirements in his area in time of emergency, whether in war or in peace, and for looking after the interests of transport itself at such times. With his knowledge of the road and rail facilities in his area, the Traffic Commissioner-cum-Licensing Authority is the obvious choice for this duty.

When difficulties arise in peace—for example, if there is a strike involving transport—manufacturers and traders and public utilities naturally do their utmost to help themselves, but they know that they can if necessary seek the assistance of Regional Transport Commissioners either directly or through the Regional Transport Committees which are usually set up. If a State of Emergency were declared at such a time the Minister might delegate some of his emergency powers to his Commissioners, as he did during the railway strike in 1955 when the Commissioners were empowered to requisition tipper vehicles for the carriage of coal. Their most recent major task was the rationing of motor fuel for goods vehicles and buses and coaches at the time of the Suez crisis.

During the war they administered the motor fuel rationing scheme and the system of permits which took the place of the licences. By this means they ensured that sufficient transport was available for essential traffics which had to go by road. They also helped to arrange for transport when shortages occurred, though in the later stages a separate Road Haulage Organisation was created to provide for the movement of Government traffic and of important long-distance traffic carried on private account. In emergency the Commissioners and their staffs are an essential part of the country's inland transport organisation and the civil defence transport plans, which the Department must make in case war should come, are based in large measure upon them.

[1] In Wales there is now an exception to this rule. On 1st October, 1958, a Special Transport Commissioner for Wales and Monmouthshire was appointed who is not a Traffic Commissioner or Licensing Authority.

CHAPTER IX

Road and Rail since the War

The Transport Act of 1947 — The Transport
Act of 1953 and subsequent legislation —
Present Problems and Responsibilities

*

THE railways were brought under direct Government control
during the Second World War and were managed by the Railway
Executive Committee, a body appointed by the Minister and consisting of representatives of the four main-line companies and of the
London Passenger Transport Board. The story of the remarkable
war-time achievement of the railways has been told elsewhere,[1] but
the price they paid for that achievement was very high. By the end
of the war there were heavy arrears of maintenance on the permanent way, in signalling equipment and at stations. A large amount
of the damage inflicted by enemy action had not been repaired:
rolling stock had suffered abnormal wear and tear and much of it
was overdue for replacement, and there was a shortage in particular
of passenger coaching stock. The financial outlook was no less
gloomy. With the falling away of war-time traffics the charges were
too low to cover costs and had to be raised substantially: the drift
of traffic from rail to road, which war-time fuel rationing and other
measures had artificially reversed, was resumed. It was clear that
some radical step would have to be taken if the best use was to be
made of the country's inland transport resources.

A number of different solutions were propounded. Just before the
war the railways, seeing that the Acts of 1930 and 1933 had not, in
their view, achieved the *modus vivendi* between road and rail which
had been hoped for, had put forward their 'Square Deal' proposals,
suggesting an important revision of previous policies and applying
for complete freedom to fix their own rates. This had been considered by the Transport Advisory Council set up under the 1933
Act and the Ministry was in fact preparing fresh legislation when
war broke out. In the closing stages of the war much thought was
again given to the problem in the Ministry of War Transport, and

[1] See in particular C. I. Savage: *Inland Transport, History of the Second
World War* (Civil Series) (H.M.S.O.)

after the war the London and North Eastern Railway put forward yet another proposal—their so-called 'Landlord and Tenant' scheme. But the coming into power of the Labour Government in 1945 left no doubt what solution would be adopted. The Labour Party had long been pledged to nationalise the railways. They had urged this policy after the First World War when it was generally thought that the newly-created Ministry of Transport would do exactly this. Later three members of the Royal Commission on Transport had recommended nationalisation in the final report of the Commission in 1931. Mr Herbert Morrison had set out the case for a public corporation in his book *Socialisation and Transport* published in 1933. Mr Ernest Bevin and two other representatives of labour had dissented from a report of the Transport Advisory Council in 1937 on the ground that national ownership of the means of public transport offered the only real solution to the road/rail problem. It was therefore no surprise that the Ministry was instructed immediately after the Labour Government came to power to prepare a nationalisation Bill.

THE TRANSPORT ACT OF 1947

The framing of the Transport Bill together with the consultations and discussions attendant upon such a measure and the task of piloting the Bill through all its stages in Parliament was the major preoccupation of the Minister and the Department in 1946 and the first half of 1947. The Act which resulted is a formidable document of 128 sections and 15 schedules but its main objects are clearly defined and simple in outline. It set up the British Transport Commission as a public authority, with its Chairman and Members appointed by the Minister, 'to provide or secure or promote the provision of' in the words of Section 3, 'an efficient, adequate, economical and properly integrated system of public inland transport and port facilities within Great Britain for passengers and goods with due regard to safety of operation . . .'. Important powers were reserved to the Minister as has already been described in Chapter 1; but it was a major principle behind the Act that the Commission should be left as free as possible to run the business on commercial lines and in matters of day-to-day administration Parliament decided not to interfere.[1] Under the Commission, a number of different Executives were set up to manage and operate, according to schemes of delegation prepared by the Commission, the various interests acquired under the Act. The Chairman and members of the Executives were again appointed by the Minister, after consultation with

[1] *Hansard*, H. of C., 4th December, 1947, Col. 566 *et seq.*

the Commission. The principal railways were vested by the Act in the Commission and placed under the management of the Railway Executive. All long-distance[1] road haulage concerns, apart from those dealing in certain specialised traffics such as furniture removals, meat and livestock, were acquired compulsorily (unless agreement on voluntary acquisition was reached first) and the vehicles and property were transferred to the management of the Road Haulage Executive. All 'A' and 'B' licensed operators not taken over (i.e. the short-distance men) had to get permission from the Commission if they wanted to carry goods for hire or reward outside a radius of 25 miles from their operating centre.[2] By these measures it was hoped to secure the 'properly integrated system'—the key phrase of the 1947 Act—of rail and long-distance road haulage and to solve the problem of the competition for goods traffic between these two forms of transport which had so long dominated pre-war inland transport.

The old-established policy of subjecting rail charges to the jurisdiction of an independent tribunal was continued under nationalisation. But the concept of integration necessarily meant that the charges of all the transport services provided by the Commission, including both rail and road, should be controlled by this one body. So the Transport Tribunal replaced the Railway Rates Tribunal, and was given wider powers and functions. The Commission's charges were to be governed by 'charges schemes' submitted to the Tribunal and confirmed after public inquiry. The schemes could regulate charges in a variety of ways: they could provide for fixed charges or for maximum charges or for standard charges with or without minimum charges, or indeed could leave charges to the Commission's discretion with or without appeal to the Tribunal. Various schemes covering passenger fares on British Railways and on the Commission's road and rail services in the London Area were in fact confirmed but on the most complicated issue—freight charges—progress was naturally much slower. The Commission were about to submit a draft scheme (covering carriage of goods by rail, inland waterway and long-distance road transport) at the end of 1951 after having discussed the principles of the scheme with Trade Associations. But by then a Conservative Government was in office with a declared policy of introducing fresh legislation. The date by which the Commission were required to submit a scheme was therefore further

[1] The tests as to what was 'long-distance' were complicated but, roughly, the term covered concerns more than half of whose operations were over distances of 40 miles or more provided the vehicles concerned went more than 25 miles from their operating centres.
[2] 'C' licensed operators were not affected by the Act—a clause imposing a 40-mile limit on the operation of 'C' vehicles having been withdrawn at the Committee stage of the Bill.

postponed by the Minister under powers given him in the 1947 Act.

Road passenger services were not directly nationalised by the 1947 Act but the Commission were given powers to prepare area schemes for co-ordinating road and rail passenger services. These schemes, whether for the simple regrouping of operators or for full-scale nationalisation, were to come into force only after an Order by the Minister. In fact the only area scheme proposed—one for the North-East of England—evoked lively opposition, not least from municipal passenger transport authorities, and was not pursued. Indeed the Road Passenger Executive which had been set up, later than the other Executives, to work on these schemes had a short life. The Commission did however acquire by voluntary agreement ownership of two of the three largest bus undertakings in Great Britain, Tillings and Scottish Motor Traction, as well as some smaller concerns and have left the company structure in being to carry on management under the new ownership. The possession of these companies, together with the part interests in other bus companies which the Commission inherited from the former main-line railway companies, gives them a big stake in public road passenger transport. In fact, of the country's 78,000 buses and trolley buses the Commission own some 24,000 and have an interest in many more.

Three more Executives were set up by the Act for the remaining interests which the Commission took over—the London Transport Executive which replaced the London Passenger Transport Board, the Hotels Executive for the railway hotels and other catering services, and the Docks and Inland Waterways Executive for the railway-owned docks and for canals and other inland navigations.[1] This last-named Executive also had powers to prepare area schemes for docks and harbours on the same principle as those for road passenger transport. But no scheme was in fact produced.

THE TRANSPORT ACT OF 1953 AND SUBSEQUENT LEGISLATION

In 1951–52 the new Conservative Government decided to modify the Transport Act, 1947. Instead of seeking the co-ordination and integration of the main national transport effort through a single authority they decided that there should be both public and private enterprise in transport and that private road hauliers should be given the opportunity of coming back into the long-distance business. There was no proposal to denationalise the railways, but instead the Government announced their intention of reorganising the railways

[1] See Chapter VII.

H

into regional groups of economic size. It was at the same time recognised that the road transport proposals would expose the railways to competition from road hauliers whose charges were uncontrolled, and it was therefore considered reasonable to give the railways greater freedom in charging than they had hitherto been allowed.

The main change introduced by the Transport Act, 1953—and the one that attracted most attention—affected the road haulage side of the Commission's activities. The Commission had to dispose as quickly as they reasonably could of most of the vehicles and other property they were using for goods transport except that part of it which had been formerly operated by the railway companies. The Road Haulage Disposal Board was set up under the Act to supervise the process of disposal. Buyers of vehicles were entitled to special 'A' licences and the 25-mile limit restriction came to an end after an interval. A levy was temporarily introduced upon road goods transport as a whole, 'C' licensed vehicles as well as 'A' and 'B', to help to make up to the Commission the loss on the sale of the undertaking. Vehicles offered in small units sold well, but when vehicles and premises were offered in units large enough for potential buyers to be able to maintain the long-distance trunk services the Commission had built up, demand proved to be relatively small. The Government decided that in the national interest it would be wrong to allow these services to be broken up and in 1956 the Transport (Disposal of Road Haulage Property) Act was passed which enabled the Commission to retain sufficient vehicles and other property to keep the services in being. The result is that some 15,000 vehicles out of the 40,000 the Road Haulage Executive had in 1952 remain at present in the ownership of the Commission and in the management of British Road Services. These maintain the important long-distance trunk routes and constitute the largest and most important single road haulage concern in the country. In addition, 17,000 vehicles perform the railway collection and delivery services. But to see these figures in perspective, the total of 33,000 goods vehicles owned by the B.T.C. compares with over 1,200,000 vehicles in private hands— 86,000 'A' licensed vehicles, 71,000 'B's and over a million 'C's. Thus it will be seen that the Commission are very far from having a monopoly of road freight traffic, though it must be remembered that the great majority of 'C' licensed vehicles are relatively small and include all retail delivery vans.

As for the other parts of the Commission's undertakings, the Transport Act, 1953, reorganised the Commission and relieved them of their duty under the 1947 Act to provide the 'properly integrated system of public inland transport and port facilities within Great Britain'. The management of the railways under a central Railway

Executive of the British Transport Commission had been much criticised as over-centralised—though it was generally recognised that the Executive had played an indispensable role in the early days of the Commission—and the Conservative Government, while not seeking to undo what had been achieved by the Railway Executive since 1947 in unifying the railways into a single system, favoured an organisation with a greater degree of decentralisation to regions. The Railway Executive and all the other Executives with the exception of the London Transport Executive were abolished. Area Boards for the railways were appointed by the Commission, and policy and management functions were delegated to them under a scheme drafted by the Commission and brought into force by Order of the Minister and affirmed by Parliament. The powers to prepare area road passenger and dock and harbour schemes were repealed.

To help the railways to hold their own in competition with de-nationalised road haulage, the 1953 Act abolished the long-standing equality and undue preference restrictions on charges and allowed the Commission to make agreed charges with traders without having to get any authority from the Tribunal and without publishing them. It also limited the scope of the charges schemes to be submitted by the Commission; road haulage charges and charges for carriage by inland waterway were excluded, so that the Commission were given the same freedom in these competitive fields as other operators. Charges schemes were to fix only maximum charges or, where that was not reasonably practicable, or was undesirable, they were to provide for 'reasonable charges'. The Tribunal could be asked to determine what was 'reasonable'. Actual charges within the maxima were left to the Commission's discretion and a charges scheme must secure that no conditions or limitations were imposed on that discretion. The obligation to publish all charges was also to disappear when the scheme came into force and the Commission were to be required to publish only maximum charges.

The Railway Merchandise Charges Scheme submitted to the Transport Tribunal in 1955 set out in detail the Commission's proposals for taking advantage of the new freedom given in the Act. In place of 'standard charges' related to a classification of merchandise primarily based on value, it substituted a system of maximum charges based on the weight and the 'loadability' or loading characteristics of the goods to be carried. It provided for a fixed charge per ton to cover terminal charges and the first 10 miles of conveyance and a mileage charge per ton thereafter. The primary basis of charging was therefore the cost to the Commission of carrying the goods, and their value was of only secondary importance. The Commission's scheme was the subject of a lengthy public inquiry by the Transport

Tribunal. Although certain modifications were made to the maximum charges proposed and certain important consignments were made subject to reasonable charges, the main principles were approved.

The scheme came into force in July, 1957, but it is still too early to judge its effect on the pattern of railway freight traffic or, indeed, its effect upon road traffic. The new system has, however, the virtue of flexibility and there is plenty of scope for the Commission to adapt it to the needs of the customer and to compete for traffic without many of the previous handicaps. Competition from road haulage (both of the Commission and of private enterprise) should ensure generally that charges are fair while in those cases where 'reasonable charges' are made, or where there is no reasonable alternative to rail, anyone who considers that the charges imposed on him are unreasonable can appeal to the Tribunal. There are also statutory provisions giving a measure of protection to coasting shipping, to independent canals and canal carriers and to independent harbour undertakings.

The requirement to decentralise the organisation of the railways and the new provisions giving greater freedom to fix charges more in accordance with commercial principles did not, however, complete the legislative framework created by the Conservative Government for the railways. In 1957 another section was added to it in the form of the Transport (Railway Finances) Act, the reasons for which were as follows. In 1955 the Commission had launched a plan for the modernisation and re-equipment of British Railways which they estimated would cost £1,200 million over the next 15 years (later revised to £1,500 million).[1] For 30 years the railways, with few exceptions—the outstanding exception being the Southern Railway's electrification programme—had not been able to undertake any large schemes of modernisation. Before the war they had difficulty in attracting capital; during the war maintenance was reduced to the level required only to keep them going; in the immediate post-war years a policy of restricted capital investment in transport deprived them of the opportunity to modernise on the extensive scale required, or even to overtake the arrears of maintenance accumulated during the war. Thus the new policy of competition between road and rail found the railways ill-equipped to take advantage of the opportunities it offered them. The railway modernisation plan took full account of the tremendous part road transport would claim in the public transport system. The object of the plan was therefore to re-fashion the railways to do the tasks which, given modern equipment, they ought to be able to do more efficiently than any other form of transport; for instance, the carriage of passengers over long distances

[1] Of this amount almost half represents replacements and normal maintenance.

or on the short daily journeys from the suburbs to work in the big cities, and the movement of bulk freight. Here the railways have an inherent advantage over other forms of transport—an advantage which is often spectacularly confirmed by the response from the public on those sectors or services where modern equipment has been introduced. The Government, after examining the broad outline of the plan (as they are required to examine all programmes of the Commission's capital expenditure), approved it in principle subject to closer scrutiny of the detail as it emerged.

A bold programme of railway modernisation was not enough in itself to bring about a satisfactory relationship between road and rail. The Commission themselves recognised that it would be some years before the programme began to bear fruit and before traffic trends could be reversed and profitable operation assured. By 1956 the financial situation on the railways had become a matter of serious concern. The accumulated deficit on revenue account since nationalisation had risen to £70 million. Nor was there any immediate prospect of being able to recoup increased costs and balance the revenue account—let alone repay past deficits. The Government decided that the whole financial situation called for review; this was undertaken jointly by the Department and the Commission. As a result, in the Transport (Railway Finances) Act, 1957, the Commission were authorised to borrow from the Consolidated Fund sums required to meet the deficits on revenue account of British Railways during the years up to 1962—up to a total of £250 million[1] —plus the interest on these advances. The Commission were also authorised to borrow moneys required to meet the interest on capital spent on the modernisation programme in the period before it was expected that it could become revenue earning. In effect the 1957 Act has, for the present, modified the Commission's obligation under the Transport Act, 1947, to balance their revenue account 'taking one year with another' and has given them a new target to break even by 1962 and an obligation eventually not only to repay in full the advances made to assist them through the difficult period of post-war railway reconstruction and development but also to make good the deficit which had accumulated at the end of 1955.

PRESENT PROBLEMS AND RESPONSIBILITIES

There are many other tasks that fall to the Ministry in dealing with road and rail transport besides the overriding one of setting the legislative framework within which these two forms of transport shall operate. Many of these duties have been dealt with in the

[1] This has since been increased to £400 million.

previous chapter; but many more may be cited. The Department advises on the private legislation of the British Transport Commission and on other private legislation affecting transport so that the Minister may report to the Committees of both Houses of Parliament that scrutinise Private Bills and Provisional Orders; it is involved in the discussions on the Economic Commission for Europe and the Organisation for European Economic Co-operation about the freer movement of traffic to, from and within Europe; it represents the Government at the meetings about the International Conventions concerning the carriage of goods and passengers by rail; it studies the reports made by the principal Transport Users' Consultative Committees[1]—particularly as the Minister is empowered to give a direction to the Commission on a recommendation of the Central Committee or of the Committees for Scotland or Wales. But, important as these duties can become, the major problem in this field remains that of watching the balance between road and rail.

The enactments described in this and the previous chapter form the framework within which current policies for road and rail transport must be devised and together they prescribe the basic principles on which the national transport system shall be developed. On the railway side they provide that responsibility for ownership and operation shall be concentrated in the British Transport Commission with an obligation to decentralise management. Public road transport is provided by a combination of public and private enterprise, the British Transport Commission retaining a substantial, if reduced, stake in road haulage, particularly in the important trunk services, and their interest in numerous provincial bus companies. In London the British Transport Commission retain through the London Transport Executive their monopoly of both road and rail passenger transport. The role of the railways has been prescribed and underwritten during the period when their equipment is being brought up to the standard that will enable them to fulfil it. Competition between road and rail has been facilitated by the removal of past restrictions on the railways' charging policy. Competition between road transport undertakings remains subject to the control of licensing.

It is the Department's business to see that policies for dealing with the problems that confront road and rail transport are devised within this framework and to give such guidance and assistance as will help the industry to fulfil as well as possible the role assigned to each part of it. On the road side, the Department's principal duty

---

[1] Set up under the Transport Acts as consumers' councils where complaints about the Commission's services and facilities may be considered and recommendations made.

is the oversight of the road transport licensing system. On the railway side, much of the Department's work arises from the particular problems of the vast and ambitious plan of modernisation and the general problems posed by a large-scale nationalised industry whose activities lie near the roots of the country's economy. The public interest in the railways requires that the Minister and his officers should be in close touch with all major developments. Without trespassing on the field of management reserved to the Commission, the Department must keep abreast of their progress in modernisation, their charges policy, their capital investment needs, their changes of organisation and the many other facets of their transport operations which provide a guide to their ability to meet their obligations and carry out the role that has been assigned to them. It is not always easy for the public to understand the fine line that separates the Minister's responsibilities from those of the nationalised industry's, and the Department has constantly to be on the alert to maintain a relationship which on the one hand takes account of the fact that the industry is accountable to Parliament and the nation and on the other protects it from unnecessary interference in its management.

Whether the right balance has now been struck between road and rail will be a matter for future Governments to decide. But in order that the Department can be in a position to advise Ministers, it must keep under review the development of current policy and attempt such projections into the future as a knowledge of present transport and economic trends permit. In attempting to forecast these trends, investigators have long been hampered by a lack of knowledge about the actual employment of road goods transport. To a considerable extent this omission was repaired by statistical inquiries using modern sampling techniques which the Ministry initiated in 1952.[1] The investigation showed that road goods transport was in 1952 carrying three times as much tonnage as the railways (900 million tons as against 300 million) and that the ton mileage performed was almost as great as that of the railways.[2] Calculations based on these and other statistics and their projection into the future lead to the expectation that road goods transport will obtain a high proportion of the increase in traffic resulting from the expected increase in national production. This growth is not likely to take place to any great extent in 'A' and 'B' vehicles where the licensing system tightly controls the number and size of lorries available and where the Licensing Authorities take account of all transport, both road

[1] As this book goes to press another sample inquiry is being conducted.
[2] See K. F. Glover and D. N. Miller: *The Outline of the Road Goods Transport Industry* (*Journal of the Royal Statistical Society*, Vol. 117, Pt. 3, 1954).

and rail, that is available. The effect of the licensing system in recent years has in fact been that the number of public haulage vehicles has remained fairly static though the size of vehicle has tended to rise. This trend will no doubt continue. But where the growth of road transport is most likely to occur, as in the recent past, is in 'C' vehicles, the expansion of which is unchecked by the Licensing Authorities. From 306,000 at the end of 1945 'C' licensed vehicles have risen to over a million. Many of these vehicles are quite small—over half are of less than 30 cwt. unladen weight—and engaged merely in local delivery services. But many are of substantial size and the statistical investigations referred to above show that 'C' vehicles account for well over half the total ton mileage of all road goods vehicles. Whether these trends are or are not in the public interest is a matter that is much argued. It may be said, however, that the advantages to manufacturing or distributing organisations of having 'C' vehicles at their exclusive disposal are to ensure that there are no delays in production, to avoid special packing of goods, to ensure that fragile goods are handled by skilled persons with an interest in seeing that they arrive undamaged and promptly, and to ensure that vehicles—some perhaps with special constructional features—are available whenever they are required. Whether all operators know what their fleets cost them, as compared with the use of public transport, is perhaps doubtful, though many certainly do. But the cost element of the transport operation itself is only one consideration to be taken into account; transport costs might be regarded as justified if the better facilities were successful in securing more than compensating economies elsewhere in the production process.

The other side of the picture is the effect which large withdrawals of traffic may have on public transport—that is, on the facilities that are available to those manufacturers and others who do not possess their own transport. Public transport cannot be economically provided in the absence of sufficient traffic. The balance between public and private transport must, therefore, continue to be watched.

This problem of the abstraction of traffic from public transport by private vehicles is already becoming serious in the passenger field, where, so far from there being an expansion, there is actually a decline in the number of public service vehicles. Rising costs coupled with the decline in traffic occasioned by present-day personal spending habits and the growth of private motoring—cars, scooters, motorised bicycles and so on—face the providers of this form of public transport with increasing difficulties. In particular the serving of the rural areas, where operations are frequently uneconomic, is a matter of serious concern. The traditional answer has been cross-subsidisation, that is to say, the maintenance of the uneconomic route by the better patronised and more paying urban services, but more radical solutions may have to be found. For a start some relaxation of the public service vehicle regulations has been allowed to make it easier for the small 'village carrier' type of utility bus to carry passengers.

The suggestions which have been canvassed for the future of inland transport are legion; for example, that the Government should go further than they have already gone in taking steps—both fiscal and otherwise—to guide traffic to that form of transport to which it is thought to be best suited, or should take steps to curtail the growing movement by road of what are traditionally the railway's staple traffics such as coal. The contrary view is that it is impossible for a central authority to judge what form of transport is suitable for any particular purpose. Apart from the sheer volume of decisions to be taken it is not possible for a Government Department to learn enough about the internal arrangements of industry and commerce and the varying circumstances of individual concerns to know which means of transport is best at any particular time; using one form rather than another may give rise to savings in non-transport costs. This school of thought advocates the maximum freedom of competition and the greatest freedom of users' choice. This, they say, will also have the advantage of driving high-cost carriers out of business as quickly as possible.

The solution adopted by the 1953 Transport Act was to restore road competition, to provide for the reorganisation of railway management, and to allow the railways a greater freedom of charging which would among other things enable them to make their charges more nearly match their costs. Later came the scheme to modernise the system, with which must be coupled the process started soon after nationalisation of closing uneconomic branch lines and curtailing facilities no longer required. The object of all these is to enable the railways to hold and develop those traffics for which they are specially well suited, to divest themselves of traffics which are costly to carry by rail and for which road transport is better suited, and to give a service of such quality and price that they will obtain a fair share in the large intermediate field of truly competitive traffics.

These are all contentious issues. The Commission in their Report for 1956 express the hope that 'they will be allowed reasonable freedom and a period of stability to press on with reconstruction and that the whole fabric of public transport will no longer be subjected to periodic and seismic upheaval on political account'. This *cri de cœur* must be echoed widely, not least in the Government

Department concerned with the upheavals when they occur. But the organisation of inland transport and the legislative framework within which it is to operate, which is one of the three principal tasks of the Ministry, is inevitably a matter of great public concern. It will be the Department's duty as heretofore to advise on what it considers to be the best arrangements in the circumstances of the time, but it will be succeeding Governments that will take the decisions.

CHAPTER X

Highways

Historical — A National Highway Authority — Classified Roads — Trunk Roads — Motorways — The Current Road Programme — Highways and Control of Development — Traffic Congestion

*

HISTORICAL

THERE is today more sustained interest in highways than in any other of the Department's activities. Thus the amount of money devoted by the Government to road improvements and the choice of individual schemes on which to start work, together with the wastefulness of traffic congestion and the problems of road safety,[1] evoke the liveliest criticism and comment in Parliament and elsewhere. Yet only 50 years ago a Parliamentary Question on highways—except one in the most general terms—was not admitted. In fact, except for the picturesque interlude of the Turnpike Trusts and the Georgian days of coaching, the roads were traditionally held to be a local interest and responsibility.

Under the feudal system responsibility for the upkeep of roads was one of the many duties laid upon landlords as a condition of the tenure of their land; and traces of these ancient obligations can still be found where a landowner is obliged to maintain a public highway crossing his land. When the feudal system broke down some other means had to be found for keeping the roads in repair. The obligation was placed upon the parish, and legal proceedings could be taken against the inhabitants if they failed in their duty. The system did not work well, for the parish was concerned only to keep the roads in good enough order for its own modest needs and saw no necessity for lavish, or even regular, maintenance for the benefit of passing strangers. But with the development of industry and commerce in the seventeenth and eighteenth centuries better roads became both a necessity and a good business proposition. In the words of Dr G. M. Trevelyan '. . . recourse was had to private initiative, in which the improving spirit of that age resided. Turnpike

---
[1] Dealt with in the next chapter.

companies were granted Parliamentary powers to erect gates and toll bars and mulct the actual users of the road in return for remaking and maintaining some particular stretch of highway. Between 1700 and 1750 as many as 400 Road Acts were passed; between 1751 and 1790, 1,600!'[1] Apart from the achievements in Scotland of General Wade, who began the construction of many miles of excellent roads in the Highlands after the 1715 rising, the Turnpike Trusts or Companies represent the first real attempt to bring some proper improvement to our highways. Competent surveyors, of whom the most eminent were Telford and Macadam, were engaged and by the turn of the century there were some 20,000 miles of turnpike road with several thousand toll gates and side-bars. The busier and more important roads were thus maintained by the trusts, whilst only those of purely local value remained the responsibility of the parish; this position was accepted when highway law was first overhauled and codified in the Highways Acts of 1835.

But the Turnpikes were not popular—nor in many instances efficient—and the principle of charging the users of the roads began to be challenged early in Queen Victoria's reign. In Wales opposition took the form of violence and the houses of the keepers were assailed and burned down in the so-called Rebecca riots.[2] About the same time the modern form of local government was evolving and the framework of highway administration was gradually altered to fit into the new system. The Trusts, many of which had in any case been made bankrupt by the growth of the railways, were steadily swept away by legislation, the last in 1895.

Although Parliament was at this time taking some notice of the general need for reforming the administration of the roads, there was no thought or suggestion by either the Home Office, which was, until 1872, the Department responsible, or after that by the Local Government Board, that the State should take a more direct hand. The pressure for this came from the first cyclists and, not many years later, from the first motorists. What had been adequate for horse and cart traffic provided an indifferent, and often thoroughly bad, surface for bicycles and cars. Dust was a special nuisance in the summer. It came more and more to be appreciated that the multiplicity of local authorities responsible for the country's roads meant that there was no consistency in the standard of a road as it passed from one authority's area to another, often several times in a few miles. Agitation was reaching a peak when Lloyd George became Chancellor of the Exchequer; he, with more foresight than most of his

---

[1] Dr. G. M. Trevelyan: *English Social History*, p. 382.
[2] For this colourful episode in highway history see Sidney and Beatrice Webb: *The Story of the King's Highway* (1913), pp. 217–20.

political contemporaries, had a vision of the future growth of motor traffic and the extensive road improvements that would be needed; in consequence the Development and Road Improvement Fund Act was passed in 1909. The part of this Act dealing with highways set up a Road Board as the central highway authority. (The rest of the Act dealt with the unemployment problem, and the association in the economic mind of roads and unemployment, which then began and which has only just been broken, has at times acted as a regrettable brake on necessary highway improvements.) The 1909 Act is important, as it marks the origin of today's administrative system. It gave the Board power to make grants to highway authorities for the improvement and maintenance of roads, although it failed to regulate the basis on which the grants should be made. When the first Minister of Transport took over in 1919 this defect was remedied and powers to classify roads so as to provide a basis for grants were obtained in the Ministry of Transport Act. Since then the term 'classified roads', indicating those maintained partly by the State and partly from the local rates, has become thoroughly familiar in highway circles and much of this chapter will be devoted to them.

Two other important statutes which, with the 1909 Act, form the basis of the system as it stands today are the Local Government Act, 1929, and the Trunk Roads Act, 1936. Under the former, responsibility for the publicly maintained highways was reallocated. As a result County Boroughs in England and Wales and large Burghs in Scotland (with a few exceptions in the case of trunk roads) are responsible for all public roads, classified and unclassified, within their boundaries. Outside these boundaries the County Council is responsible for all the classified roads (though there are arrangements whereby urban districts with a population of over 20,000 can claim to maintain these roads); the non-county boroughs and urban districts in England and Wales and the small Burghs in Scotland are responsible for the unclassified roads within their boundaries, but elsewhere in the county the County Council is responsible for unclassified as well as for classified roads. These 1929 arrangements still hold good except that the Minister is himself the highway authority for the main trunk routes by virtue of the Trunk Roads Act, 1936. The gradual centralisation of highway matters culminated in this Act; it was a recognition that a national policy for highways could be made effective only if the Minister had under his direct control the most important routes of the country. Further, only in this way was consistency in types of road surface, treatment of bridges, the need for widening, by-passing and so on, likely to be achieved. Under the Act the Minister became the highway authority for some 4,459 miles of the principal routes and under the Trunk Roads Act, 1946, a further 3,585 miles were added.

Thus today's system emerges. There are 190,030 miles of public roads in England, Scotland and Wales. These are looked after by nearly 1,300 highway authorities, ranging from Urban District Councils through County Councils to the Minister and the Secretary of State for Scotland[1] with their responsibility for 6,322 and 1,949 miles of trunk roads respectively. The current expenditure on roads is over £120 million annually, over half of it from the Exchequer.

And yet, if the administrator of today were to start again from scratch he might not devise or even imagine the present scheme of things which, like so many other features of our political and economic life, is the result of gradual growth influenced by chance and accident. It certainly provokes, at times, demands for a more clear-cut organisation such as, for example, a public corporation. But this would be a drastic step, taking yet more responsibility away from local government.

A NATIONAL HIGHWAY AUTHORITY

In general it seems unlikely that the creation of a public corporation or, as some have urged, a National Highway Authority, would achieve more than can be done as well or better under the present arrangements. If, as would be necessary, it were to have the same range of duties as the Ministry now has in respect of the construction and maintenance of roads, such an Authority would need either to have extensive powers to spend Exchequer funds or have its own sources of revenue, for example from tolls or rates or loans, independently of the Exchequer. In either case a constitutional change of major importance would be involved in that it would deprive Parliament of the right, which it now has where Ministers are responsible, to call to account the Authority responsible for the selection of road improvement schemes and for the spending of large sums of public money on roads. Nor can it be imagined that an Authority could more easily secure a continuity of funds for road construction by borrowing because, in point of fact, there is nothing at the present time which prevents borrowing for road building purposes if the Government of the day consider it desirable. A separate Authority with no source of income other than the Exchequer—except when tolls were levied to recover part of the cost of certain major projects—

---

[1] Following the recommendations of the Royal Commission on Scottish Affairs the Minister's responsibilities for Scottish roads were transferred to the Secretary of State for Scotland on 1st April, 1956. The figures in subsequent paragraphs are for Great Britain as a whole; procedure in Scotland is the same as in England and Wales.

would be able to borrow only to the extent that the Government were prepared to allow, having regard to their view of its effect on the general financial situation and the amount of Exchequer revenue which could be set aside in future years for the servicing of the loans.

Apart from these difficulties, it might perhaps be argued that the setting up of an independent Authority would be justified if it would result in an appreciable acceleration in building or improving roads. There are some who have suggested that such a result would follow because the Authority could be freed from Civil Service restrictions and detailed Treasury control in respect of establishments, contracts and financial procedures. They consider that the taking away of executive responsibility from the Minister (and the Civil Service) would make possible a more businesslike approach to the practical and engineering problems involved in the carrying out of the roads programme. Against this argument there is the constitutional difficulty that the responsibility for making statutory Trunk Road Orders and Compulsory Purchase Orders, which are forms of delegated legislation, cannot suitably be transferred from a Minister, who is answerable to Parliament, to an independent authority not so answerable. If the making of Orders must remain with the Minister, then the Authority would have to put forward its proposals to the Ministry for checking, and points of difficulty requiring discussion would certainly take time and involve some duplication of staff. The establishment of a new organisation would also increase the demand for technical staff, for which so far the demand always exceeds the supply. As regards the system of grants for classified roads, which is set out in the following pages, it may also be doubted whether the local highway authorities would accept an arrangement whereby these grants were settled by an independent organisation not directly responsible to Parliament. And if final decisions were to rest in all cases with the Minister, then both the Authority and the Ministry would again be duplicating technical and administrative staff.

CLASSIFIED ROADS

Since the power to classify roads was first obtained in the Ministry of Transport Act, 1919, there have been alterations in the method of classification and in the rates of grant. But at the time of writing the figures are as follows—19,734 miles of Class I road to which the Exchequer contributes 75 per cent of the cost of improvement and maintenance, 17,600 miles of Class II attracting 60 per cent and 48,849 miles of Class III roads eligible for 50 per cent grants. This leaves 95,576 miles of unclassified roads for which the local highway authorities are entirely responsible. The Class I roads represent the more important roads connecting large centres of population and other roads of major importance to through traffic. Roads which are important links between Class I roads and between the smaller centres of population are placed in Class II. Class III (an additional category introduced in 1946) are minor roads that nevertheless have more than local traffic value. The unclassified roads are those of local interest only, though they may be most important streets in themselves.

Such is the broad statistical picture of classified roads. In its essentials the system is settled and is not likely to be altered in the foreseeable future. In its details, however, the system can always be altered—and frequently is. It is always open to highway authorities to represent that a stretch of road merits reclassification, that unclassified roads should be upgraded to Class III, or that Class I's should become trunk roads. But before such a proposal can be accepted it is usually necessary to take a traffic census of the vehicles using the road to make sure that the proposal stems from an increase in through traffic.

Let us now follow the method by which local highway authorities obtain Exchequer grants for work on their classified roads. This is different—and it is an important distinction—for (i) maintenance and minor improvement work[1] and for (ii) works of major improvement and new construction. Grants for the former are allocated annually. Some months before the financial year begins each County Council[2] puts in its estimate of requirements to the Department's Divisional Road Engineer, who is on the staff of the Chief Highways Engineer of the Ministry. There are now, for England and Wales, nine D.R.E.s locally resident, who cover together the whole country and each of whom possesses, with his subordinate engineers, a thorough knowledge of road requirements throughout his division and maintains close contact with the Surveyors to the local highway authorities. After such screening of the County Council's proposals as they think necessary, each of these officers puts forward a consolidated requirement for all the counties in his division. On the basis of these figures the annual estimates are framed and discussed with the Treasury. Before the Second World War it was generally possible to let County Councils have as much grant money as they asked for

---

[1] Broadly speaking major improvements involve acquisition of new land beyond existing highway boundaries, whereas minor improvements do not.

[2] Under the Local Government Acts of 1929 the separate grants for the maintenance of classified roads in County Boroughs, Metropolitan Boroughs and large Burghs in Scotland were ended as part of a general reorganisation of the financial relationship between central and local government which, broadly, substituted inclusive block grants for the previous individual grants for each type of service.

and were prepared to match by the appropriate provisions from their rates. But this has not been so in the more difficult times since the war, when the sum total of their demands has always exceeded the total which the Chancellor of the Exchequer has been able to make available, and sometimes substantial reductions have, with great reluctance, had to be imposed. Once the allocations are made the Authority is given a very free hand in spending the money, in accord with the recommendations of the Local Government Manpower Committee in their report of 1950.[1]

The system for major improvements is necessarily different from that for maintenance. Each scheme has to be considered separately, although the advantage of planning as far ahead as possible and arranging schemes in at least provisional programmes is generally recognised. The Divisional Road Engineers have authority to approve, within the limit of the funds that can be made available to them, schemes costing less than £25,000. All other schemes are submitted to the Ministry's Headquarters with the Divisional Road Engineer's recommendations on them.

The precise degree of control which the central Government should exercise over the local highway authority in these matters has long been the subject of argument and frequently of criticism. The County Surveyor is a properly qualified engineer and the road engineers of the Ministry would certainly not claim that they, as a class, were themselves better technically qualified. What then can this duality of control—even trinity of control, counting the scrutiny at Headquarters—hope to achieve? If the local engineers have selected, after much thought and weighing of priorities, a particular scheme and a particular method of doing it, how can the Divisional Road Engineer (let alone London) expect to improve on the suggestion? In any case, as the local authority are contributing a sizeable proportion from the rates, is there not already sufficient stimulus to economy? There is force in such criticisms and it is, in fact, the aim of the Minister to confine control to the minimum consistent with his duty to Parliament. After all, the responsibility for their roads rests by law with the highway authorities and, even though the central Government may have a major financial interest, the Department cannot dictate to the authorities how they shall carry out their duties. Certainly so far as maintenance is concerned the local authorities, as already indicated, have a very substantial degree of freedom. But a claim for complete freedom could hardly be entertained. On the total mileage of all classified roads the Exchequer is paying about half the cost; it is not, therefore, just a Departmental matter, but essentially one of Parliamentary control. Parliament votes large sums

[1] Cmd. 7870.

I

to roads and must be satisfied, with the help of the Public Accounts Committee, that it gets its money's worth. Indeed the purpose of control goes wider still. The grant from the Exchequer is not merely a form of financial help; it is also a powerful instrument of policy. After many years of short commons on road works it cannot yet be envisaged when the amount of money available is likely to meet all the demands and in such circumstances the rate and character of the national investment in roads must be ordered by a central authority, giving preference to those schemes which, for reasons of safety, industrial development, town and country planning and so on, are particularly desirable in a given place at a given time. Nor does the influence of the grant system end in determining relative priorities; by examining schemes submitted for grant the Department is able to exercise some control over the standard of technical design and can ensure that reasonable uniformity is observed in adhering to standards which experience has shown to be the best. The criteria applied are to a large extent based upon the findings of Committees which include the Ministry's engineers and representatives of local government engineers. The whole system, indeed, establishes a close partnership between the Ministry and local authorities.

The results of the grant system as they have emerged over the last 35 years have certainly been beneficial for maintenance. The standard of structural strength and surfacing of our roads, even on the most insignificant through routes, is uniformly high and has long been the subject of favourable comment from visiting motorists. As for road improvements, the deficiencies, and the more or less complete absence of work for many years, have been all too obvious. Even so it is as well to remember that before the war many important projects were carried out, such as the Great West Road, Western Avenue, Eastern Avenue and the new London–Southend Road, the By-passes of Barking, Dartford, Croydon, Eltham and Sidcup, the North Circular Road, East Lancashire Road, the Edinburgh–Glasgow Road, the new Birmingham–Wolverhampton Road and the Helsby–Queensferry Road in Cheshire. And now, after the long gap, improvements to classified roads are under way again—the County of London section of the Cromwell Road extension, the Dartford–Purfleet Tunnel, the Swansea East Side Approach Road, the Whiteinch tunnel in Glasgow, the inner relief road in Birmingham and many others.

TRUNK ROADS

Even though the Minister is himself the highway authority for trunk roads and the Exchequer pays all the costs, the partnership with local authorities continues. For convenience and economy of administration many of them are appointed as the Minister's agents. Clearly it would be extravagant to maintain staffs and machinery to do work which the local authorities can conveniently and economically do with the resources of manpower and equipment which they have to maintain for their own roads. At all stages, however— planning, construction, maintenance, finance and so forth—there is full consultation and contact between principals and agents.[1] At the same time there are important differences between the procedure which the Minister has to observe in planning the construction and improvement of trunk roads and the procedure which applies to local highway authorities. The latter, perhaps because they are subject to a measure of control from the Ministry, are free from many of the statutory formalities to which the Minister himself is subject. It is as though Parliament has said 'We can trust the Minister to look after the councils, but who is to look after the Minister?' Before constructing a new length of trunk road or altering side roads connecting with trunk roads the Minister is bound by statute to publish a draft Order indicating the line of the new road or the alterations proposed. This draft has to be referred to interested local authorities and is open for three months to objections from them and from other affected parties. If there are any substantial objections a public inquiry may have to be held and much time must thus elapse before an Order can be made. Beyond this, land acquisition often involves the further complications and delays of the statutory procedure applying to Compulsory Purchase Orders. What is therefore in effect, though not in form, the same objection, can twice hold up progress towards carrying out a trunk road improvement. The same procedure and the same delays apply to the planning of trunk road motorways, of which more is said later. Nevertheless the procedure under which the final Orders are made by the Minister, both under the Trunk Roads Acts and for compulsory purchase, are criticised— as are other aspects of land acquisition—on the ground that the Minister is judge in his own cause. The reply is that he remains answerable to Parliament, which is the only proper tribunal for determining a conflict between the needs of the community as a whole and the interests of an individual.

Although much of the detailed work on trunk roads is delegated to the local authorities acting as the Minister's agents, nevertheless much work requires to be done by the Ministry's staff at headquarters as well as in the divisions. There is, for example, a special Lands Branch which deals not only with the formalities of land acquisition

---

[1] Moreover roads in County Boroughs and large Burghs in Scotland, which form part of trunk routes, remain classified roads—with a few exceptions which have little local traffic value.

but also with managing land between the date of its purchase and the date of its inclusion in a trunk road scheme. During this interim period every effort is made to make good use of the land. Thus the Minister may find himself temporary landlord of a number of agricultural tenants and of shopkeepers and of a surprising variety of other tenants, bringing with them all the problems with which tenants confront landlords everywhere.

MOTORWAYS

Until the passing of the Special Roads Act, 1949, pedestrians and all other forms of traffic, within reason, were free to pass along the 'King's Highway'. This Act gave the Minister (and other highway authorities) power to construct roads which would be reserved for particular classes of traffic—ranging from motor vehicles of various kinds to 'pedal cycles, animals ridden, led or driven, and pedestrians'. These powers are now being used to construct new roads reserved for motor traffic, like those which exist for example in America, Italy and Germany. The new roads are carried over or under existing roads and at important junctions there are fly-overs and under-passes, with connecting roads to keep traffic flowing smoothly. No frontage access—except from service stations and other essential places—is permitted. The roads are for the exclusive use of motor traffic and only in exceptional cases and under special arrangements is any other traffic allowed on any part of them.

The cost of these roads is formidable. Each mile of new motorway costs on average some £300,000; this average figure excludes, however, the cost of individual engineering works, such as bridges, which may cost as much as a million or more each. It has, therefore, been seriously debated whether the cost might be met by the user paying his way by toll, as has been done with much success in America. These roads are, however, primarily intended to relieve the existing roads as much as possible and, remembering the opposition that the Turnpikes aroused, not to mention the existing level of vehicle and oil fuel taxation, such a proposal could hardly be expected to be welcomed in this country or to be considered appropriate. Nor would the collection of tolls be cheap where the number of points of entry would be so much greater than in the wider open spaces of the United States of America. On the other hand there is clearly justification for a toll to pay back some or all of the heavy first cost of a comparatively short, but very expensive, bridge or tunnel which saves the road user a long detour. On this principle tolls are collected for use of the Mersey Tunnel and have been authorised for the Dartford–Purfleet Tunnel, now under construction, as well as for the projected Forth Road Bridge.

THE CURRENT ROAD PROGRAMME

The difficulty is to decide which of the many pressing needs should be first met. The determination of relative priorities requires the wisdom of Solomon, but even if the Minister were thus generously endowed he could hardly hope to escape criticism. Although considerable help is gained from traffic censuses and other studies, there can be no entirely satisfactory system of assessing the degree of national interest in carrying out a scheme in one part of the country as against a similar scheme in another, any more than there is an entirely reliable method of calculating the true economic value to the country of a particular road or bridge scheme. But research is in hand on both aspects of this problem and some helpful results will almost certainly emerge.

The main framework of the current road programme has been built round five major projects:

(i) An improved trunk road from London to the north-east. This is based on the present Great North Road, the 270 miles of which from London to Newcastle will eventually be dual carriageway throughout.

(ii) A new motorway from London to the north-west. This consists of some 70 miles of motorway from the south end of the St. Albans By-Pass to Dunchurch, east of Birmingham, with a link to over 90 miles of motorway from north of Birmingham to the Preston By-Pass, whence the motorway is planned to continue northwards via the Lancaster By-Pass to Shap.

(iii) Improved roads from London to the south-east. This is by means of the Medway Towns motor road and improvements to the two trunk roads from London to the south-east coast, with by-passes and relief roads in built-up areas.

(iv) A road from the Midlands to South Wales. This includes 21 miles of motorway in the Ross Spur, with improvements to the existing trunk roads further west. More of the pattern will be filled in by a motorway from Birmingham to Bristol and the Severn Bridge and its approach roads.

(v) A road from London to London Airport and onwards. This involves a short length of double-decker road at the London end and provides for motorway standards to west of Maidenhead. Eventually this road will extend to the West of England and South Wales.

Urgently needed as they are, these major projects, together with other improvements designed to speed traffic across the country cannot but lead to disappointment and frustration if, when the traffic reaches its destination, congestion and delays are made the worse by the ease with which it got there. Careful consideration is therefore being given by the highway authorities in the larger built-up areas to what can be done to help the traffic in them. This presents extremely difficult problems; in particular, any major road construction in an industrial and commercial district involves disturbing very expensive property, and, if residential areas are affected, homes must be found for the people who have to move. But this is the kind of intractable problem which all concerned with the roads of this country—the Minister and the local highway authorities alike—aim to solve.

Broadly speaking, the types of scheme which command priority at present are those which will help to speed up traffic on the principal industrial routes and those designed to promote road safety; categories which often, of course, overlap. Included among the less costly improvements is a programme for strengthening weak bridges, of which there are several hundred on the main trunk routes alone. The canal and railway companies naturally built bridges only strong enough for the traffic anticipated at the time. Many have never been modernised and impose severe limitations upon 'abnormal indivisible loads', which move on the roads because other forms of transport cannot be used or are more expensive. Level crossings are another incubus from the age when road traffic was sparse. Plans exist to get rid of some of those that cause major hold-ups and a number of such schemes, as for example Pelham Bridge in the City of Lincoln, have been completed.

HIGHWAYS AND CONTROL OF DEVELOPMENT

There has long been a clash between the importance of keeping the main routes clear and safe and the need for housing and other development. Not long after the first new roads and by-passes were built between the wars the lack of any form of control over adjacent development began seriously to impair their usefulness for the purpose for which they were built. Frontagers were able to exercise their common law right to have access to the highway, and the by-passes tended to become as heavily built up and as much used by local traffic as the roads they were built to by-pass. Such was the origin of the Restriction of Ribbon Development Act, 1935, which removed the right of frontagers to develop. The powers are now embraced in the Town and Country Planning Acts. The grant system for classified roads is also used to the same end; it is a condition of any grant for the construction of a new classified road that access will be restricted according to the needs of the road. The Department imposes similar restrictions for trunk roads. The appeal of aggrieved parties lies to the Minister of Housing and Local Government or the Secretary of State for Scotland.

On the Development Plans prepared by County and County Borough Councils (large Burghs in Scotland), the Ministry's principal interest is in trunk roads. Their development as proposed over the initial twenty-year period of the Plans has been set out for the benefit of local authorities and would-be developers so that they shall know how they stand.

TRAFFIC CONGESTION

The administrative system for regulating traffic on the roads differs significantly from that for building and maintaining the roads themselves. Indeed it is important to realise what the Minister is not responsible for. Most correspondents (and they are many) live under the mistaken impression that it is the Department's duty to solve all the problems of traffic congestion in towns and villages all over the country. This is not so. On trunk roads the Minister certainly has the responsibility for all measures of traffic regulation, traffic signs and so forth, but outside the London Traffic Area on all roads other than trunk roads his position is entirely different. The initiative has always rested with the local authorities, which for this purpose are, in England and Wales, County Councils, County Borough Councils, Municipal Borough Councils and Urban District Councils with a population of 20,000 souls or over.[1] The Minister can act as a court of appeal, since orders made by local authorities may require his confirmation or, when they do not, may be varied or revoked by him; he also has effective control over much of what is done because he controls the grant contributions from the Exchequer. Generally speaking, however, it is fair to say that outside London, on roads other than trunk roads, the responsibility for dealing with traffic congestion is a local and not a national responsibility, as indeed it should be.

In the London Traffic Area, roughly speaking a circle of 25 miles radius based on Charing Cross, and thus a good deal wider than the Metropolitan Police District, the Minister is, under the London Traffic Act, 1924, the traffic authority. This Act recognises that the interests of the Capital as a whole are wider than the interests either of the Boroughs or even the County Councils of which it is composed. It is necessary to look at London traffic as a whole and it would be unreasonable to expect the ratepayers, or the individual Councils with responsibilities in the London Traffic Area, to take that kind of

[1] In Scotland since 1956 traffic control has been the responsibility of the Scottish Home Department.

standpoint. The Minister therefore makes the traffic regulation orders in London which, elsewhere in the country, are the functions of the local authorities. Even so the Minister is far from being a traffic dictator in London. So that he should have an adequate means of testing public opinion before such orders are made he is under a statutory obligation to consult the London and Home Counties Traffic Advisory Committee[1] about them. This Committee consists of some 45 persons representing the police, the local authorities, the trade unions concerned with transport, British Railways, the London Transport Executive and various categories of road user, and its advice on traffic regulations is almost invariably taken. It is also important to realise that in their area the Metropolitan Police have a special responsibility for traffic control on the ground and for enforcement of the Minister's orders; and they have adopted a useful practice whereby they experiment with temporary traffic regulations under their own powers before thought is given to making the regulations permanent. Additional powers to conduct these experiments, subject to the Minister's consent, were taken in the Road Traffic Act, 1956. Again, no permanent signs or signals can be put up without the consent of the local highway authority, which is always responsible for their cost or the cost of their maintenance either in whole or in part. Thus, apart from the practical necessity for the Minister to carry the Advisory Committee with him, it is difficult for him to make improvements in London traffic control unless agreement is reached first with the police and the boroughs concerned. At a complicated site like Marble Arch, three or more boroughs may be involved (in this instance, Westminster, St Marylebone and Paddington) as well as the Minister of Works who is responsible for routes through the Royal Parks. Thus, while the Minister is nominally the traffic authority, he is not in effective control, and above all, there are so many interests to be consulted that it is quite impossible to secure quick action, however great the need may be.

These complications do not arise in quite the same measure in the rest of the country. The troubles which do arise stem more from the fact that traffic regulations, necessary to prevent congestion, tend to be unpopular with local Chambers of Commerce and the individual shop-keepers likely to be affected, as they often limit the parking of cars outside their shops. Before 1956 local authorities could have a long row to hoe in getting their Orders. All of them had to come to the Minister for confirmation and inevitably some time elapsed before objections, already voiced locally, had again been heard centrally. But an important change was made in the 1956 Road Traffic Act. The Minister no longer has to confirm Orders dealing

[1] See also page 104.

with waiting restrictions on one-way streets, except on trunk roads. He can still vary or revoke the Orders or hold public inquiries but the new law increases considerably the autonomy of local authorities and shortens substantially a procedure which was previously too dilatory.

The forms of traffic regulation which the Minister and the other authorities concerned with traffic most frequently employ are as follows:

(a) one-way-street orders—useful to prevent congestion in very narrow roads, and, when there are compensating routes, to improve the traffic flow in busy city centres;

(b) no waiting regulations—essential on main traffic routes to keep them free for moving traffic; these regulations always include exemptions to provide for reasonable access for loading or unloading goods or taking up or setting down passengers;

(c) unilateral waiting regulations—useful to keep parked vehicles to one side of a street only; they often have the effect of turning that side of the street into a virtual car park. They are not suitable when traffic is heavy or for narrow streets as the loading and unloading of vehicles on the opposite side, usually permitted, could cause a complete blockage.

(d) weight prohibitions and road closures—these may be needed for a variety of reasons, usually connected with public safety;

(e) establishment of street playgrounds in congested city areas, where children with no access to parks can play safely.

In addition there is the ever-growing need to provide parking space for cars. In the London Traffic Area, but not elsewhere, it is the Minister who has power to appoint authorised street parking-places, where alone (up to now) motorists have had a positive right to park for the time allowed. Outside the London Traffic Area this is a function of local authorities and the Minister is not concerned. The responsibility for confirming any bye-laws rests with the Home Secretary or the Secretary of State for Scotland. These powers are provided by the Public Health Act, 1925, and the Restriction of Ribbon Development Act, 1935, which also make the provision of parking-places off the highway an exclusive function of local authorities, even in London. Here these powers have scarcely been used, except to provide temporary bombed site car parks, now rapidly vanishing. Outside London, where land costs are less, this system has worked reasonably well and it is rare for a local authority to show reluctance to provide open car parks on or off the street if they are needed.

The 1956 Road Traffic Act enables local authorities to apply to the Minister for orders so that they can charge for parking on the highway—usually by means of parking meters. The Minister is given certain default powers for the Metropolitan and City Police areas only. The main purpose of parking meters is to restrict street parking to those places where it will have the least adverse effect on moving traffic and also, by imposing a time limit, to increase the turnover of parked cars, thereby improving the use made of available kerbside space. They have proved successful in doing this in a number of other countries, notably the United States of America and New Zealand. Parking meters have now got off to a good start in Westminster, where the first scheme was launched in July 1958, in the north-west corner of Mayfair.

The 1956 Act also widens the powers of the police to tow away vehicles left on the highway so that any vehicle left in breach of statutory regulations is liable to be towed away in the driver's absence. This method of enforcement has proved salutary in other countries and is assuming considerable importance in London.

Speed limits, a most important form of traffic regulation, are dealt with in the next chapter, but there remains one other important form of traffic device which should be mentioned, namely, traffic signs, including traffic lights. Except on trunk roads, where the Minister is the highway authority, their erection is the responsibility of the local highway authority, but to secure uniformity throughout the country the forms which they may take, and in some cases the places in which they may be put, are controlled by the Minister. He also has the last say in many respects through the grant procedure. The system of signs giving warnings or directions to traffic is not precisely that used either on the Continent of Europe or in America and there is no general agreement whether it is as good as that of a number of other countries. In particular on most warning signs words are used to supplement the conventional sign—'School', for example, in addition to the symbol of the torch, now being replaced by a silhouette of children on the road. Many countries omit words altogether because they do not assume that every driver knows the language of the country in which he is driving. As regards direction sign-posting, with the English inheritance of vast numbers of country lanes and the division of responsibility between a large number of highway authorities, it may be that signs throughout the country are not as complete or thorough as on some Continental routes, but the system is a sound one and new regulations, which should improve it, have recently been made. On the new motorways, however, an altogether new series of traffic signs will be necessary and a Committee was appointed in 1957 to consider what form they should take. It may well prove that the new motorway signs will point the way towards further improvements for direction signposting generally.

Traffic congestion in our cities and on our main roads is bound to increase with the ever greater number of cars in circulation. There are already over 7 million vehicles on our roads and before 1970 this may well have doubled. Present methods of traffic regulation and control will therefore need continual review and strengthening if traffic is to be kept moving at a reasonable pace. By now nearly every city and town in the country has its waiting restrictions and its car parks, but still congestion gets worse. No single method can provide a cure; the problem, except on trunk roads and in the London Traffic Area, is primarily a local one in the solution of which the Minister is only a partner. Time alone will show whether these present methods of control, both in and out of London, with the present division of responsibilities, will be adequate to meet the insistent demands of traffic. Time has already shown that no methods of control are a substitute for adequate off-street parking-places and for highway improvements.

CHAPTER XI

Safety in Inland Transport

Railway Safety — Inspection of New Works —
Accident Inquiry — Road Safety — The Road
— The Vehicle — The Individual

*

RAILWAY SAFETY

'DOES anybody mean to say that decent people, passengers who would use their own carriages and are accustomed to their own comforts, would consent to be hurried along through the air upon a railroad, from which, had a lazy schoolboy left a marble or a wicked one a stone, they would be pitched off their track, into the valley beneath; or is it to be imagined that women, who may like the fun of being whirled away on a party of pleasure for an hour to see a sight, would endure the fatigue and misery and danger, not only to themselves but their children and families, of being dragged through the air at the rate of twenty miles an hour, all their lives being at the mercy of a tin pipe or a copper boiler, or the accidental dropping of a pebble on the line of way?'[1]

Sentiments such as these led to the safety provisions of the first Regulation of Railways Act of 1840 when the President of the Board of Trade was given powers to appoint Inspecting Officers of Railways. The first holder of the post was Lieut-Col. Sir Frederick Smith of the Royal Engineers, and all Inspecting Officers have been drawn from the Corps in unbroken succession since that date. The staff has never been large and today consists of the Chief Inspecting Officer and three Inspecting Officers together with one Senior and three other Railway Employment Inspectors. Compared with the much larger staffs employed on inspection and other duties for the safety of ships, aircraft and road traffic this may at first sight seem somewhat surprising. But the intrinsic safety of railway travel, on fixed lines and within a fenced track, was recognised long ago—despite the writer of the article in *John Bull* and his like. This has meant that the State has been able to exercise its responsibility for safety on the railways with a comparatively light hand.

[1] *John Bull*, 15th November, 1835.

INSPECTION OF NEW WORKS

The 1840 Act and subsequent railway legislation—the latest being the Road and Rail Traffic Act, 1933—gives the Inspecting Officers power to examine new passenger lines or alterations to them and to report on their construction and equipment. It is interesting to note that George Stephenson, that robust exponent of private enterprise, strongly supported the Government over the earlier Acts so as 'to prevent wild and visionary schemes being tried at the great danger of injury or loss of life to the public'.

Traditionally the standards which the Inspecting Officers require for new works are codified in a public document entitled 'Requirements of the Minister of Transport for Passenger Lines and Recommendations for Goods Lines'. These Requirements were first issued in simple form in 1858, and have been revised periodically in close consultation with the railways to take account of developments in railway working. The last revision in 1950 was particularly thorough as there had been so much progress in signalling since the previous issue in 1928. At the same time they are nothing like an elaborate treatise on railway engineering and signalling: important basic standards are prescribed but otherwise much discretion is left to the responsible engineers on the job. In any case the requirements have no statutory backing and may be relaxed at the discretion of an Inspecting Officer to meet any special conditions.

The normal procedure before a new work is begun is for the plans to be submitted to the Minister for approval. These are examined by an Inspecting Officer and sometimes discussed with the railway officers. The Minister gives provisional approval subject to inspection as soon as practicable after the work is finished. Finally the Minister's formal approval is given, subject where necessary to compliance with the Inspecting Officer's requirements. Contrary to what most people imagine, new works on the railways are coming into operation all the time and in 1957 more than 78 modernisation schemes and alterations on passenger lines were submitted for the Minister's approval.

Once new works have been approved the Minister has no jurisdiction over their maintenance, the responsibility for which rests with the British Transport Commission. Nor has he any jurisdiction over the construction of rolling stock (except on electric tube lines) or over the qualifications of the operating staff. Today, despite the contrasting situation in shipping, aviation and road transport, this rather loose form of control goes unquestioned and indeed it is very doubtful whether a more rigid, and consequently more costly, system would bring any improvement. In the early years of railways some voices were raised that State control should be strengthened but successive investigations advised against it. The Royal Commission of 1865 said: 'We believe that no other mode of locomotion ever used by man can show more satisfactory results and we are therefore not prepared to suggest any alteration of the present law.' Another Royal Commission was appointed in 1874 and, although it made a number of recommendations, including the compulsory adoption of absolute block working[1] and the interlocking of points and signals, which eventually took shape in an important Act in 1889, it endorsed the view of the earlier Royal Commission as follows:

'Upon full consideration we are not prepared to recommend any legislation authorising such interference with railways as would impair in any way the responsibility of the companies for injury or loss of life caused by accident on their lines. To impose upon any public department the duty, and to entrust it with the necessary powers, to exercise a general control over the practical administration of railways, would not, in our opinion, be either prudent or desirable. A government authority placed in such a position would be exposed to the danger either of appearing indirectly to guarantee works, appliances and arrangements which might practically prove faulty or insufficient, or else of interfering with railway management to an extent which would soon alienate from it public sympathy and confidence and thus destroy its moral influence and with it its capacity for usefulness.'

These findings accord closely with the tenor of those of the Royal Commission on Unseaworthy Ships of the same year, but there the Plimsoll agitation of the time overbore the Commission's recommendations, with the result that the Board of Trade took on a much greater amount of direct work in the survey of ships. But the principles enumerated by the Royal Commission on Railways prevailed and there is certainly no reason to depart from them today when the safety of railway travel is even greater despite the increase in train speeds and traffic density.

ACCIDENT INQUIRY

The duties of the Railway Inspectorate which mainly come before the public gaze are those for holding accident inquiries. As in the case of inspection, the powers date back to the Act of 1840 when the railway companies were first required to submit returns of all accidents involving personal injury. In the same year Sir Frederick Smith held the first inquiry, though in fact the statutory provisions on inquiries were not enacted until 1871. Today reports are made to the Minister of all accidents to passenger trains and goods trains on, or affecting, passenger running lines, of all mechanical and structural failures of

---

[1] The maintenance of a space interval, instead of a time interval, between trains.

certain defined classes, including broken tyres, axles and rails, and of all accidents to persons on the railway, except that those to railway servants have to be reported only if the victim is absent from duty for more than three days. The train accident reports are examined by an Inspecting Officer and accidents to the staff by a Railway Employment Inspector. Where necessary, questions are asked and full information is obtained from the railway management. Formal inquiries are held for the more serious train accidents, usually whenever there are passenger fatalities, but also in any other case where the cause is obscure or other circumstances warrant a detailed investigation and published report.

Two types of inquiry were authorised by the 1871 Act; first, a formal investigation in which a legal officer is appointed to hold the inquiry with an Inspecting Officer to assist him, such an investigation being held in Open Court and witnesses being examined on oath; second, an Inspecting Officer's inquiry in which the Inspecting Officer is appointed by the Minister to carry out the investigation. The second is not a court of law and evidence is not taken on oath nor is the Inspecting Officer bound by the strict rules of evidence.

The formal investigation has seldom been ordered. The last one was that into the Tay Bridge disaster in 1879 when in a fierce gale on the night of 28th December part of the bridge collapsed and a train passing over at the time fell into the river with the loss of all its 75 passengers and crew. The normal type of inquiry is undertaken by an Inspecting Officer who usually opens the proceedings and hears the evidence in the presence of the Press and members of the public, though both may be excluded if there is a chance that a witness might prejudice himself in possible future criminal proceedings were he to give his evidence in public. The Inspecting Officer is not concerned with criminal negligence nor with civil liability; his sole object is to find out the cause of the accident and to make recommendations to prevent a recurrence. His inquiry is quite independent of the railway management's private inquiry, but the evidence taken at the latter is always placed at his disposal. Railway officers and representatives of the Trade Unions attend to assist the Inspecting Officer, but his findings are his own independent responsibility. He hears the evidence and examines the witnesses, after which he asks the Railway Officers and Trade Union representatives if they have any questions to suggest. On completion of the examination of witnesses the public proceedings are closed but protracted investigations frequently have to be undertaken before a final conclusion is reached. The Minister is required by statute to publish the report and it is invariably sent to the railway management for their observations on the Inspecting Officer's recommendations. These cannot be enforced by law, but thorough investigation and discussion with the Railway Officers usually result in their being accepted. Reliance is thus placed on the co-operation of a responsible railway management with the Inspectorate in the pursuit of a common objective.

The Railway Employment Inspectors hold numerous inquiries into accidents to railway staff. These are conducted on somewhat similar lines to the train accident inquiries, except that Press and public are not usually present and as a rule the reports are not published. They are, however, sent to the railway management and to the Trade Unions and a reference is made to the more important cases in the Chief Inspecting Officer's Annual Report. These Reports, which have been published annually since 1840, are a mine of information about railway working and about the accidents which have occurred during the year.

Although the railways have a splendid record for safety, improvements are continually being sought and put into practice. Great advances have been made in signalling during the current century by the adoption of colour light signals in place of semaphores—with advantages in visibility and simplicity—by the introduction of track circuiting which is an additional control for the prevention of signalmen's mistakes, and by the development of power signalling which enables large and complicated layouts to be controlled safely and more efficiently from one centre in place of manual operation from a number of scattered signal boxes. In addition, the extension to all main routes of automatic train control should reduce still further the risk of overrunning signals by giving an audible indication to the driver of the aspect of the distant signal and an automatic brake application in the event of his failure to act upon a caution signal. Many of these improvements, as well as strengthening of the permanent way, contribute to the efficiency of the whole system, and their further extension is part of the modernisation plan for the railways, but much of the work—and a great deal of expenditure—is attributable to the search for even greater safety.

ROAD SAFETY

This is one of the most difficult subjects with which the Ministry[1] is is concerned. With the other forms of transport the different elements can be better controlled, the vehicle is in charge of a highly skilled and experienced professional and aids to safe navigation are highly developed. But the human being on the road, whether as driver, cyclist or pedestrian, is infinitely various, not only in skill but also in

[1] Most road safety matters in Scotland have been, since 1956, the responsibility of the Scottish Home Department.

temperament and physical fitness. The casualty figures—over 5,500 killed and more than 268,000 injured during 1957[1]—are sufficient evidence. It is also a subject on which most people tend to be self-appointed experts. There is a constant stream of suggestions to the Minister of varying value and practicability—suggestions, for example, for a 'Dodgem' type bumper, which would completely encircle a vehicle, for rubber steering wheels or for putting cats' eyes on dogs' collars. At the same time therefore as they plan ahead in conjunction with the Department's highway engineers and the Road Research Laboratory of the Department of Scientific and Industrial Research, with which close contact is maintained, the officers engaged on this difficult task have also to cope with a considerable pressure of day-to-day business. In the face of the mass of information and advice, much of it conflicting, the formulation of acceptable policy is not easy. The Minister has therefore appointed a Departmental Committee on Road Safety, under the Chairmanship of one of the Parliamentary Secretaries and representing all the different classes of road user as well as the police, local authorities, the Royal Society for the Prevention of Accidents, the Road Research Laboratory and the Ministry.

In the result many legislative and other measures have been taken. These may best be considered in three stages—the road, the vehicle and the individual. But first it should be noted that, despite the figures quoted above, the situation might be even worse. In 1934, before the effects could be felt of the Road Traffic Act passed in that year, the casualty figures were over 7,000 dead and over 230,000 injured. They then dropped and it was not until 1955 that the 1934 total of casualties was again passed. By then there were more than twice as many vehicles on the road and the population of the country had increased by 4 million. And road deaths since the Second World War, as distinct from total casualties, have remained considerably fewer than in the 1930's. Great Britain is the only country for which reliable figures are available where this has happened.

THE ROAD

The work of highway improvement and maintenance and the measures to relieve traffic congestion, which have been described in the previous chapter, of course have an effect on road safety. But, in addition, many special measures have been taken to counteract the dangers of 'the rolling English road . . . that rambles round the shire'. The frequency with which accidents occur at particular places is

[1] The figures for road casualties in this chapter relate to Great Britain as a whole.

observed and, within the limit of the available funds, alterations are made to these so-called 'black spots'. It may be quite a minor improvement such as the installation of traffic signs, or resurfacing to prevent skidding, or the banking of a corner, or merely the erection of a few black and white posts with cats' eyes to mark an unexpected bend in the road; or it may be something quite large, such as the construction of a roundabout or a new section of road. Some spectacular results have been achieved; for example, after the installation of a roundabout at Sawley Crossroads, south-east of Derby, where 29 accidents had occured in seven years, there were no accidents at all in the 18 months following completion of the work; again, before the road surface of wood blocks was replaced by an improved surface on a 1¼ mile length of Finchley Road, Hampstead, 90 skidding accidents were reported during a period of four winter months; after the new surface was laid there were only two skidding accidents over the same four months the next winter when the rainfall was about the same. The installation of traffic signals not only aids safety and eases traffic flow but also brings about substantial economies in police time and wages. Before the war the Bank of England complex of junctions required a police sergeant for 40 hours and constables for over 700 man hours each week. Signals, which cost £8,500 to instal and £650 a year to maintain, are an obvious economy.

A number of devices have been developed to protect the pedestrian —guard rails, for example, as well as subways and school crossing patrols. In 1951 a new type of uncontrolled pedestrian crossing, marked with zebra stripes and lighted beacons, was introduced to replace the old Belisha crossings, which were too numerous and were largely disregarded by motorists and pedestrians alike. There was some resistance at the time to the reduction by two-thirds of the existing number of crossings but the policy has justified itself by the results. Zebra crossings are now generally respected and their use is increasing; they have had a marked effect on road behaviour and pedestrian casualties fell by 9 per cent in 1952 as compared with the previous year. They have now risen again beyond the 1951 figure, but not nearly so much as have those for the other classes of road user and far less than in proportion to the number of vehicles on the road. To all the measures mentioned in this paragraph the Government contributes financially.

A great deal can also be done through better lighting. Twice as many accidents occur during night time as during the day in relation to the traffic volume, and better lighting can reduce the casualty rate significantly. The central Government has little direct influence here since there is no power to make grants, except on trunk roads where half the cost is met by the Government.

Apart from physical improvements to the roads themselves, and in what is oddly termed 'street furniture', there is one particular measure affecting traffic on the roads which is of the highest importance; that is the general speed limit in built-up areas. Up to 1930 there was a universal speed limit on all roads of 20 mph, which by then had come to be entirely disregarded and was abolished. In 1934, since accidents were still rising, it was decided as an experiment to introduce a 30 mph speed limit, but only in built-up areas. The accident figures at once showed that this was a wise course. Built-up areas were defined by reference to the existence or otherwise of a system of street lighting. In the heart of our cities this has worked well enough, but on the outskirts and in small towns and villages, where the law provides means of removing anomalies, local opinion often demands speed limits in places where motorists would not regard them as reasonable and would be unlikely to obey them. Cases of this kind often raise strong passions and can be settled only after a public inquiry. Up to the beginning of 1957 the 30 mph speed limit had to be renewed annually by Parliament, but it has now become permanent, and speed limits are no longer automatically imposed whenever street lighting is introduced on trunk and main roads. The effect will be to enable borderline cases, of which there are many, to be considered more freely on their merits. An experiment is also being conducted into an intermediate or differential speed limit of 40 mph on main traffic routes on the outskirts of residential areas in the London Traffic Area. If the experiment is a success the 40 mph limit will be applied, if Parliament agrees, to suitable roads in other parts of the country. It is suitable especially for modern arterial roads, where for the modern car with its high speeds and good brakes a limit of 30 mph is unreasonable and commands no respect but equally where, owing to the presence of pedestrians, unlimited speed is dangerous.

THE VEHICLE

Many regulations are in force governing the construction, equipment and use of motor vehicles. Maximum lengths, widths and laden weights are laid down; various items of equipment such as lights, rear-reflectors, pneumatic tyres, mirrors and safety glass and a speedometer are compulsory on all, or most, vehicles; and the towing of trailers and other matters requiring safety precautions are dealt with. Independent braking systems must be provided and there are requirements for these and other parts of the vehicle to be maintained in proper working order. With the increase in the number of different types of vehicle and in the endeavour to promote safe working, the regulations have become extremely complex. Fortunately, although his safety largely depends upon them, the ordinary vehicle owner need not know all of them in detail. But they are all of fundamental importance to manufacturers, and discussion with the motor industry's trade associations is therefore frequent and a proportion of the industry's research station costs are borne by the Government.

In a rather special category are speed limits imposed on certain particular classes of motor vehicle. These are in addition to the general speed limit in built-up areas. For example, goods vehicles and buses are restricted to a speed of 30 mph both inside and outside built-up areas, while vehicles towing trailers, or with non-pneumatic tyres or falling into certain other categories, are subjected to still lower speed limits. Until May, 1957, the speed limit for heavy goods vehicles was 20 mph but it was so widely disregarded as to be practically a dead letter. These speed limits are designed to keep a reasonable balance between the often conflicting requirements of road safety and road traffic and may be varied by the Minister by regulation, subject to prior approval by Parliament. The general pressure nowadays is always towards increasing maximum speeds in view of the technical developments in braking and other equipment, but speed limits are a matter on which public opinion can be very sensitive. Experience shows also that occasionally extraneous factors have to be taken into account such as working conditions of drivers of commercial vehicles. The Minister has special powers to relax these speed limits on the new motorways and, with Parliament's approval, has experimentally removed almost all speed limits and raised the remainder to 40 mph.

Headlamp dazzle is an outstanding problem which it is difficult to cover fully by legislation. As the regulations stand at present they require that lamps fitted with bulbs exceeding 7 watts in power shall be permanently deflected or be capable of being deflected so as not to dazzle a person standing 25 feet away. The other essential point, of course, is that drivers should dip their lamps with proper consideration for other road users and keep them correctly focused and aimed. Aim is most important, since, if lamps are even as little as 2° above the proper setting, they can be a menace. The testing of headlamps together with that of other lights and of brakes and steering will be covered when the new vehicle testing scheme is set up. The Minister was given powers to enforce the testing of vehicles over 10 years old under sections 1 and 2 of the Road Traffic Act, 1956, and a practical scheme is being worked out. Meantime, some experience of the problems involved in actual testing has been obtained by the opening of a pilot testing station at Hendon.

The testing of passenger vehicles plying for public hire has been in operation since 1930. Certifying Officers and Vehicle Examiners on the staff of the Department examine all buses and coaches before they are brought into service and periodically thereafter. If the vehicle is constructed and equipped according to the special regulations applying to these vehicles, the Certifying Officer issues a Certificate of Fitness, if he is satisfied with the condition of the vehicle, rather in the way that Passenger Certificates are issued to passenger ships. Without the Certificate the public service vehicle licence cannot be issued.[1] And if at any time it appears to a Certifying Officer or Vehicle Examiner that the vehicle is in an unsatisfactory condition he can forthwith suspend the p.s.v. licence. These officers also have power to enforce the mechanical fitness regulations upon goods vehicles, which they can prohibit from the carriage of goods, but there is no periodical inspection and no certificate of fitness. As for trams and trolley buses, the inspection of new routes—and inquiry into accidents—is the responsibility of the Railway Inspecting Officers. This naturally followed when tramways developed from railways and trolley buses from trams.

The examination of taxis is not governed by the Road Traffic Acts but is carried out by local authorities (in London the Commissioner of Police) under powers adopted locally or obtained by Special Acts.

THE INDIVIDUAL

The individual feels the impact of authority most directly through the driving test and 'L' plate procedure and through the police. Driving tests, which necessitate a large organisation—850 driving examiners at 330 centres all over the country—were instituted by the Road Traffic Act, 1934, and no doubt contributed to the reduction in accidents which took place after it came into force. With this in mind many hold that the system should be extended to those who have never been tested, to those who have reached the age of say 65, and to any drivers who have been involved in an accident. The difficulty with all these suggestions is that, whereas it is known they would require a very great increase in staff, it is doubtful whether they would do good.

The influence of the police upon the road user is, of course, enormous. The attitude of driver or cyclist changes immediately in their presence. In particular the effect of mobile police patrols is remarkable. The classic instance is pre-war Lancashire where 'courtesy cops' reduced the accident rate by no less than 44 per cent as compared with the year before their introduction, including an

[1] See page 102.

18 per cent reduction in deaths, while casualties in the rest of the country went up by 3 per cent. These results were obtained with only four-fifths of the number of prosecutions of the previous year. The patrols undoubtedly proved their worth and the Minister would much like to see further increases in their number.

The impact of authority is felt less directly—but felt none the less—in the efforts which successive Governments have made in recent years by propaganda campaigns to bring home to the individual his responsibilities as road user. Shortly after the war the Royal Society for the Prevention of Accidents were asked to set up a special area organisation, of which the Government paid the whole cost. Local authorities were also encouraged to set up Road Safety Committees on which the police, the local education authority and the Royal Society for the Prevention of Accidents all sit and towards whose activities the Government make grants. These Road Safety Committees, as every road user will know, are extremely active in drawing attention to local casualty figures and in encouraging road safety activities of all kinds. Their propaganda, together with that issued nationally, has done much to create a sense of awareness of road dangers. A notable example of the effect of recent propaganda has been the way in which motor cyclists and pillion riders have very sensibly taken to the wearing of crash helmets. The latest issue of the Highway Code has also been effective. It has not the force of law, but breach or observance of the Code may be used in evidence in the Courts. Above all, concentration upon child education has paid rich dividends. Just before the 1939–45 war casualties to child pedestrians and cyclists under the age of 15 amounted to some 42,000 each year, of which about 1,000 were fatal. In 1957 the corresponding figures were about 36,500 and 550—despite the increase of nearly one and a half millions in the number of children under 15 and the steep rise in the number of vehicles. Stress is also being laid upon the special vulnerability of the young cyclist and upon the attention which these riders, as well as their parents and relatives, should pay to their riding skill and thorough knowledge of the Highway Code and to proper maintenance of their machines. The Ministry and others concerned are now planning to develop existing child cycling proficiency schemes into a nation-wide organisation capable of training and testing 300,000 child cyclists a year. Looking further ahead—because the changes must be rung fairly frequently if the propaganda is to be effective—it may be best to concentrate on the techniques of driving, riding or even walking upon the roads. Certainly most people's driving can be improved and, if it could become more a matter of pride to the individual to drive well, it would be a great step forward.

To conclude, road safety is a subject with innumerable aspects. Now one line of attack, now another is tried. Some have achieved noticeable results—the 30 mph speed limit, for example, and zebra crossings. But the depressing fact remains that, after a temporary drop, the accident figures, following the continual increase in the number of vehicles, start to rise again. There is, therefore, no official complacency. Within the limitations of the funds available, new measures are being thought out and applied all the time. A noteworthy experiment has been that at Slough where from 1955 to 1957 new road safety ideas were tested and scientifically measured for their effectiveness.

These are some of the things which the Government and the Ministry and other authorities do to reduce the appalling tale of injury and loss of life on the roads. But none is more conscious how little he can do than Ministers and their advisers. While authority can help and guide and adjure, the main remedy lies in other hands —the hands of every man, woman and child who uses the roads. At sea, on the railways, in the air, elaborate precautions in the construction and maintenance of equipment of all kinds, and the handling of vehicles and other devices by highly skilled operators, can ensure a high degree of safety. On the road everything depends on the individual. The most perfect vehicle in the hands of a driver, however skilful, who is momentarily careless or inconsiderate, may be a deadly peril. Equally a stupid or thoughtless action by a pedestrian may lead to an accident to himself or others which the most skilful and careful driver cannot avoid. The responsibility lies with every individual, and that is why the most hopeful work being done is the education of the children in road dangers and the way to avoid them and in the need for constant care and consideration for others.

PART FOUR

Civil Aviation

CHAPTER XII

Air Policy

The State and Civil Aviation — The Ministry
and British Civil Aviation — International Work
— Relations with the Air Corporations —
Relations with the Independent Airlines —
Commonwealth and Colonial Civil Aviation
— Private Flying

*

THE STATE AND CIVIL AVIATION

GOVERNMENT in all countries has played a much greater part in
the shaping and control of civil aviation than in other transport
industries. This might in any case have happened, because safety,
which is one of the chief traditional reasons for Government regulation of industry, is an extensive and complex problem for aviation,
whilst the provision of radio navigational facilities and of major
airports are undertakings of such wide extent that, in most cases,
only Governments can deal with them. However, all Governments
have gone much further than this, and have regarded civil aviation
policy generally as their responsibility because of its international and
political character and of the exceptional economic problems in its
development. National security also demanded that Governments
should assert sovereignty over their own air space and should control
the passage of aircraft over their territories. Moreover, civil aviation
was both a potential ancillary to defence in war and an essential
complement in peace to a successful aircraft manufacturing industry,
while national pride as well as commercial foresight in many countries engaged the keen interest of Governments in the development of
national airlines.

On the commercial side air transport has not been able unaided to
develop efficiently and extensively. As a young and technically complicated industry it required heavy, and often speculative, investment
in equipment and offered its rewards only in the long term. Its
travelling public had to be created; its cost was high and its risks
obvious. Also few countries (with the United States of America the
obvious exception) offered large or easy opportunities for domestic
air services—those with large areas often having a sparse population

or poor living standards, and those with a promising social development being usually too small and already furnished with well-developed road and rail transport systems. For most countries, therefore, it was, and is, impossible to maintain powerful airlines without living primarily off international traffic. But it is precisely here that competition tends to be fiercest and this has been artificially intensified since, from the early days, Governments gave support, direct and indirect, for one reason or another, to their own airlines. With the rapid growth of air travel since the war to confirm its earlier promise as a major world industry, Governments have attached more and more weight to the economic benefits, as well as to the uncommercial advantages, of successful national airlines, and in their cause have employed much more extensively than before 1939 their control over the use of the air.

While all these factors have varied in weight from time to time and country to country, they have universally resulted in an exceptionally close relationship between government and industry. On the technical and safety side Governments with the full support of industry have co-operated with one another. They have done this mainly through the International Civil Aviation Organization (ICAO), the specialist agency of the United Nations set up by Governments 'to develop the principles and techniques of international air navigation and to foster the planning and development of international air transport'. On the commercial side, political, economic and military considerations have led Governments to assume a close responsibility for civil aviation policy, helping their airlines by subsidy, financing airports, navigation facilities and aircraft development, taking an active part in regulating international competition through their control over traffic rights in their territories, and generally deciding or controlling the main principles of the nation's air transport effort.

In these ways and for these reasons the United Kingdom's air policy and the basic structure of its air transport industry have assumed their present forms. After the First World War the industry was left to 'fly by itself'—a praiseworthy but short-lived policy; when the first air service from London to Paris failed before competition from heavily subsidised French airlines, the Government began to subsidise its own industry, and from this beginning the present close partnership between airlines and the State has developed here as elsewhere. The international nature of the industry and the fierceness of competition, universally Government-supported, inevitably led not only to the evolution of a policy of Government help, whether direct or indirect, but also to the concentration of the national effort into a limited number of air lines as the 'chosen instruments' of Government policy to win the maximum share of world trade.

This principle of civil aviation policy is independent of political doctrines, as the experience of other countries shows. In France both a nationalised corporation (Air France) and selected independent companies are used as chosen instruments, each being allotted a sphere of operations where it does not compete with the others. In the United States of America, where airlines are not State-controlled (although, as elsewhere, the State has materially assisted in their development), world-wide operations are confined to three airlines (Pan American Airways, Trans-World Airlines, North-West Airlines), which again are kept as far as possible from international competition with each other. In the United Kingdom the same approach had resulted in 1939 in the creation by Act of Parliament of a chosen instrument in the British Overseas Airways Corporation which, as a corporation under public ownership and control, absorbed the Government-subsidised but privately-owned Imperial Airways and British Airways. So British organisation followed the general pattern of civil aviation development in all countries and ante-dated the post-war nationalisation of certain other important industries.

In domestic as well as in international air services, most Governments have intervened to produce the orderliness necessary for the development of a safe and efficient industry, to secure the provision of essential services, even if some of them are not economic, or to ensure that internal air transport played the right part in civil aviation policy generally. Governments in countries of continental size have naturally been able to afford their domestic air transport freer scope for purely commercial operation than smaller countries, but all exercise considerable control. In Australia the responsibility for the major domestic routes is shared between nationalised and private companies. In the United States of America, competition and development on domestic routes is closely controlled by the Civil Aeronautics Board, and Pan American Airways, the chief international carrier, is debarred entirely. Within the United Kingdom the problem has been chiefly the uneconomic nature of most of the routes, and Government policy since the war has therefore been to secure a reasonable spread of services by preventing a concentration of competition on the few lucrative routes.

Whatever practical variations may be made from time to time, the basis of civil aviation policy is likely to remain the allocation of the major tasks to a very few large airlines as 'chosen instruments'. The present structure of civil aviation in the United Kingdom conforms to this policy, with the two Corporations carrying the chief responsibilities for regular scheduled services, BOAC the long-haul operations and BEA the domestic and short-haul European operations. But this does not mean that there is no room for other airlines or other activities, and thus private companies are able to provide charter flights, pioneer special air transport services such as car ferries, operate scheduled services which do not conflict with those of the Corporations and develop particular activities such as crop-spraying and aerial photography.

THE MINISTRY AND BRITISH CIVIL AVIATION

The functions of the Ministry in relation to both the Corporations and the independents are complex as well as close. In all cases it is responsible for negotiating with other Governments for the traffic rights necessary for international operations. In the case of the two publicly-owned Corporations the Minister has a general responsibility for seeing that they are efficient and economic, while at the same time ensuring that their managements are given as much freedom as possible to enable them to discharge their commercial responsibilities to the nation. While the Minister has no similar responsibilities for the independent companies, nevertheless, as they have an important part to play in British civil aviation, the Ministry must do what it can to enable them to play it as effectively as possible, within whatever political directions Governments may give about the relative roles of the Corporations and the independents. Also, the Ministry and the Ministry of Supply do what they can to see that the air transport and the aircraft manufacturing industries complement and assist each other to produce the optimum result for British aviation as a whole.

INTERNATIONAL WORK

The Government's responsibilities for the international needs of British air transport fall into two main groups—the first arising from legal, technical and safety matters and the second from national control over the freedom of the air. The first group includes customs, immigration, the provision of airports and air navigation facilities as well as more general questions of international air law. As these are matters of common interest to all Governments, they are, in the main, dealt with through the International Civil Aviation Organization. The United Kingdom has a permanent member, a senior official of the Ministry, on the Council of the Organization. ICAO has a valuable record of achievements in the operational and technical field and has brought about a high degree of standardisation throughout the non-Communist world on such matters as the procedures for telecommunications, air traffic control and air information services;

the qualifications for aircrew, air traffic control officers and maintenance personnel; and specifications for aerodrome lay-out and lighting, for the length and bearing strength of runways, and for navigational aids. Not only has ICAO laid down the standards, but by means of regional air navigation conferences has kept under review the provision by States of the technical facilities required for air-line operation. ICAO has also made some progress towards the unification of international aviation law on such matters as the liability of operators to passengers, consignors of cargo and third parties on the ground and also in easing the flow of international air travel by reducing formalities and paper work. But in economic matters the Organization has been less successful. In particular, all attempts so far to conclude a multilateral agreement on the exchange of traffic rights have failed. ICAO's greater success in the technical field is understandable, for there is a common interest in the standardisation of the procedures and equipment for airline operation throughout the world, whereas on economic matters the interests of different countries vary widely depending amongst other things on the competitive strength of their airlines.

The failure of ICAO to achieve a multilateral agreement establishing in the air anything similar to the freedom which a ship enjoys to carry passengers and goods to and from any port in the world has left international air transport subject to an intricate complex of traffic rights which have to be negotiated bilaterally between countries. The rights which an airline needs for international services are known as the 'five freedoms', a concept which since the war has been accepted as indispensable to discussions and negotiations between Governments about traffic rights. Two of these so-called freedoms are merely the right to fly across the territory of a State without landing and the right to land solely for such matters as refuelling and repair. These do not normally involve the Ministry in much negotiation, since they are the subject of a multilateral agreement, the International Air Services Transit Agreement, which was promoted by the United Kingdom at an International Civil Aviation Conference in Chicago in 1944 (which also established the present ICAO). Most, although not all, countries important in civil aviation have signed this agreement. The remaining freedoms are those conferring commercial or traffic rights and require negotiation foreign country by foreign country, since they confer the right to pick up or put down passengers, mail and freight and to carry them either between an airline's own country and a foreign country or (most controversial and difficult to negotiate) between two foreign countries. Some Governments insist upon their bilateral agreements exchanging these traffic rights being in great detail, even specifying such matters as the number of flights which the airlines of the two countries may mount upon particular routes or the amount of traffic of different kinds which they may carry and so on. Most countries, however, have accepted as a pattern the bilateral air services agreement which the United Kingdom and the United States of America concluded at Bermuda in 1946. An agreement of this sort specifies the routes which the airlines of the two countries may fly, lays down procedure for designating the airlines which are to fly them, sets forth the broad principles to be observed by those airlines in the interests of fair competition and orderly development, and finally provides for fares to be agreed. Fares are in the first place discussed and agreed collectively by the airlines themselves, meeting in their own International Air Transport Association, but their resolutions whether on fares, rates or associated commercial matters require the approval of Governments. It is, however, unusual for Governments to reject the major resolutions of IATA, since consultation between Governments and their airlines before and after such meetings usually ensures that the final proposals of the airlines are acceptable.

The broad principles of the Bermuda kind of agreement are designed on the one hand to avoid hampering the commercial freedom of airlines to develop quickly and efficiently, and on the other hand to provide criteria to judge whether an airline is promoting wasteful competition by putting on more services than the traffic requires, or relying excessively upon traffic which does not originate in, or is not destined for, its own country. The Government of either country has the right to challenge the operations of the airlines of the other country over any of the routes covered by the agreement and, by reference to these principles and the facts of the case, to call upon the other Government either to show that the complaint is unjustified or to remedy it. The negotiation of these agreements is chiefly concerned, however, not with the text, since that tends to follow more or less standard forms based on the Bermuda Agreement, but with the schedules which specify the routes which the airlines of each country may operate through the territory of the other and the points at which traffic rights may be exercised. But even when an agreement has been signed between the United Kingdom and another country the work of the Ministry is far from finished. Problems of interpretation may arise and, more frequently, since operational requirements are constantly changing in a rapidly developing industry, amendments to route schedules will be necessary especially as the introduction of a new point in a long distance route in one agreement may very well require consequential amendment of agreements with other countries through which the route passes. In the negotiation of these agreements the Ministry has the advice and assistance of various other departments, particularly the Foreign Office, Commonwealth Relations Office and Colonial Office, as well as that of the airlines.[1]

In addition to negotiations concerned with formal bilateral agreements the Department is constantly at work obtaining traffic rights for United Kingdom airlines from countries where no formal agreement has been concluded, traffic rights which are wanted for a particular limited purpose or for specified periods of time, or rights which for some other reason are most conveniently dealt with by informal or temporary authorisation; and, of course, dealing with similar claims from foreign Governments on behalf of their airlines.

Obviously the Ministry's object in negotiating traffic rights must be to obtain the best possible exchange of rights in the interests of the country's airlines; but it is often far from easy to assess the relative merits of long-term advantages and short-term gains. There may indeed sometimes be strong arguments for granting traffic rights to another country where there is little or no case, as a matter of pure traffic right trading, to do so. The United Kingdom fundamentally believes that liberal principles, which it has traditionally upheld on the sea, giving the maximum possible freedom from Government control and interference over international traffic rights, would be in the best interests of efficient world air transport. Although attempts since the war to achieve this by means of a multilateral agreement binding all nations have failed, and the United Kingdom has been forced back upon separate bilateral negotiation with individual countries, nevertheless the hope that ultimately liberal doctrines will be generally accepted remains a strong influence on United Kingdom policy. In the same way the concept of non-discrimination is important. While there can be no legal obligation to treat all countries alike, it is often difficult to deny to one country rights that have been given to another, whose case for them—pure bargaining apart—may be no better and perhaps less good. Again the United Kingdom has been ready, in the right circumstances, to deal generously with countries that have less to offer to us than we to them, in recognition of the importance of their contribution toward world air transport.

RELATIONS WITH AIR CORPORATIONS

While the international activities of the Ministry are on behalf of all United Kingdom operators, naturally it is the two Corporations which are mostly concerned because of their predominant place in British aviation policy. Consequently, too, the Ministry's dealings with the Corporations in other matters are many and comprehensive. The position of the Corporations as the two chosen instruments of

[1] In a number of posts overseas an officer of the Department serves as Civil Air Attaché or Representative.

British aviation policy is established by Section 24 of the Air Corporations Act, 1949. This section reserves to the Corporations and their associates all scheduled services touching the United Kingdom (with the small exception of circular tours and, of course, the properly authorised services of foreign airlines), which means in effect a virtual monopoly of those services which are open to the public generally and which operate regularly. But any United Kingdom operator whatsoever can provide non-scheduled services—that is, broadly speaking, charter flights since they are not available to the public generally, or flights, such as journeys organised for special occasions, which, even if they are open to anyone, do not form a regular service. It is in the sphere of non-scheduled services that the independent private companies were, after the Second World War, expected to find their main occupation. In more recent years they have also expanded their activities in scheduled operations as associates of one or other of the Corporations.

The exceptionally close relationship between the Minister and his chosen instruments, which was inevitable in any case, is made closer by the public ownership of the Corporations, which imposes upon the Minister special responsibilities to Parliament and to the nation. He has both specific powers and certain general statutory authority but the working link between the Ministry and the Corporations is much stronger than is required by any formal statutory powers. In fact, the important part which the Government must of necessity play in matters vital to the Corporations has inevitably called for constant, informal dealings between the Ministry and the Corporations on all matters of major policy. Formal statutory provisions give the Minister authority which Parliament has required him to exercise over the affairs of the Corporations. These have been set out in Chapter I but it may be convenient to restate the major points here particularly as, in a number of instances, the control over the Air Corporations is closer than it is over the British Transport Commission. The Minister appoints the Chairmen and all members of the Boards; the Corporations are required to submit to him every three years a programme of proposed services with corresponding estimates of receipts and expenditure; they are also required to give him in advance for each financial year an estimate of their proposed capital expenditure during that year; he has power to call for such additional information as he may require; he can give to the Corporations directions of a general nature in the national interest; he has to lay before Parliament in respect of each financial year the Reports and Accounts of the Corporations; and, if a profit has been made, the Minister, with Treasury approval, and after consultation with the Chairman of the Corporation concerned, has the power to direct how it shall be applied. During the period in which the Corporations were entitled to subsidy, the Minister and the Treasury also had to decide whether a grant was to be made from public funds to subsidise the year's programme and, during the course of the year, whether any grant decided upon should be revised. The Minister was also entitled, during that period, to receive from the Corporations before the beginning of each financial year their programme of services together with estimates of revenue and expenditure. Both Corporations became self-supporting before the end of the subsidy period which lapsed at March 31, 1956.

The Air Corporations Act, 1949, gives the Corporations power, with the consent of the Treasury, to raise capital by the issue of stock, both capital and interest being guaranteed by the Treasury. With similar consent they may also borrow temporarily by way of overdraft or otherwise. Under the Finance Act, 1956, however, for a temporary period, the raising of capital by the issue of stock has been replaced by issues from the Exchequer. It will be seen, therefore, that the formal degree of financial control over the Corporations is considerable. Although neither Corporation has in recent years required an annual grant, and the statutory provisions for making grants has lapsed, the profits made by the Corporations, in common with those of almost every major airline, remain slender and precarious. The Minister's active interest in the finances of the Corporations, therefore, remains undiminished. He is responsible (as he is not in the case of the British Transport Commission's services) for the ultimate approval of fares and freight rates and has, in this respect, a dual obligation—to the Corporations to see that they are not too low and to the public to see that they are not too high.

Despite the control which the Minister is required to exercise over the Corporations, particularly in financial matters, it is a key principle of relations between the Ministry and the Corporations that their managements, like those of other nationalised industries, should be left full discretion in the day-to-day conduct of business and the exercise of essential commercial judgment. The planning of routes and services, aircraft maintenance and other engineering arrangements, passenger and freight-handling procedures, sales, advertising and labour relations are all matters in which the Ministry considers it has a positive responsibility not to interfere, though there are some exceptions to this wide general statement. For example, the Minister has a statutory responsibility for making pension schemes for Corporation employees, though these are normally settled in the first instance by the National Joint Council for Civil Air Transport which the Corporations and Trade Unions set up as joint negotiating machinery to deal with terms and conditions of employment, including the health, safety and welfare of employees and matters of mutual interest to management and labour. Again the ordering of new aircraft is very much a commercial matter but it also intimately concerns the Government because of the heavy capital investment required (a BOAC order in 1958 for 35 aircraft with spares amounted to some £70 million) or because currency questions arise or because of its impact on the aircraft manufacturing industry. Indeed, the aircraft requirements of the Corporations have had an important place in aviation policy. The policy has been to 'fly British' but exceptions have had to be made, particularly in the case of long-haul aircraft for BOAC when no suitable British aircraft was available at the time. Immediately after the last war, the aircraft manufacturers in the United States of America had the advantage that, unlike our companies, they had continued during the war to produce types suitable for development as civil aircraft and hence the United States airlines were quickly able to re-introduce modern international air services. For some time, therefore, the aircraft manufacturers in the United Kingdom desperately needed help from the Government to recover from war-time preoccupations, so that they could produce transport aircraft that would enable the Corporations to face growing competition on the international routes, particularly from the United States of America. That phase is now passing and, more recently, the manufacturers have undertaken the development and production of aircraft required by the Corporations on a 'private venture' basis without any financial assistance from the Government.

RELATIONS WITH THE INDEPENDENT AIRLINES

Naturally the relations between the Ministry and the independent private operators are less complex. While there are differences of opinion about the exact role of the independents in relation to that of the two Corporations, all Governments since the war have agreed that while the Corporations must undertake the main task, the independents have a part to play; and all have agreed that British aviation must not weaken its international effort by competing with itself to the advantage of its foreign competitors. The private companies in active business owned between them in 1957 about 180 multi-engined transport aircraft, and, as their opportunities and activities have expanded, so they have begun to acquire more modern aircraft, and they now own or have on order Viscounts and Britannias. In the earlier years after the war their chief task was intended to be the provision of the non-scheduled services which Parliament excluded from the monopoly given to the Corporations and their associate companies. This field they have developed considerably, but in recent years they have also taken an increasing part in the provision of scheduled services (as associates of the Corporations) and in air trooping for the Service departments.

The operation of scheduled services by independents started on a small scale in 1949 but their opportunities were greatly expanded in 1952 when the Government permitted them to undertake scheduled services if, in general terms, they were either on routes not served by the Corporations or of a kind which would not seriously affect the services of the Corporations. Every application for such a service is submitted by the operator in the first place to an independent statutory body, the Air Transport Advisory Council. The Council hear the case for it (and any objection against it) and, after considering its operational and economic aspects, including the probable effect of the new services upon existing ones whether provided by other independent operators or by the Corporations, they advise the Minister whether or not an application should be approved. These arrangements have allowed the independent companies to pioneer new types of service, such as the car ferries and the air/coach services, which combine the advantage of air travel over the Channel with the cheapness of road travel, but the biggest development recently has been in 'inclusive tour' services catering for (and themselves creating) the enormous increase in holiday traffic by air to Europe. Many of these new services are on international routes and so require foreign traffic rights. But the independent companies, notably those in which shipowners have a major interest, also operate scheduled services on long-haul routes, particularly to Africa where, since 1952, they have developed all-freight services and, for passengers, the colonial coach services which, by offering a lower class of travel at cheaper fares, have met a demand for air travel between the United Kingdom and Colonial territories that was not being catered for by the more luxurious standards of the Corporations' services at more expensive IATA fares.

COMMONWEALTH AND COLONIAL
CIVIL AVIATION

For purposes of international civil aviation, as in other matters, the countries of the Commonwealth are separate States. It is, of course, the policy of the Ministry and the Commonwealth Relations Office to work for the very best understandings with them.

In 1945 the Commonwealth Air Transport Council was formed with a permanent secretariat in London. There are also regional councils. The Southern Africa Air Transport Council comprises the United Kingdom, the Union of South Africa, the Federation of

Rhodesia and Nyasaland, Ghana and British territories in East and West Africa, while the members of the South Pacific Air Transport Council are Australia, New Zealand, Canada, the United Kingdom and Fiji. In addition to Commonwealth co-operation through Governments there is considerable commercial co-operation between United Kingdom and other Commonwealth airlines. BOAC and Qantas Empire Airways operate the 'Kangaroo' route between London and Sydney in partnership with one another, each bearing its own operating costs and pooling the revenue, and it is hoped to extend the partnership arrangements as other routes between the United Kingdom and Australia are introduced. The Air Services Agreement signed by the United Kingdom and Australia early in 1958 provided for a number of new routes between Australia and the United Kingdom, including a route westabout from the United Kingdom to Australia through the United States of America and across the Pacific Ocean. Similar partnership arrangements exist on the 'Springbok' route to South Africa between BOAC, South African Airways, Central African Airways, and more recently East African Airways.

The Ministry, together with the Colonial Office, co-operates closely also with the Colonial Governments to promote the fullest development of civil aviation in Colonial territories to the mutual benefit of the United Kingdom and the Colonies. The United Kingdom Government is responsible for negotiating traffic rights for colonial airlines and watching their interests in foreign negotiations generally; and it has played its part in a policy whereby the territories of West, East and Central Africa have developed international airlines of their own, all having close operational and commercial relations with BOAC. Through subsidiary companies locally managed, BOAC also are more directly responsible for air transport in the West Indies, Bahamas and Aden. Hong Kong has two airlines, Cathay Pacific Airways, a wholly private company, and Hong Kong Airways, in which BOAC and private interests share, which operate on international routes stretching from Japan to India. But perhaps the most interesting as well as the most recent illustration of Commonwealth and Colonial civil aviation policy is the present Malayan Airways, in which BOAC and Qantas join with local private interests and Governments and which operates under contractual agreements involving the Governments of the newly independent Federation of Malaya, of the self-governing colony of Singapore and of the British territories in Borneo.

PRIVATE FLYING

It would be wrong to conclude without a reference to the Ministry's concern for private flying and gliding. It has been Government policy since 1945 to give what help it can to flying and gliding clubs short of direct general subsidies. It has been possible to relieve flying clubs and gliding clubs of part of the duty which they would otherwise have to pay on petrol. Moreover, private and club pilots, through a scheme introduced with the co-operation of the Royal Aero Club, are able to use a large number of State aerodromes by payment of a modest fixed annual fee instead of the normal landing charges. The Air Ministry has also helped by establishing a scholarship scheme under which selected cadets of the Air Training Corps and of the RAF section of the Combined Cadet Force are trained up to the standard of a private pilot's licence by the flying clubs at Air Ministry expense. Gliding is encouraged by exempting gliders from the normal requirements for registration and certificates of airworthiness. In dealing with private flying and gliding, the Ministry has had the full co-operation of the Royal Aero Club, the Association of British Aero Clubs and Centres, the Popular Flying Association and the British Gliding Association, the enthusiasm of whose members ensures that this small part of the civil aviation scene will remain a very live one.

CHAPTER XIII

Aerodromes

Development of Aerodrome Policy — The
London Area — Administration — Aerodrome
Development — Finance — Licensed Aerodromes
— Aerodromes Overseas — Conclusion

*

IN 1957 the United Kingdom handled a total of over 6 million air travellers; over 85 per cent of them, carried in more than a quarter of a million planes, used aerodromes run by the Ministry of Transport and Civil Aviation. According to the Civil Aviation Act, 1949, an aerodrome is 'any area of land or water designed, equipped, set apart or commonly used for affording facilities for the landing or departure of aircraft'. This sounds refreshingly simple but in providing for the safe and timely travel of so many people and aircraft the Ministry is engaged in a large and highly specialised business, with a background of constant, rapid and to some extent unpredictable change: for the air transport industry has proceeded by a series of giant steps rather than by gradual development. In less that 40 years, progress has reached forward from converted military aircraft adapted to carry a two-passenger payload on short-stage flights to the high-speed turbine aircraft of today carrying 100 passengers and more, while small grass airfields have been replaced by long concrete runways, and simple radio aids by the complicated navigational devices described in the next chapter. Moreover, the history of the transport industry can show nothing else to compare with the speed of growth of air travel. In 1937 about 166,000 air passengers passed through the London area; the comparable figure for 1957 was over 3½ million. Today the Ministry must provide for the needs of passengers flying for week-ends to Paris or on business to Santiago da Chile, and of aircraft bound for Montreal, Manila or Manchester. On its aerodromes you may find news stands and engineering workshops, nurseries and electronic installations, industrial canteens and high-class restaurants, pony rides and propeller turbines. The Ministry's aerodrome duties are also unusual in that they involve the exercise of important regulatory functions in addition to wide executive responsibilities; as well as operating its own aerodromes, the Ministry licenses others. To see how it has come into this complex inheritance from its predecessors, the Ministry of Civil Aviation and, before that, the Air Ministry, it is necesary to look back briefly at the story of civil aerodromes.

DEVELOPMENT OF AERODROME POLICY

In 1939 the Government had responsibility for only three civil aerodromes, two near London and one, Lympne, on the South Coast. Elsewhere the provision of aerodromes was left to local authorities and others. There was no central planning of aerodrome development and the only assistance the Government gave to aerodrome owners was to provide air traffic control, telecommunications and meteorological services. When the Second World War ended and civil aerodromes were urgently needed it had to be decided how many must be provided and where, and how they should be operated and administered. Since it seemed likely that few local authorities would be able to meet the high cost of providing the large and elaborate aerodromes called for by post-war aircraft, the Government decided that the State should be responsible for the principal international airports and for the main aerodromes required for the planned network of internal services; and that these should be operated directly by the new Ministry of Civil Aviation. Otherwise the field was left open to local authorities and others to operate aerodromes under licence, as before the war. The Ministry's aerodromes—except London Airport—are used not only by scheduled service operators but also by charter operators, flying clubs, private owners, manufacturers and the Royal Air Force to the extent that their use by scheduled services allows. London Airport caters for some incidental charter flying but otherwise only for airlines whose main business is to operate scheduled services.

The number of aerodromes operated by the Ministry has been gradually reduced, as the shape of air services has become clearer, from 35 at the beginning of 1948 to 25 ten years later. Of these, four serve London, including the recently opened Gatwick; one is the transatlantic airport of Prestwick; eight are for social services in the Highlands and Islands of Scotland and in the Scilly Isles; and the remainder for important centres in England, Wales, Scotland and Northern Ireland. In addition there are places such as Edinburgh (Turnhouse) where the Ministry operates civil enclaves at RAF aerodromes.

THE LONDON AREA

The heaviest air traffic in Europe is in the London Area which is naturally the magnet for overseas air services, long and short; it has a special significance for foreign airlines most of whose passengers bound for the United Kingdom want London to be their first port of call; it is a junction at which overseas passengers change from one air service to another; and it produces much outward traffic. In this crowded and heavily built-up area the Ministry must provide adequate aerodromes as close as possible to London, with bad-weather alternative aerodromes not too far away, and site them so that the increasing traffic in the air over south-east England can be handled safely and expeditiously. After the Second World War, the Government decided to develop London Airport at Heathrow as the premier airport in the United Kingdom and to make it capable of taking the largest amount of traffic which could regularly be dealt with at one airport in the kind of weather normally encountered in England. London Airport first became available for civil aviation in 1946—with one runway and a makeshift collection of huts, tents and caravans. With such small resources it could not handle all the traffic offering and most short haul air services were based on Northolt, which was borrowed for civil aviation from the Air Ministry and used until 1955 when the first stages of development at London Airport were completed and the airport was ready to fill its intended role. At the same time five other State-owned aerodromes in the London Area (Blackbushe, Bovingdon, Stansted, Croydon and Gatwick) were available to the Ministry as civil aerodromes. Since then the capacity of London Airport and of the system of air traffic control in the area have become strained. London Airport must be further developed and, in addition, other aerodromes must be used: but the original five were too many and were badly placed. They produced a network of routes which made efficient air traffic control difficult, and they were uneconomic. Only two of them will be retained, as bad weather alternatives and to take spill-over traffic from London Airport. One is Gatwick, which, after a full public inquiry called for by strong local opposition, the Government decided to develop as the main alternative to London Airport: the other is Blackbushe. Stansted will be held in reserve, Bovingdon has been handed back to the RAF and Croydon is being closed.

ADMINISTRATION

With aerodromes scattered from the Shetlands to the Scillies it is obviously essential to decentralise control. In 1947 the country was first divided into four Divisions, which were reduced to three in 1956. Each Division is under a Controller who is responsible for the supervision and executive management of the Ministry's aerodromes and most of the other civil aviation outstations (such as the Air Traffic Control Centres and Radio Stations which are dealt with in the next chapter) in his Division, except in the case of the aerodromes serving London where a special organisation, described below, is in force. Between them, the three Divisional Controllers are responsible for about 70 different establishments. The day-to-day running of each aerodrome falls to an Aerodrome Commandant who is responsible to his Divisional Controller for the efficient operation of his aerodrome, subject to Headquarters responsibility for policy and planning.

An Aerodrome Commandant may be responsible for the running of one major aerodrome or a group of smaller ones. Under his control come the business side of the aerodrome; the Air Traffic Control organisation at the aerodrome; telecommunications services; the Aeronautical Information Service, which provides pilots with the latest information about the aerodromes and the navigational facilities along their proposed routes; the aerodrome Fire Service; the aerodrome Constabulary; mechanical transport ranging from snowploughs to forklifts; and the aircraft marshallers, baggage porters, cleaners, drivers, fitters, telephone operators—a wide range of staff. He is responsible for ensuring that the facilities of the aerodrome are efficiently run for the benefit of those who travel or send mail or freight by air and of the airlines who carry them. The Ministry's job is to provide and maintain the aerodrome and the requisite ground technical services; the airlines, who provide their own staff for the purpose, have to maintain and fly their aircraft and look after their passengers, guiding them through the traffic buildings, the Customs and other controls, and to and from the aircraft. At some busy aerodromes (notably London Airport) the need for economy and for avoiding congestion has led the Ministry to undertake, on repayment terms, the loading and unloading of freight and baggage from aircraft, the operation of buses carrying passengers between the passenger building and the aircraft, and the provision of such facilities as aircraft steps, destination boards, cabin cleaning and other apron services for the airlines. In addition to his responsibility for the operation of his aerodrome the Commandant also has the duty of watching the operation of aircraft to see that flying regulations (that properly licensed crews are carried, that aircraft are not overloaded and are certificated as airworthy, and so on) are complied with.

The airports serving London handle so much traffic and present such great problems of organisation, operation and administration that a General Manager has been appointed to take charge of them. Under him are the Commandants and a Deputy General Manager responsible for such matters as the handling of passengers, ground transport, the police and commercial matters.

The conduct of the Ministry's aerodromes is obviously a matter of concern to local interests, and the Minister has a statutory obligation to make arrangements to consult them on matters of local significance. For this purpose Aerodrome Consultative Committees have been formed, usually convened by the principal local authority in the area. These Committees have given the Ministry much useful advice and assistance in the many matters in which the aerodrome authority and its neighbours have a common interest.

AERODROME DEVELOPMENT

Aerodromes must keep in step with changes in aircraft performance and with the growth of traffic. Runways must be long enough and strong enough to permit the operation of all aircraft likely to use them. There must be runways in as many different directions as are necessary to prevent strong crosswinds from interrupting flying (modern aircraft are fortunately becoming less susceptible to crosswinds, and where three or four directions might previously have been necessary one or two should now suffice). The amount of traffic may dictate, as at London Airport, two parallel runways in each direction to be used simultaneously. Taxi tracks at a busy aerodrome must be such that large numbers of aircraft may be safely and economically directed along them by the Ministry's airport staff, even in bad weather. Aprons, on which the aircraft embark and discharge their passengers and cargoes, have to be designed to meet ever-changing requirements as aircraft grow larger, as multi-wheel undercarriages necessitate wider turning circles, and as turbine engines present special clearance problems arising from the blast from their engines. Today's aircraft may need parking stands between 140 and 220 feet wide. Thus where a number of aircraft are handled simultaneously, they need a great deal of space. This in turn must be used in such a way that the movement of passengers and goods and the manœuvring of aircraft and of many vehicles and appliances becomes as well-ordered and synchronised as possible. And, of course, all aerodrome development must aim at reducing disturbance to the neighbourhood to a minimum, must provide clear approaches for aircraft in accordance with internationally agreed standards, must prevent interference with radio aids to navigation and must provide for future extensions.

The proper design of terminal buildings is another vital factor if the aerodromes are to be run efficiently. The Control Tower, the focal point of an aerodrome's operation, with its view from on-high of the landing grounds and approaches, is one example of a highly specialised and complex building. Equally specialised in their way are the passenger and freight buildings. Not only must they cater for the swift and comfortable reception and dispatch of passengers, often through Customs and other controls, but they must also be able to deal expeditiously with freight, passengers' baggage and mail. The buildings must also, with an eye to the future, be capable of extension and adaptable to constantly changing needs. Here the Ministry has been greatly helped in recent years by distinguished architects whose work may now be seen at London Airport, Gatwick, Renfrew and Edinburgh.

One particular difficulty is to make the best use of the passenger buildings in getting large numbers of comparatively small groups to and from the aircraft. The problem is quite different in scale from that which confronts shipowners and port authorities. For example, at Dover, the busiest passenger seaport, nearly 2 million passengers passed through in 1957 from about 7,400 ships; but in the same year over 3 million passengers were dealt with at London Airport from no less than 116,101 aircraft. These factors create problems of passenger handling which up to the present have been met by shepherding each planeload through the airport buildings and controls and thence by bus to the aircraft. The need for such close control over the movement of passengers grows less as more and more become seasoned air travellers. Future plans for several of our airports envisage the passenger walking unescorted through the controls and along piers between buildings and aircraft. The demand for economy in building and speed of transit for the passenger is a spur to greater simplicity in airport design and in passenger handling. Nevertheless, with new designs of aircraft constantly bringing new terminal problems, it may be some time before airports achieve the simplicity of the seaport or of the railway platform. Meanwhile, airport terminal planning and design offers great scope for the imagination and ingenuity of the administrative and professional men engaged in it.

Normally in the past civil engineering and building works have been carried out through the agency of the Air Ministry's Directorate-General of Works. But sometimes, as at Gatwick, independent consultants have been engaged. And whilst the State provides the Control Towers, passenger buildings, fire stations, and so forth, the airlines themselves normally build their own hangars and workshops, taking a ground lease from the Ministry.

FINANCE

The Ministry's aim is to make as many as possible of its aerodromes pay their way as soon as this can be done. In this country no aerodrome is yet used to its full capacity so as to produce its full potential revenue, but when aircraft movements are growing at great speed all the time ground facilities must be provided in advance of need, and initial development and maintenance, which must be provided however small the traffic may be, is costly. If an aerodrome is approaching the time when it would be fully used, another must be in course of building, and indeed nearing completion, to cater for the growth of traffic in the same area. The need to be looking always to the morrow and to provide in advance for traffic which will come along later means that it will be some years before the airports in this country, and indeed those of the rest of the world, show a full return on the very large capital invested in them. In 1957–58 expenditure, excluding capital charges, was about £4 million with a further £2 million on aerodrome technical services. Revenue was £4 million. The concentration of London's air traffic into a smaller number of aerodromes should eventually go far towards putting them on to a sounder economic footing (at London Airport total operating and technical service expenditure in 1957–58 was £2·86 million and revenue already £2·81 million). But, at the other extreme, it is difficult to see how some of the smaller aerodromes, such as those in the Scottish Islands, can ever pay their way. Like the air and shipping services in the area, they may have to be maintained indefinitely at a loss as a social service to isolated communities.

Revenues fall into four main categories: user charges imposed on airline operators when their aircraft and passengers use the aerodrome; rents and comparable charges; revenue from concessions and from the visiting public; and other miscellaneous receipts. Their relative importance may be judged from the following analysis of gross revenues at London Airport in 1957–58:

	£
User Charges	
Landing fees	1,164,000
Passenger Service Charge	303,000
Apron Services Charge	390,000
Rents and comparable Charges	
Aircraft Housing and Parking Fees	68,000
Rents	558,000
Concessions and Public Admission	
Concessions	147,000
Public admission and car parking	89,000
Miscellaneous	
Space heating	46,000
Other	50,000
	2,815,000

It will be seen that landing fees are the most important source of revenue. They are charges for the use of runways, taxi-tracks, aprons and technical services which are the most expensive items on the aerodrome and those for which it is most difficult at the present stage of development to make a fully economic charge. The charges must be kept broadly in step with those at aerodromes on the Continent, and in settling them the Ministry must, as an international obligation, avoid discrimination between different air service operators. The scale of landing fees is the same for all the Ministry's aerodromes and is fixed after consultation with the airline operators and the owners of licensed aerodromes. The broad aim of the charging policy is to obtain a yield of approximately 5 per cent of the income derived by an aircraft carrying a normal load over an average distance. The fee for any particular aircraft is accordingly related to its weight, with rebates for very short journeys and surcharges for unusually long ones. The other user charge, the passenger service charge (5s. for each passenger leaving for overseas) is levied as a contribution towards the cost of the passenger-handling facilities at the aerodrome.

Concession revenue deserves a special mention, for the concessions —restaurants, bars, buffets, banks and shops in the traffic building, car hire services, catering and amusements in the public enclosures and so on—represent not only a growing source of revenue but also important amenities for the public. In some parts of the world the routes on the aerodromes by which passengers must walk to and from aircraft seem to be designed not so much for speed of transit as to ensure that passengers pass as many shops as possible on the way—a technique known in the Western Hemisphere as 'maximum concession exposure' and designed primarily with an eye to airport revenues. But in this country the Ministry believes that its first duty is to help passengers through the aerodrome as quickly as possible. In dealing with concessions, therefore, its primary aim is to encourage those that will give useful service to passengers and visitors with the production of the highest possible revenue for the airport as a secondary, though important, aim.

It is hardly likely that the taxpayer or the competing transport interests would tolerate a situation in which the major airports would for ever fail to pay their way and would continue to be a burden on the economy. But it would be wrong to infer from the experience of the last few years that the airports must continue to lose money. The prospect that traffic may increase by three or four times in the next 12 years and many times more thereafter, bringing with it steadily mounting revenues, including those from rents and concessions, points to a different conclusion and suggests that the heavy capital investment in these relatively early days of air transport will in the end find full economic justification.

LICENSED AERODROMES

Although the main transport aerodromes in the United Kingdom are State-owned, there remains, as in the case of air services, considerable scope for private and municipal enterprise. Anyone who wishes may operate an aerodrome, but, so that the Minister may discharge his general duty for air safety, the operator must hold a licence from the Ministry if his aerodrome is to be generally used by aircraft carrying passengers for hire or reward or for instructional flying. The licences may be either for public use or for private use. In the former case the aerodrome is open without discrimination to all suitable aircraft; in the latter it is available only to the licensee and persons specifically authorised by him.

Before a licence is granted, the Ministry satisfies itself that the site possesses certain minimum physical characteristics, and that there are available adequate fire, rescue and medical services. The site itself is usually inspected by the Ministry's technical officers. There are today between 60 and 70 licensed aerodromes, varying in size from small grass fields, used mainly by flying clubs, to busy international airports like Manchester. Some are used for scheduled services but most of them support a variety of other types of flying. Many are owned by local authorities, and one independent airline, Silver City, has built an aerodrome of its own in Kent—Ferryfield—for its ferry service of cars to and from the Continent. Some assistance is given to the operators of aerodromes licensed for public use by the free loan of technical equipment.

There is one notable case where the Ministry and a local authority are partners in developing one of the busiest aerodromes in the country—Manchester Airport. As a major airport, both for internal, continental and more recently for transatlantic services, Manchester was originally among those which the Ministry proposed to acquire and operate. But the Manchester City Council were anxious to retain control of the aerodrome which they had established with so much enthusiasm and foresight, and arrangements were made for them to retain and operate it, while the Ministry provides all the technical services and makes a substantial contribution to the cost of approved major development.

AERODROMES OVERSEAS

The Ministry's interest in aerodromes is not confined to the United Kingdom. In most territories under United Kingdom sovereignty, protection or mandate, aerodromes and ground facilities are the immediate responsibility of the local Governments, although the Ministry speaks for them in ICAO. The advice of the technical branches of the Ministry is also at the service of any colony which may seek it, as most of them do. Colonies are generally expected to shoulder the cost of their own civil aviation needs, but few of them would be able to pay for the elaborate services required by a trunk route which happens to pass through, even if it were reasonable to expect such altruism. The Commonwealth Development and Welfare Fund may help with capital expenditure required for the purposes of the colony itself, but where the development is required not for the colony but for the needs of through traffic the Ministry may make a contribution and, in doing so, may take credit for the economic benefits that flow to the colony from the existence of the trunk service. If the RAF use the ground services, the Air Ministry may also help financially. Special arrangements apply in Fiji, one of the few aeronautical stepping-stones across the Pacific. There the United Kingdom shares the cost not only with the colony itself but also with the Governments of Canada, Australia, and New Zealand through the South Pacific Air Transport Council, which has already been referred to. In many colonies aerodromes were constructed and equipped with ground facilities to meet war-time needs; for example, in Africa along the routes to the Middle East, and in Asia along the routes to Burma and the Pacific islands. In some places, particularly at Singapore and Hong Kong, our former enemies left a legacy of aerodromes.

In Bahrain and Sharjah, British protected States in the Persian Gulf, the Ministry, by agreement with the Rulers of the territories, directly controls the two principal aerodromes and operates them with the assistance of contractors. Elsewhere in British protected territory in the Persian Gulf, Kuwait for example, the local authorities provide and administer aerodromes at their own expense and with their own resources but receive advice from the United Kingdom which is responsible internationally for their civil aviation affairs.

CONCLUSION

The growth of air transport continues and with it more aerodrome development will be needed. It is possible to make a reasonably good guess at the requirements of fixed-wing aircraft for the next few years, though the faster and larger turbo-jet machines pose problems of noise and of length and strength of runways which introduce a new and serious element of uncertainty. There is also uncertainty about the future of some of the smaller provincial aerodromes, both State

M

and municipally owned, which are used mainly by short haul air services. These are the most likely to be affected by the coming of the helicopter as a means of commercial transport. The helicopter, though still in its infancy, is already presenting the Ministry and local authorities with a new problem—that of providing alighting-places near city centres. Such technical advice as is possible at this stage is given to local authorities. But when so little is known of the probable operational characteristics and requirements and of the commercial possibilities of a large helicopter the planning can be only very tentative. In any case it will be some time before helicopters are in general use as truly commercial vehicles. In the meantime air traffic using conventional aircraft increases steadily and aerodromes must be developed to keep pace. While the total capacity of the country for handling air traffic must continue to increase, few new aerodromes are likely to be required; indeed, the present number may well be reduced. The problem now is to know how existing aerodromes, whether State, municipally or privately owned, should be enlarged or developed, and to determine the part the State should play at transport aerodromes other than its own.

It is unlikely, too, that the organisation described in this chapter will remain unaltered. The growing and changing air transport industry will need adaptation and change in the ground organisation that serves it and this part of the Ministry's work will continue to be interesting and challenging. Perhaps the problem will be simplified for our successors by the development of aircraft with vertical take-off and landing. But the time for that is not yet.

CHAPTER XIV

Operational and Technical Services

The operation of a flight — Air Traffic Control
— Radio Aids to Navigation — Communications
— Other Technical Services — Aircraft Noise —
Some problems confronting the Ground Services

*

To the casual observer, an aeroplane sweeping across the sky must appear the least earth-bound and most detached object imaginable. But in fact it is connected with the ground by a number of invisible links, and the successful accomplishment of a flight is a triumph of co-ordinated effort which begins before the aircraft takes off and does not end until after it has landed. The cunning of the designer and manufacturer of the aircraft, the organisation of the airline, and the skill of the pilot and his crew all play their part; but no less important is the provision and operation of the technical services on the ground. The modern transport aircraft must be guided to its destination almost regardless of bad weather and, in busy areas, its progress and landing must be controlled and directed to avoid collision with other aircraft. The more numerous, the more complicated and the faster aircraft become, the more important and complex are the ground services needed. The way in which these services have come to be provided by the Ministry has been set out in Chapter II.[1] Apart from the Meteorological Service, which is run by the Air Ministry, all the technical services at the aerodromes are the Ministry's responsibility. They are described in this chapter under three headings—Air Traffic Control, Radio Aids to Navigation and, thirdly, the Means of Communication between ground and aircraft and between stations on the ground, without which none of the rest could work. But first, a few general words on what happens before and during a flight.

THE OPERATION OF A FLIGHT

Long before an aircraft takes off from a major aerodrome the captain and some of his crew will have visited the Meteorological Office at the aerodrome to find out what the weather is likely to be *en*

[1] Pages 38–40

route, at the destination and at aerodromes to which they may be diverted. They will also have visited the Ministry's Briefing Room, where the Aeronautical Information Service will have supplied information on the serviceability of navigational aids and aerodromes and on anything unusual on the route such as military air exercises. Important messages about the flight will already have passed between stations along its route, ranging from those about commercial matters to those which touch on safety. Once the aircraft is airborne there will be messages about the progress of the flight and about changes in the weather or in the tracks and altitudes to be followed. A special aeronautical communications network on the ground connects each important aerodrome in the United Kingdom with an Air Traffic Control Communications Centre, which in turn is linked with other Control Centres at home, in Europe, and beyond, and there are constant exchanges of information between them. Aircraft generally maintain contact with the ground stations by radio-telephony or wireless telegraphy throughout the flight and the exchange of messages ends only after the aircraft has landed, when the arrival signal is dispatched to the aerodrome of departure and to the air traffic control authorities who would be responsible for starting search and rescue action if the aircraft were overdue. All the time the aircraft is on its journey it will have the advantage of radio aids to its navigation, such as those described later on.

AIR TRAFFIC CONTROL

The Air Traffic Control system provided by the Ministry is designed to regulate traffic in the air near aerodromes and in other places where there is dense flying. Its purpose is not only to provide for the safety of air navigation but also to increase the rate at which aircraft can use aerodromes and air routes and so to avoid unnecessary and expensive delays. The overriding factor in Air Traffic Control is that, once airborne, an aircraft can neither stop nor reverse; it must go on at high speed. The Air Traffic Control Officer cannot freeze the situation and think things out; indeed he has to anticipate the future traffic situation in the air and to issue instructions accordingly. Jet aircraft intensify the problem because their long climbs and descents are more likely to cross the routes of other aircraft and their very high speeds require that decisions must be made very quickly. Difficulties are increased in what are known as 'Instrument Meteorological Conditions' (IMC) when Instrument Flight Rules (IFR) apply. When a pilot is flying in cloud or poor visibility he cannot see other aircraft in time to avoid them, so all aircraft using busy air routes or aerodromes in bad weather are required to fly under the instructions of Air Traffic Control, who keep them well separated. In fact, even in good weather most pilots avail themselves of this separation service. Away from busy areas the Rules are less strict, and at low heights outside busy areas they are still less stringent, so as to avoid unnecessary restrictions on light aircraft which do not normally fly high or very fast and are very manœuvrable.

The Air Traffic Control system in the United Kingdom is based on relatively narrow corridors, called 'Airways', along the main routes, and 'Control Zones'. In Instrument Meteorological Conditions aircraft are normally allowed to enter these airspaces only with a clearance from Air Traffic Control and, once there, must follow its directions. Airways are 10 miles wide and extend from about 25,000 feet down to 5,000 feet or less, depending on the locality, leaving sufficient space for uncontrolled aircraft to fly underneath. To accommodate new types of jet aircraft which fly very high it will be necessary to extend the controlled airspace much higher. Control Zones surround the busier aerodromes and extend down to ground level in order to protect aircraft during take-off and landing. Aircraft flying along the Airways are controlled by Air Traffic Control Centres which communicate direct with aircraft and are themselves connected to other Centres, including some overseas, by direct landline. For the last stage aircraft on and near aerodromes are controlled by Approach and Aerodrome Control Units on the aerodromes.

Before an aircraft takes off on a busy air route the Air Traffic Control Officer has begun the process of separating it from other aircraft by assigning to it particular altitudes, a time for take-off from the runway, and sometimes particular routes. Once an aircraft is airborne, the problems of navigation and Air Traffic Control in busy areas become closely allied. Modern aircraft may be approaching each other with combined cruising speeds up to 1,000 knots (over 550 yards per second) and measures for preventing collisions are important even in good weather. To keep aircraft apart, the traffic is channelled along the Airways, which are divided into sections or 'blocks' by radio beacons that serve as reporting points. The Control Officer's calculations for spacing the aircraft at safe intervals are based on position reports transmitted by the pilots, on radar plots and on his own information. In busy terminal areas extensive use is made of radar, enabling the controller to know the exact position of aircraft at all times and so permitting separation standards to be reduced and traffic to be expedited. The pattern is constantly altering and the Control Officer must be able to anticipate situations before they arise. The problem of arranging aircraft in sequence for landing and take-off at the smallest safe intervals at which they can be fed in or out by the Air Traffic Control Centre is no light task for the

Approach and Aerodrome Controllers at busy aerodromes when often numbers of civil aircraft may be waiting to take-off or land in the shortest time practicable.

If by some mischance an aircraft becomes overdue, Air Traffic Control has the important duty of alerting the search and rescue organisation provided jointly by the Royal Navy, the Royal Air Force, the Coastguard and the Life-boat Service.

RADIO AIDS TO NAVIGATION

There are many radio devices available to aircraft, some of which enable the pilot to fix his position and find his way and some of which guide him to the runway when he is approaching his destination, and the various complex systems of radio aids in use on the ground are constantly being improved. In addition to aids installed for internal and European flying, the Ministry provides and operates special aids for use by aircraft crossing the Atlantic.

Some of the better known navigational aids in use in the United Kingdom today are the Decca system, directional and non-directional beacons and means to guide approaching aircraft to their runways in bad visibility, such as the Instrument Landing System (ILS). Any description of these highly technical devices would be more appropriate to a treatise on electronics than to a book of this kind. But it may be of interest to choose one of them and explain as simply as possible how it is used. Let us take Ground Controlled Approach (GCA)—a radar approach aid.

The essence of GCA is that the pilot of an aircraft approaching an aerodrome to land is 'talked down' by the Radar Controllers on the ground. The pilot has simply to listen by radio telephone to the Controllers and be guided by the navigational instructions he receives until he comes to the point where he can see the runway. On the ground the Controllers follow the movements of the aircraft on radar screens. The aircraft is identified on the screens and is directed by one of the Radar Controllers to a position on the final approach to the runway, where the aircraft is handed over to the Precision Controller who, from a range of five or six miles from the runway, talks the aircraft down by transmitting continuous instructions and information, keeping the aircraft at the correct angle of descent and in line with the centre of the runway. The final stages of the Precision Controller's talk-down might run as follows:

GCA Precision Controller to Pilo

'$3\frac{1}{2}$ miles from touchdown . . . Heading 285 is closing you to the centre-line from the left . . .

3 miles from touchdown . . . On the glidepath[1] . . .

. . . Cleared to land . . .

2½ miles from touchdown . . . Turn left, left 5 degrees—heading 280, I say again heading 280 . . . on the centre-line . . . You are slightly below the glidepath now—40 feet too low . . .

2 miles from touchdown . . . Check your critical height[2] . . .

. . . 30 feet low . . . 20 feet low . . . back on the glidepath now . . .

1½ miles from touchdown . . . Turn left, left 3 degrees—heading 277—slightly right of centre-line, closing . . . On the glidepath . . .

1 mile from touchdown . . . Turn right 3 degrees—heading 280 . . . On the centre-line and on the glidepath . . . ½ mile from touchdown . . .

On the centre-line, on the glidepath—Precision approach completed—Out.'

On completion of the approach the aircraft is about 400 yards from the beginning of the runway at a height of about 100 feet; from here the pilot will land visually. A pilot will not attempt his approach unless he is sure of being able to complete the landing visually. Should he find, on reaching his critical height, that the weather is so bad that he cannot continue his approach visually, he will automatically break off and either remain in the vicinity in the hope of an improvement or make for another aerodrome where the weather is better.

There are at present some 260 communications and navigational installations in operation in the United Kingdom. These are calibrated and regularly checked by aircraft of the Ministry's Flying Unit, a small fleet of specially equipped aircraft which operates from Stansted in Essex. Some of these aircraft are also used to carry out the air examination of candidates for pilot's licences and for other purposes such as flights by operations officers and aerodrome lighting trials and inspection.

COMMUNICATIONS

No scheme of air traffic control or aids to navigation can work unless there are means of communication, not only between the ground and the aircraft but also between the different stations on the ground. All these are provided by the Ministry.

Within the United Kingdom the aerodrome control stations are each directly connected with their parent Air Traffic Control Centre

[1] The 'glidepath' is the imaginary path through the air which would give the aircraft its correct angle of descent to the runway.

[2] The 'critical height' is the height below which the aircraft must not descend unless it is able to continue the approach by visual reference to the ground or lighting aids.

which, in its turn, is connected with its neighbours. In the language of civil aviation the word 'neighbours' is an elastic term and includes aeronautical stations sometimes several thousand miles apart. Thus the Civil Aviation Communications Centre at Croydon is the focal point within the United Kingdom for landline and radio communications between civil aviation stations in this country and abroad, not only on the Continent but thousands of miles along regular airline routes. The system serves other aeronautical interests besides Air Traffic Control and employs radio and landline teleprinters, point-to-point radio and direct telephones. It handled some 20 million messages in 1957. In the United Kingdom it is possible for aircraft and Air Traffic Control to communicate directly and instantly with each other on Very High Frequencies except when the aircraft is flying low in certain areas. To achieve this has called for skill in designing and siting the various stations, in selecting and allocating frequencies and in integrating transmitters and receivers at Control Centres, aerodromes and relay stations. The success of the United Kingdom is leading other countries to provide in the same way for important areas where there is an appreciable volume of air traffic.

OTHER TECHNICAL SERVICES

As has been seen, even with the most effective radio aids available today, pilots usually still have to complete their landings visually. Approach and runway lighting is, therefore, of special importance for operation in bad weather and at night. The centre-line and bar approach lighting system, which is installed at most of the Ministry's aerodromes, was developed by the Ministry in collaboration with the Ministry of Supply, and a full scale (3,000 feet) experimental installation was installed at London Airport as far back as 1948, following the production of the basic design by Mr E. S. Calvert of the Royal Aircraft Establishment. It has been recognised internationally as an outstanding contribution to air operation and has been adopted in many countries. The system consists of a line of lights, beyond the end of the runway and in line with its axis, with shorter lines of lights crossing it at right angles at intervals of 500 or 1,000 feet and decreasing in length towards the runway. The approaching pilot gets a clear indication of the line on which he should fly and of the position of the end of the runway: in addition, the cross-bars indicate the plane of the horizon when this is obscured by poor visibility. The pattern as a whole therefore enables him to orientate himself immediately in relation to the runway.

On the ground, a complex system of lighting of runways and taxi-ways is required at all large aerodromes for the guidance of aircraft before take-off and after landing. This is operated from the Control Tower.

Among the most important of the many ancillary services is the Aerodrome Fire Service, which is responsible not only for aircraft fire fighting and rescue but also for general fire prevention at the Ministry's aerodromes. Its staff undergo regular training and refresher courses at the Ministry's Fire School at Cardiff.

An important part in improving ground services is played by the Ministry's Operational Research Branch, which was set up to apply scientific methods to the study of the operations for which the Ministry is directly responsible. Among other things, it has conducted experiments directed towards improving the air traffic control system; it makes periodic estimates, by sampling, of the delays to aircraft when landing or taking-off and tries to locate the basic causes; and it applies scientific methods to the measurement of aircraft noise. It also studies the rate of flow of passengers and baggage through the Airport Controls and analyses the results to see whether any modification of method of layout is desirable. Far more is involved than a mere matter of time and motion study, although this is extensively used. The aim is to apply detailed and scientific study to possible future difficulties before they arise and to find the lines of a solution. Finally, the Ministry gives advice on all these technical matters to the authorities controlling aerodromes and navigation facilities on British routes overseas and acts in an advisory capacity to the Colonial Office.

THE PROBLEM OF AIRCRAFT NOISE

The growth in the size and number of aircraft using civil aerodromes and in particular the introduction of jet engines have inevitably increased the amount of disturbance caused by noise to residents near busy airports and air routes. The problem has been to find ways of reducing and controlling the noise without reducing the safety of flight itself or crippling air transport operations. It has been accentuated by the increasing power of engines used in large modern transport aircraft.

The Ministry has devoted more and more attention to the problem over the last few years both at its own aerodromes and in collaboration with the Ministry of Supply. For long-term measures the Ministry of Supply has initiated and supported a programme of basic and applied research particularly directed at reducing the noise from existing and future turbo-jet engines. The results of this work have already been applied to designs for ground mufflers to reduce the noise when engines are being run for maintenance purposes on the ground; and there is good reason to hope that the development of such devices as jet nozzles will bring about a useful reduction in the noise from aircraft in flight. This is a field in which there are still many unknowns and the work of research will need to go on for a long time.

Concurrently with the long term measures for discovering means of reducing noise at its source, the Department is constantly devising, testing, and putting into effect day-to-day arrangements for mitigating its effects. The Operational Research Branch, which has already been referred to, and the Department of Scientific and Industrial Research measure, record and analyse noise levels in areas where nuisance has been experienced or is expected, and compare them with the prevailing background noise levels from other sources. In the light of this knowledge about the intensity and distribution of aircraft noise measures are devised by planning the layout of buildings, particularly in the maintenance areas, so that they may act as acoustic shields for nearby communities. Large experimental walls were built at London Airport to explore the effects of acoustic shielding: the results were good and the knowledge gained has been applied elsewhere. In such work as this, where the United Kingdom has been well in the forefront of progress, there is constant exchange of experience with other countries in Europe, the Commonwealth and the United States of America.

The incidence of noise due to helicopter operations in built-up areas has not been overlooked and extensive trials have been carried out to estimate the usefulness of particular forms of silencers and also the way in which the noise will be affected by buildings alongside a route. The noise generated by comparatively small helicopters used in air services so far has not proved very difficult to deal with, but the much bigger helicopters of the future present new problems which are being examined.

SOME PROBLEMS CONFRONTING THE GROUND SERVICES

The United Kingdom is a small country with only limited air space about it, and already the air is becoming congested, particularly in the South East, by the mass of civil and military flying. The problem is made more difficult by the increasing use of turbo-prop propulsion, soon to be followed by jets in large numbers. The Ministry is in constant consultation with the Air Ministry about ways of dealing with the problem of trying to fit a quart of civil and military aircraft into a pint of sky. A similar problem exists on crowded long-distance routes, particularly on the North Atlantic. Part of the solution here may be to give the aircraft an accurate means of knowing its exact position all the time probably by using the British Dectra system which shows great promise of providing the answer.

During the next few years the increase of traffic and the introduction of jet aircraft on a large scale, with their high rates of climb and descent and much greater speeds, will impose even greater burdens on the Air Traffic Control system. A great contribution to the solution will be made by the increased use of radar, electronic computers and improved methods for the transmission and display of information on aircraft positions and flight plans; but before the final solution is found a large programme of research and development will be needed, not only for equipment but also for the procedures and techniques to be used.

It is clearly necessary in all these matters to work towards international standardisation of those items of the ground services that require aircraft to carry special equipment in the air. If each country were to use different aids an aircraft on a long international flight, crossing six or seven countries, would be loaded with several kinds of heavy and expensive equipment to the exclusion of many passengers. Ideally, there should be a standard system of navigational aids comprehensive enough for use at a busy major international aerodrome but capable, by the elimination of the more delicate and complicated aids, of use also at a small aerodrome in a remote district. The standardisation of a complete system in some areas and component features in others can be achieved only if the system itself is unlikely to be changed for many years. The cost of introducing a universal system would be very high, and on this account alone the system would have to last for 15 to 20 years, even if it were possible to ignore the long gap between international agreement on the installation of a new system and its being put into service. A high degree of standardisation is, however, so important that it might be worth paying a heavy price for it, even though part of the price might be delay in taking early advantage of later improvements in navigational aids. The Ministry is engaged, as of course are other member states of the International Civil Aviation Organisation, in continuous research, planning and negotiation on this difficult subject.

Thus the constantly growing volume of commercial flying and the ever-increasing demands of modern aircraft require a corresponding advance and expansion in ground technical services; and new designs and increased speeds of aircraft, and possible complications due to the commercial operation of helicopters, will have profound effects on the ground services needed. But there is a sense of excitement and of exhilaration in facing the fascinating problems that are on the horizon.

CHAPTER XV

Safety in the Air

The Rules of the Air — Aircraft and the Air
Registration Board — The Operator — The Crew
— The Investigation and Prevention of
Accidents — The Search for Safety

*

THE very nature of aircraft and the rapidity with which modern
technology develops make the pursuit of safety a task demanding
constant vigilance and anticipation and raise problems which are
technically more difficult and complex than in other forms of transport. Nevertheless, by the very fact that they are either technical, and
can be solved by scientists and engineers, or operational, where
they are in the hands of highly trained and skilled pilots, crews and
ground staffs, they are not so intractable as the problem of road
safety. Air safety can be tackled only by close co-operation between
the men who build the aircraft, those who operate them, the crews
and engineers who fly and maintain them, those who provide the
aerodromes and the technical and navigational services, and the
authority which lays down safety requirements and regulations. It
would be easy to produce requirements so severe as to make it
economically impossible for aircraft to fly at all; or alternatively, the
entire responsibility might be left with the operator, without any
kind of regulatory protection for the travelling public. Neither
extreme is possible and the problem is to find the right mean between
them.

By the end of the First World War, it was apparent that an acceptable standard of safety in the air must be founded upon international
agreement. The first steps were taken by European States in the Paris
Convention of 1919 (air safety thus found its way into an effective
international convention before marine safety, curiously enough)
and by the Americas in the Havana Convention of 1928. Towards
the end of the Second World War, with the expansion of long-distance
routes, it became clear that some international agreement covering
the whole world was required and in 1944 the two Conventions were
replaced by the famous Chicago Convention. Annexes to this Convention dealing with many technical matters, including measures to

further safety, were worked out in great detail by the International Civil Aviation Organisation and are kept under constant review by that body.

The Minister is by statute charged with the general responsibility for safety in the air, and a variety of Orders and Regulations under the Civil Aviation Act, 1949, provide him with the necessary instruments. These statutory instruments are also the means of implementing agreements reached at ICAO. Although they are often necessarily very detailed, the principle on which they are framed is to lay down minimum standards but not to interfere with the final responsibility of the operator and the pilot-in-command for the safety of the individual aircraft. There are many operating variables in which the operator or his pilots must have a considerable say. Among them are weather minima—that is, the lowest horizontal and vertical visibility in which an aircraft can safely take off and land. The Regulations place on the operator the responsibility of specifying minima for his aircraft and require the pilot-in-command to comply with them. In setting his weather minima, the operator must take account of a number of factors including the standard of training of his crews, the handling and performance characteristics of his aircraft, the aerodrome topography and the landing aids available. Even so, the mandatory requirements laid down for the safe operation of aircraft remain numerous and complex, but their details are outside the scope of this book. The requirements for aircraft engaged in public transport are, of course, stricter than those for other aircraft, while the regulations governing private flying are limited in the main to what is necessary to protect other users of the air and persons and property on the ground. The basic requirements are known as the 'Rules of the Air', and apply to all aircraft.

THE RULES OF THE AIR

The Rules of the Air, contained in a Schedule to the Air Navigation Order, 1954, define the responsibilities of pilots whilst airborne. They include rules for the prevention of collision and for the showing of lights. These follow the same principles as those which apply at sea but are more complicated because of the high speed of aircraft and the existence of a third dimension. The situation arising from flight in low visibility or when in or near cloud is dealt with by the Instrument Flight Rules which are described in Chapter XIV. Protection of persons and property on the ground is provided by airspace restrictions and by making reckless or dangerous flying, or the dropping from the air of objects which might be a source of danger, offences against the law.

It is convenient to consider the way in which the Minister discharges his responsibility for the promotion of air safety, in addition to the issue of the Rules of the Air, under four heads: aircraft, operators, aircrew, and the investigation and prevention of accidents.

AIRCRAFT AND THE AIR REGISTRATION BOARD

The Minister is responsible for laying down standards of airworthiness for aircraft, but his administrative functions are delegated by statute to the Air Registration Board, which was constituted for this purpose in 1937. This Board, which resembles in some respects Lloyd's Register of Shipping, is a non-profit-making incorporated body. It has 18 members, two appointed by the Minister, 12 representative of constructors, operators and insurers of aircraft, and four co-opted. The Board ensures that aircraft are designed and built to high standards; that only approved materials are used; and that during their subsequent life aircraft are, by a proper system of servicing and inspection, maintained in sound condition. It formulates and publishes technical requirements for the design, construction and maintenance of aircraft, engines, components, accessories and equipment; it arranges for the inspection of aircraft and the approval of engines and equipment; and it recommends to the Minister the grant of certificates of airworthiness. The Board also administers a system of licensing for aircraft maintenance engineers. But the power to suspend certificates or licences remains the direct prerogative of the Minister.

Save in exceptional circumstances, no civil aircraft may fly unless it has a valid certificate of airworthiness. It must, if it has been made in this country, have been designed and built in accordance with the British Civil Airworthiness Requirements by constructors approved by the Air Registration Board. To establish that the airworthiness requirements are met by a new type of transport aircraft, the integrity of the structure in respect of static strength and fatigue resistance must be proved by a series of ground tests, and a comprehensive flight test programme, in which the Board's test pilots participate, has to be completed. These flight tests cover the range of conditions in which the aircraft is to be operated, ensure that its handling characteristics are satisfactory and establish its performance. The information on performance, with suitable safety margins incorporated, is recorded in a 'flight manual', which forms part of the certificate of airworthiness of the aircraft. In addition to what the Board require before they will recommend to the Minister the issue of a certificate of airworthiness, there is a set of requirements designed to ensure the aircraft's continued airworthiness. The constructor has to produce comprehensive data about the aircraft in the form of a maintenance manual. The operator must lay down, and have approved by the Board, a maintenance schedule, involving a series of progressive inspections to be made at stated intervals and to be certified by licensed engineers. The modification, overhaul and repair of aircraft are similarly controlled.

The operator is also required to prepare comprehensive instructions for the loading of aircraft, as regards both amount and distribution of weight. The weight and performance of the aircraft have to be regulated for the route and the meteorological conditions. In the case of the larger modern aircraft the performance and weight have to be such as to ensure safety even if one engine fails and, for long over-water flights, even if two engines fail.

Radio equipment must be approved by the Minister just as other equipment which may affect safety is approved by the Air Registration Board. The manner of installation must be approved by the Board and the radio station in the aircraft must be inspected periodically, in accordance with an approved maintenance schedule, by a qualified radio engineer.

THE OPERATOR

The air navigation regulations are so framed as to place clear responsibilities on the operator for the safety of his aircraft, as distinct from those which he shares with the captain. He is, of course, responsible for everything concerning his base organisation, including compliance with the requirements for aircraft maintenance, loading, and equipment. He must also provide detailed instructions to his flight crews in the form of an operations manual. This manual contains guidance on the operation of the aircraft on all stages of the proposed flights and includes the procedure to be followed in an emergency. The aircrew licensing system, described later, ensures that the crew have the necessary basic qualifications but, because of the difference between various types of operation and routes which may be flown on regular airline flights, the operator must ensure that his crews are competent for the particular work upon which he employs them and that they maintain that competence. The regulations, therefore, require an operator to check his crews periodically. For example, he must satisfy himself periodically that his pilots and flight engineers can carry out not only the manœuvres used in normal flight but also emergency procedures such as flying with one or more engines out of action.

THE CREW

All members of the aircraft's crew, pilots, navigators, flight engineers and radio operators, must be licensed by the Minister. The crew to be carried varies from aircraft to aircraft according to the complexity of its operation and the route to be flown. The minimum crew necessary is determined at the aircraft's certification stage and is laid down in the certificate of airworthiness. The Air Navigation Regulations prescribe the conditions in which additional crew members must be carried, but the Minister has power to vary the crew laid down by the Regulations where special circumstances apply.

There is a graduated licensing system for pilots, the technical and practical flying qualifications varying in severity according to the size of aircraft which the licence permits the holder to fly and whether it is for private or public transport. The Ministry officers carry out the technical and practical flying examinations for the initial issue of professional pilots' licences except those to test the pilots' knowledge of aircraft, which are undertaken by the Air Registration Board as it has specialist staff available for the purpose. For similar reasons the Board also conducts examinations for the issue of flight engineers' licences. The examinations for navigators' and radio operators' licences are conducted by the Ministry. As flying may impose considerable physical and mental strain on the crew, and good sight and hearing are obviously of great importance, a high standard of medical fitness is demanded and a periodical medical examination forms part of the crew licensing system.

Before a pilot may fly in controlled air space in bad weather, when the Instrument Flight Rules apply, he is required to have an Instrument Rating in his licence, to obtain which he must pass a special examination. The Instrument Rating must be renewed every year after a flight check of the pilot's continued efficiency. It is clear that for the safety of the aircraft and everybody on board the pilot-in-command must be fully aware of his responsibilities and must discharge them meticulously. The Air Navigation Regulations recognise this and lay down rules which govern his actions before and during flight. He must, for example, check that the aircraft has sufficient fuel, is properly loaded and is in every way fit for flight. He must also plan his operation carefully in the light of weather reports, the route to be followed and possible alternative destinations. He must fly carefully in accordance with the Rules of the Air and at all times take whatever action is possible to avoid hazard.

Good flying instruction is essential to safety, and special qualifications are required from pilots who wish to practise as instructors. The Minister is responsible for the grant of Instructors' Ratings and in practice such ratings are given to pilots with appropriate flying experience who hold certificates of competency as flying instructors from the Guild of Air Pilots and Navigators.

THE INVESTIGATION AND PREVENTION OF ACCIDENTS

The careful investigation of accidents in order to discover their causes and to prevent their recurrence plays an important part in the search for safety in the air. This responsible task is the province of the Ministry's Air Accident Investigation Branch under the Chief Inspector of Accidents, staffed by officers with wide technical knowledge and experience. All aircraft accidents which occur in the United Kingdom or which occur elsewhere to aircraft registered in the United Kingdom and which result in death or serious injury or substantial damage to the aircraft must be notified to the Ministry. Any accident which occurs in the United Kingdom whether notifiable or not, may be investigated by the Chief Inspector of Accidents, if he thinks fit, although normally he investigates only the more serious accidents. In appropriate cases a formal public inquiry is ordered by the Minister. In England and Wales these inquiries are held by a Commissioner and Assessors appointed by the Lord Chancellor, and the preparation and presentation of the evidence becomes the responsibility of the Attorney-General assisted by the Treasury Solicitor and the Chief Inspector of Accidents. There are analogous arrangements for holding public inquiries in Scotland and Northern Ireland. All reports of Commissioners and of the Chief Inspector of Accidents are carefully studied within the Ministry. If necessary, Regulations are amended and any lessons to be learned are brought home to those concerned so that all possible remedial measures may be taken. The Department also obtains and classifies information about minor accidents not investigated by the Chief Inspector and carefully watches statistics for significant trends. A close liaison is maintained with the Safety Committees of the larger air operators who maintain their own organisations which assist in the official investigation of accidents to their own aircraft.

If an accident to a British aircraft occurs outside the United Kingdom and in the territory of a State which is a member of ICAO, the inquiry is normally conducted by that State. When the accident is serious, one of the Ministry's Inspectors attends the inquiry officially as an accredited representative, with advisers to assist him, and invariably their presence is accepted and welcomed. In countries where there are no expert staff, as in some of the colonies, the Inspectors are occasionally appointed temporarily to be Inspector of

N

Accidents for the colony. At all times, therefore, Inspectors of Accidents must be ready to leave for the furthest corners of the earth at any moment of the day or night.

Apart from these possible trips abroad, the work of investigating the causes of accidents may sound, from this account, dull and boring. That the finding and piecing together of fragments of a crashed aircraft may involve hours of concentrated, and often frustrating, labour is undeniable, but the attempt to reconstruct the course of events and, by experiment and deduction, to find, for example, the cause of a structural failure may be more exciting than any thriller. The outstanding case was the inquiry into the cause of the loss of the Comet I near Elba and of the second near Naples. The second fell in very deep water and recovery was out of the question, but near Elba, where the depth though still great was manageable, by the combined efforts of the Royal Navy, the Italian authorities, and the local Italian fishermen, by the use of under-water television and other modern inventions, and by persistence with older devices like nets and trawls, much of the wreck was recovered. As each piece came up it was identified by the Ministry's Inspectors on the spot and flown immediately to Farnborough where it was fitted by the staff of the Royal Aircraft Establishment into its place in an enormous jigsaw puzzle. The operation at sea was aptly and graphically described by Earl Mountbatten, then C.-in-C., Mediterranean, as trying to find the contents of a bag of peas, scattered over a one acre field, in a fog, using a helicopter hovering a 100 feet in the air. Nevertheless, over 70 per cent of the aircraft structure was recovered before the search was called off—an almost unbelievable feat.

At Farnborough the work was not confined to fitting together the fragments and examining the result. At the same time as this was going on, a huge tank was built round the fuselage of a Comet I, and machinery was erected to increase and decrease the pressure inside, simulating the effect of ascent to 40,000 feet and descent from that height—very much speeded up—while the effect on the wings of movement and buffeting was simulated in the same way. The result was that the fuselage gave way while the wings were still intact, and the piece which blew out was found to resemble very closely one of the pieces recovered from the Elba Comet. Further work established beyond reasonable doubt that the cause of the disaster was the structural failure of the pressure cabin brought about by fatigue. That the sequence of events indicated by the tank test was right was confirmed by the finding of marks on one of the wings of the Elba Comet which could only have been made by a fragment of the fuselage being shot across it while the wing was still in position.

This is no more than a condensed and inadequate summary of a great feat of detection carried out by those who recovered the wreck and by the scientific and engineering staff at Farnborough who, with the Inspectors of Accidents, interpreted the results and did the independent tests. The story is told in the Report of the Formal Inquiry under Lord Cohen.[1] But anyone who reads that fascinating Report must face the risk of being driven irresistibly to read also the exciting evidence upon which the conclusions are based.

Was the result of all this work worth more than the obvious value of knowing why these tragic accidents had happened? Undoubtedly it was. The most valuable outcome was the impetus given to research and development work in respect of pressure cabin design and testing. The water tank test, which was first used to explore the fatigue characteristics of the Comet, has formed the pattern for testing several other new types of aircraft and many practical design lessons have been learned in this way. Also programmes of research aimed at providing a better fundamental basis for design were started at Government establishments and in the industry; the results of this work are now beginning to bear fruit. Among other results a new, bigger and better Comet is carrying passengers across the Atlantic. Thus the price paid so tragically for being far in advance of the rest of the world in producing a commercial jet-propelled aircraft has been repaid by a great increase in knowledge for the benefit of our own and of other countries.

This was only one—albeit the classic example—of the many investigations carried out when accidents happen. From nearly all of them lessons are learned which can be applied to prevent similar happenings in the future, and it is this, and not the desire to apportion blame, that justifies the time and effort devoted to the work. The fact that so much has been written about accident investigation does not mean that this branch of the Department's work is more important than the devising and enforcing of safety rules or the survey and maintenance of aircraft under construction and in service. The exciting and the humdrum work together to the same end and the one is not more important than the other.

THE SEARCH FOR SAFETY

In quite a different way the Air Safety Board under the Chief Aeronautical Adviser plays an important part in the search for safety. This Board, appointed by the Minister as a standing advisory body, keeps a watch on all matters that concern the safety of British civil aviation, including the efficiency of the ground services provided in the United Kingdom for civil aircraft of all nations. The Board works

[1] Civil Aviation Publication No. 127 (H.M.S.O., 1955).

not only with the technical departments of the Ministry but also with the Air Registration Board, the Ministry of Supply, aircraft manufacturers and operators, and the aircrew organisations.

Finally, the variety and complexity of the Air Navigation Regulations, together with the large number of aircraft operators, demand a system of inspection to ensure that the operating code is being carefully applied and to give operators advice on safety requirements. This involves a field organisation working within the Ministry's civil aviation Divisional Organisation, mentioned in Chapter XIII. The emphasis of these inspections is on help and advice rather than on policing.

Travel by air, like other branches of the transport industry, has its own particular problems to face in the search for safety. The vulnerability of the aircraft itself, the fact that it cannot stop to await safer conditions and the complications due to operating in three dimensions all require precautions that have no counterpart elsewhere. The need has been met by the complex organisation and by the ingenious scientific devices described in this and the preceding chapter, and there is every reason to suppose that, even in the face of greater problems which will come from the rapidly growing numbers of aircraft and from higher speeds, standards of safety can still be improved. But the flight of an aircraft is a combined operation which can be successfully completed only through the care and co-operation of all concerned. The price of safety, as of freedom, is eternal vigilance.

PART FIVE

Organisation, Common Services and Conclusion

CHAPTER XVI

Organisation and Common Services

Organisation — Effect of Amalgamation —
Establishment — Finance and Accounts —
Economics and Statistics

*

ORGANISATION

THE published estimates of the Ministry of Transport and Civil Aviation for 1958–59 provide for a total of some 15,500 employees. The persevering reader will by now be acquainted with the extent and variety of the Department's work and so will have some clue to what all these people do—a very large number of very different jobs requiring many different qualifications. There is, indeed, a remarkable number of so-called 'Departmental classes', that is classes peculiar to the Ministry and not common to the whole Civil Service. The Ministry differs from most others in its accumulation of almost 50 of these Departmental classes—coastguards, air traffic controllers, airport hands, firemen and policemen, marine surveyors, inspectors of ships' provisions, highway engineers, and many others. In all, these special classes account for nearly 5,000 persons. The second special feature, which is shared with a number of other Departments, is the extent to which the staff is deployed all over the country. As is shown by the table on the following page, three-quarters of the total numbers work outside headquarters at ports and aerodromes, in great cities, in isolated places such as coastguard and aircraft radio stations, and overseas.

The fact that so much of the work must be done on the spot and not at headquarters is one of the two main determining factors in the Department's organisation. The other, as will already be evident, is the great diversity in the character of the work, which makes it necessary to divide the Ministry into separate blocks each dealing with a particular aspect of each form of transport. The resulting organisation is set out in chart form on pages 218 and 219. It will be seen that under the Minister and the Permanent Secretary come three Deputy Secretaries—one responsible for shipping and ports, one for inland transport, one for civil aviation and a fourth officer, the Controller of Civil Aviation Ground Services, is responsible for

Number of staff and employees		Type of Office	Number of offices or out-stations	Principal duties
Non-Industrial	*Industrial*			
462	—	Marine Survey Offices	26	The survey of merchant ships.
336	—	Mercantile Marine Offices	28	Statutory functions relating to ships' crews.
18	—	Sea Transport Offices	2	Movement of Forces' personnel and stores.
76	460	Sea Transport Stores	6	Holding, issuing and recovering stores and equipment required specially for vessels in Sea Transport service.
74	43	Sea Transport Offices and Stores Overseas	6	
16	—	Sea Transport Survey Offices	2	Planning and supervising locally the fitting out of troopships and the maintenance of troop fittings.
530	—	H.M. Coastguard	155 (excluding auxiliary stations)	Life-saving around the coasts of the United Kingdom.
2,359	—	Traffic Area Offices etc.	12*	Licensing of goods vehicles, bus services, of buses and coaches and their drivers and conductors; enforcement duties; driving tests of would-be drivers of all motor vehicles.
401	—	Divisional Road Engineer Offices	9	Professional and technical matters relating to trunk and classified roads and bridges.
33	—	Finance Area Offices	10	Examination of local highway authorities' accounts in connection with payments made by the Ministry.
332	27	Civil Aviation Divisional Offices	3	Administration and operation of technical and other services (such as air traffic control and telecommunications), and management of state-operated aerodromes.
3,584	2,753	Civil Aviation Aerodromes and Outstations	70	
43	—	Shipping and Civil Air Attachés, Advisers and Representatives overseas	8	

* In addition there are 204 centres where driving tests are regularly conducted, apart from 126 others where tests are conducted from time to time as need arises. There are also over 200 Vehicle Examiners stationed throughout the country.

the State-owned aerodromes and the ground technical services. Each Deputy Secretary's command is for the most part divided between Under Secretaries in charge of Groups of Divisions and subdivided again into Divisions or Directorates each in charge of an Assistant Secretary or an officer of equivalent rank. Ordinarily it is to this level —the Division or Directorate level—that the heads of the different outstations report. Moreover they report direct; the work is too diverse in character to permit of Regional co-ordination. No one could usefully try to supervise the work of Marine Surveyors, Divisional Road Engineers, Traffic Commissioners and Aerodrome Commandants—to take only a few examples—at Regional level. There is however a regional representative of the Department in Wales.

Finally there come the central or so-called 'common service' Groups of Divisions—Establishment, Organisation and General; Finance and Accounts; Economics and Statistics—each in the charge of an Under Secretary. These Groups, which serve the whole Ministry and whose heads report direct to the Permanent Secretary, are dealt with in this chapter. But before describing their work a few words on the effect of the amalgamations which the Department underwent in 1941 and 1953 may not be out of place, for these occasions have radically affected the Ministry's organisation and, in particular, the work of the central Divisions.

EFFECT OF AMALGAMATION

The merger of the Ministry of Transport with the Ministry of Shipping in 1941 to form the Ministry of War Transport created a very large Department whose staff, at the height of the war, numbered some 25,000. With offices all over the world, it directly controlled the surface transport of the country and at sea of half the world beside. It was a powerful mixed team of civil servants, business men and others drawn temporarily from many walks of life. The swift dismantling of this machine together with the simultaneous concentration upon the transport problems of peace, and notably the issue of nationalisation, taxed to the full the energies of those who were left. At the same time the task, with which quite substantial progress had been made during the war, was continued of welding into a single Ministry two Departments with relatively few points of contact except in relation to the work of the ports and apart from special common tasks such as the transport by land and sea of the military forces for the invasion of Europe in 1944. By transfers of staff and by the growth of social activities, the sense of belonging to, and working for, transport rather than simply for shipping or inland transport was rapidly built up.

Since 1953 this painful process has been going on all over again. The moulding of the separate Ministries of Transport and of Civil Aviation into one organisation could not be expected to take place without a good deal of thought and planning and without some degree of heart burning. The effect of Departmental mergers— Pensions with National Insurance; Agriculture and Fisheries with Food; Transport with Civil Aviation—may, for those not directly involved, seem comparatively insignificant. The work goes on much as before and the total number of staff is pretty much unchanged— unless quite fortuitously some substantial block of work is discontinued about the same time, as happened in one of the other cases when the remaining forms of food rationing were stopped. But the effect of these mergers on the minds of the staffs concerned is by no means negligible. Many have to leave the offices to which they have become accustomed and others will be transferred to different kinds of work that may at first seem strange and unfamiliar, while those belonging to classes common to the two Departments will find their names on a combined staff list with unknown consequences to their prospects for the future. In the higher reaches of the Department the effect is felt most intimately. There is one Minister instead of two with all that means in responsibility and in load of work. The same is true for the Permanent Secretary and for the Principal Establishment and Organisation Officer and the Director of Finance.

ESTABLISHMENT

The general nature of Establishment work will be familiar to students of public administration, but the effect of the latest amalgamation and of having so many different grades to deal with is to throw a special burden on this part of the Ministry. Staff—many of them with special skills—have to be recruited, trained, posted, transferred, given leave, documented, promoted and eventually pensioned. Moreover, building adequate career structures for some of the more specialised classes presents a real problem. In the lower grades substantial numbers are needed, often with high technical qualifications and ability; but the higher posts may be few, and the chances of changing from one class to another are usually limited. The provision of career prospects which will attract the right type of entrant and maintain morale is therefore one of the most important that those responsible for staffing have to face.

The Establishment group of divisions has to deal also with matters other than pure staffing. Among them are Organisation and Methods on which a small staff is continuously engaged in a planned survey of the different Ministry offices and is available to undertake any specific investigation which may be dictated by swift changes in work loads or by an opportunity to take advantage of new methods or office machinery. Office services, including accommodation, registries, typing services and other similar common requirements involve much work in a large Ministry with many out-stations but call for no special comment. The Ministry, however, prides itself on the amount of care and attention given to training schemes for its staff. They range from basic courses for new entrants to supervisory courses for the middle grades and supervisors' conferences for senior staff and also include some vocational courses for technical staff.

In a Ministry with so many widely different interests and duties, it is necessary to have some central division to deal with problems of common concern and with matters that do not fall within the province of any of the more specialised divisions. The General Division supplies this need and deals among many other things with such matters as the legislative programme, with the scrutiny of Parliamentary Bills and documents to see whether they affect any responsibility of the Ministry, and with general matters affecting the nationalised industries for which the Minister is responsible, including appointments which it falls to him to make.

Under the Principal Establishment and Organisation Officer, but having a particularly close link with the Minister, comes the Information Branch. In a Department so concerned with matters which interest the public, this Branch is naturally a busy one. It issues the Press Notices and other official announcements relating to the work of the Ministry, answers general inquiries, particularly from the Press, arranges for Press conferences and organises publicity campaigns, for example on road safety, by way of radio, films, posters and exhibitions.

FINANCE AND ACCOUNTS

The combination of the two Finance and Accounts organisations of the former separate Ministries makes a unit which is responsible for four Votes totalling, for the financial year 1958–59, £88 million, all in Class IX of the Parliamentary Estimates. Vote one is almost entirely devoted to the salaries and expenses of the Ministry. It amounts to over £10 million after bringing to account receipts from fees for licensing of public service vehicles and goods vehicles, including payments for driving tests, and receipts from fees for services under the Merchant Shipping Acts and for other miscellaneous services. Vote two, for roads, accounting for by far the largest single item of the Ministry's total expenditure, amounts to nearly £70 million, a figure that is a reflection of the greatly increased highways programme. This represents expenditure on the trunk roads and percentage grants to highway authorities for classified roads as well as for traffic signs, pedestrian crossings and other safety measures. The Vote also includes some £3 million for payments to local authorities to reimburse them for expenses incurred in collecting motor vehicle excise duties and fees for driving licences and in registering vehicles, an agency service which they and the Ministry carry out for the Treasury. Vote three, Transport (Shipping and Special Services), is only for a net sum of £374,000 for 1958–59. The largest part of the expenditure, that on trooping (£7 million) and emigration shipping services (£1·6 million), is self-balancing as the costs are recovered from the Service Departments and the Commonwealth countries concerned. There are further receipts which cover the expenses of a few Government-owned ships which are operated commercially pending disposal. The balance of the expenditure in this Vote is mainly for the civil defence of railways and ports. Vote four, Civil Aviation, covers capital expenditure at the aerodromes owned by the Ministry and expenses of aerodrome maintenance, air navigational aids and meteorological services. In 1958–59 estimated expenditure on these items amounts to £10·7 million out of a total Vote of £12·6 million. On the credit side there are substantial receipts estimated to amount in all to £5·6 million from landing fees, rents, concessions and other sources.

In addition to the Appropriation Accounts a number of other accounts are kept, the more important of which are presented to Parliament after examination by the Comptroller and Auditor General. They include the accounts of the General Lighthouse Fund, the Marine and Aviation Insurance (War Risk) Fund, and the Seamen's Savings Bank Fund.

These facts and figures make it clear that the range of duties of the Finance and Accounts Divisions is very wide. Although the chief concern is with the expenditure of the Department and the revenue collected, advice is also called for on general financial questions which arise in the course of the Department's business, even though Government funds may not always be directly involved. For example, advice is required about the Minister's supervisory responsibilities for a number of transport undertakings, such as dock and harbour authorities incorporated under statute, many of which are required to make returns to him; the exercise of his powers to sanction loans required by local authorities for harbours or municipal transport; and his appellate jurisdiction over fares charged for road passenger services.[1] Other financial questions arise from legislation proposed by the Ministry and by other Departments or from

[1] Page 103.

Private Bills. More important still are the Minister's wide responsibilities in relation to the British Transport Commission and the Air Corporations, many of which are concerned with finance.

Most of the work is connected in some way with the annual Parliamentary estimates. Their preparation means collecting and examining much material to ensure that the Department asks for adequate, but not more than adequate, moneys needed for approved services. Once the necessary funds have been voted a close and continuous review of expenditure must be kept to see that it is held within the limits and used for the purposes authorised by Parliament. In addition, there must be constant effort to obtain the best value for money and to avoid uneconomical or wasteful expenditure and, by the adoption of adequate safeguards and sound procedure, to prevent fraud or irregularity. In all this work the Finance and Accounts Divisions owe a special responsibility to the Permanent Secretary as Accounting Officer responsible to Parliament through the Public Accounts Committee, before whom he is required to appear each year to render account of his stewardship. Since it is impossible for him to exercise financial control in detail, he must to a considerable extent delegate his functions to the officers appointed to assist him in carrying out this responsibility. In all staffing matters he is entitled to rely on the Principal Establishment and Organisation Officer; in other financial matters on the Director of Finance. The special responsibility devolving in this way upon both these officers is recognised by the method of their appointments which require the approval of the Prime Minister.

ECONOMICS AND STATISTICS

The remaining services which are provided centrally and on which all sides of the office can draw are those for economics and statistics. The collation of figures indicating the nation's transport resources and the nature of its employment is, of course, an essential prerequisite to the determination of policy. Studies are constantly made of traffic growth and the use of facilities. For example, extensive studies are made from time to time to guide the Department in deciding the size and layout of the international airports to serve London and the speed with which the facilities ought to be provided in order to cope with the traffic expected to develop. These estimates have to take into account not only general trends and total demands but also such complications as seasonal and daily peaks which may be the determining factor in deciding what facilities are needed. The work of analysing proposals for alterations in air fares and rates, the Minister's responsibility for which was referred to in Chapter XII, is also carried out in this part of the Ministry. Until recently, another important duty was to examine and advise upon the annual budgets produced by the Air Corporations in support of their requests for grants to balance their accounts. Such grants are no longer made, but appraisal of the proposals for capital investment by the Corporations, aircraft being the main item, continues as a major responsibility —and a specially difficult one in these days of rapid progress in the design and the performance of aircraft. On each application to start a new regular air service the Ministry also supplies, for the benefit of the Air Transport Advisory Council,[1] a brief study of the traffic on the proposed route, no small task when applications are running at the rate of about 700 a year.

On the inland transport side a number of returns are published— the annual census of vehicles, for example, and the annual booklet containing public road passenger transport statistics. Road accidents statistics are compiled in great detail and variety with the aid of mechanical sorting equipment. This is also the part of the Ministry which must take the credit for repairing the gap in knowledge which previously existed about the employment of road goods transport and which has been referred to in Chapter IX. As a result of the special inquiry in 1952, using modern sampling techniques, it is now known fairly accurately how large the contribution of road vehicles is to our internal transport resources as a whole. In terms of tonnage the goods carried by road amounted in 1952 to over 70 per cent of the total internal and coastwise movement of goods and in terms of ton mileage to nearly 40 per cent—almost as much as the railway contribution and nearly twice that of coasting ships. Much other important knowledge was gained by this statistical inquiry—of the effect, for example, of differences in the nature of the traffic upon the amount of work which a vehicle can do in a given period.

In the case of shipping, under arrangements agreed upon at the North Atlantic Treaty Organisation, detailed records of all British registered ocean-going tonnage and its movements are kept in a form that can be readily used in emergency and estimates are made of the amount and types of shipping that might be required in certain eventualities and of the immediate and prospective availability of tonnage. Statistics of United Kingdom and world merchant fleets, including the employment of United Kingdom coasting ships, are also maintained, together with particulars of arrivals and departures at United Kingdom ports, and an annual return of shipping casualties and deaths is compiled and published.

It is interesting to note that the business of collecting statistics as a basis for policy is dealt with somewhat differently on the shipping

[1] Page 165.

and inland transport sides of the Ministry as distinct from the civil aviation side. Following the practice of the old Ministry of Transport, statistics on shipping and rail and road transport are collected by the Statistics Division. The various operating Divisions then draw upon the results and use them for the formulation of policy. In other words the economic appraisement of the statistics produced is often the job of the operating division concerned. On the civil aviation side much of this is done by the Economics Division. There are advantages in both systems. In the one, those who are actively involved in the formulation of policy do the economist's job along with their own more normal tasks; under the other there is the advantage of specialisation. Both systems continue side by side in the combined Ministry, at any rate for the time being. Unison is not invariably or necessarily superior to harmony.

CHAPTER XVII

Some Reflections on the Future

*

THE preceding pages have illustrated the diversity of the problems facing the Ministry and the tenuousness of the thread that binds the different aspects of its work together. The responsibilities and the activities of the Department have been laid upon it by slow development over many years, and the pattern that emerges is characterised by complexity rather than uniformity, a complexity that arises as much from the intrinsic peculiarities of each form of transport as from the political and economic climate prevailing at the time when the various responsibilities were undertaken. Indeed, a consistent pattern is scarcely to be expected since each part has been and is being continually adapted to meet changing needs and changing circumstances. For the Department must at all times keep under review each individual aspect of its operations on the basis of things as they are and in the light both of present needs and of probable future tendencies.

What that means is simple enough to understand in such technical matters as preparing for the advent of nuclear propulsion of ships or providing navigational aids for the jet age in commercial air transport, but what does it mean in respect of general far-reaching questions of transport policy? It is perhaps worth considering the question for a moment because it involves thinking about what the Department exists to do and what are the limitations on its sphere of activity. Some things clearly it cannot usefully do. When a subject is a matter of political controversy it obviously is idle for the Department to spend much time considering whether a particular policy advocated by one party is better than another policy advocated by its political opponents. Which policy will be adopted will be decided not by a nice weighing of merits but by the political colour of the Government in power. What then can the Department contribute on such issues, for example, as the conception of the 'integration' of a large part of the inland transport system, which is the basis of the Labour Government's Transport Act of 1947 on the one hand, and a greater degree of free competition as adopted by the Conservative Government in the Act of 1953? What the Department can and must do, when changes are determined by political considerations, is to advise on the form which the changes should take, with a view both to securing the best ultimate pattern and to minimising the damage which must almost certainly arise during a transition from one form of organisation to another.

When dealing with issues which are the subject of political controversy, the Department is concerned, therefore, not with propounding broad theories of transport policy, but with the practical application of policies imposed from outside. For this purpose, as for all the Department's work on policy matters, the main requirements are a good working knowledge of the industry, access on a basis of confidence to those who control and operate transport and who have, therefore, the practical knowledge which is indispensable in arriving at solutions which will work, and some familiarity with academic studies in the field of transport theory. While a great deal of work has been done academically on transport subjects in this country, other countries, particularly the United States and Germany, have studied them much more systematically and the Department is therefore much interested in and encouraged by the action of the Institute of Transport in securing the endowment of a Readership and Research Fellowships at Oxford University in the economics and organisation of transport.

Many other matters which are not the subject of political controversy are settled, in essence, by considerations outside the control of the Department. For example, a question which is continually cropping up in one way or another is the extent to which transport should be looked upon as a service available to the public irrespective of the financial results of running particular parts of it, or, on the other hand, as one in which the facilities should be provided only where the charges will cover the cost of providing them. In this country, the accepted general principle is the same for all kinds of transport. Clearly every private enterprise undertaking must pay for itself or go out of business, and the publicly owned British Transport Commission are equally under obligation to pay their way, in the words of the 1947 Act, 'taking one year with another'. The Air Corporations are in the same general position. Within that framework, however, a great many services which cannot pay for themselves are, and will continue to be, provided by transport undertakings, privately owned and publicly owned; but while they will provide many such services in the public interest the extent to which they do so must be decided by the interested parties in the light of the facts of each individual case. For its part the Department must watch what is happening and be prepared with suggestions if action

o

appears to be called for. A particularly difficult example of the changing shape of public transport services in 1958 is the decrease in passenger travel by bus, due mainly to the increased use of private cars and other vehicles, and to some extent to changes in social habits such as the increase in watching television. This problem has already been touched on in Chapter IX.

It is this kind of problem—the problem which arises from the compulsion of events and changes in social habits, or others which arise from advances in scientific knowledge, or from changes in the international climate such as the growth of the spirit of nationalism —that inevitably involves the great bulk of the forward thinking of the Department. The most obvious examples are in the field of scientific and technical advance. At sea the application of nuclear power to the propulsion of merchant ships is a case in point. It is, of course, already a proved success for naval purposes but at a cost which would be prohibitive for commercial use. Nevertheless, although at the time of writing the advent of nuclear-powered merchant ships in significant numbers seems a long distance ahead, their appearance has been anticipated by putting in hand studies connected with the ships themselves, with the precautions which should be taken and the requirements that should be imposed by the ports to which they may go and with the special provisions that may have to be made about their navigation, particularly in crowded or restricted waters. All these matters must be thrashed out, first nationally and then internationally, well before the ships themselves are ready to sail the seas.

In the air, where developments are so rapid as to be almost frightening, the Department is directly concerned, for example, with the problems of air traffic control presented by the big jets and with the airport facilities they require. But it is also concerned with the future provision of suitable and competitive aircraft for our civil airlines. Plans and designs for the jet age are well ahead, but what of the next stage? Is our research into aircraft development of the right quality and quantity, and in the right directions, to keep, and perhaps to increase, the lead we have taken in producing the first turbo-prop and turbo-jet civil aircraft? Should we spare more or less resources on research into the design and economics of supersonic aircraft and on their development? Should we put more effort into solving the problems of vertical take-off and landing—an advance that is potentially of the greatest interest to the Department with its responsibilities for costly airports? These are questions affecting more than one Department of State as well as the research establishments of the Government and of the industry. The Department concerned with the operation of civil aviation cannot alone answer the questions, but it must ask them and take its part in devising the machinery to keep the progress in answering them under continuous review. Similarly, in the matter of aids to navigation in the air and of control of aircraft from the ground the drive for improved technical devices and procedure for the next stage but one in dealing with increasing numbers of aircraft flying at ever-increasing speeds must be a major preoccupation. Outstanding here is the application of electronic information handling, computing and display equipment unheard of a few years ago.

These examples arise because of spectacular and revolutionary advances in the application of scientific knowledge—advances comparable in the range of their effects to the discovery and application of the power of steam a century and a half before. But examples of this kind are by no means the whole story. Much more numerous are problems posed by the changes that arise from the steady but slower improvements that are continually taking place, for example, the evolution of fully automatic flight, the possible effect on the fire risk in ships arising from the use of light metals which melt at a lower temperature than steel, the institution of automatic barriers at railway level crossings and the constant pressure towards the use of bigger and faster buses and lorries.

More difficult to anticipate and also less easy to deal with are the problems that arise from the political and economic policies and actions of other countries. Naturally, these mostly affect shipping and air transport operating internationally. One example is the growth throughout the shipping world of flag discrimination, that is the practice of some Governments of securing by one means or another that preference is given to ships flying their own flag in the carriage of goods to and from their ports, even to the extent of requiring by law, and sometimes in commercial treaties, that fixed percentages of exports must be so carried. Apart from the economic waste arising from the inevitable use of more ships than the trade requires and the delays involved in waiting for a ship of the right flag to present itself, such requirements are bound to have a seriously adverse effect on the shipping interests of all other countries. Effective action against this practice is not easy but the Department must watch for tendencies in this direction and initiate such action, through the diplomatic channel or otherwise, as seems best in each particular case.

Again, a most serious problem is the growth of fleets under flags of convenience which are immune from the control exercised by the Governments of all traditional maritime nations in the fields of safety of ships and protection of crews and which enjoy almost complete freedom from taxation. Financial reserves for building up such fleets and for their other commercial purposes bear no taxes at all. The competition of ships with such advantages is clearly a menace to the shipping of other countries and gives serious anxiety also to the Trade Unions representing officers and seamen. Some help in meeting this competition has been given in many maritime countries by tax concessions to their own shipping industry, but the problem bristles with difficulties and the Department is in close touch with colleagues in other maritime countries and with the shipping industry about it.

In the air, nations of all sizes and economic wealth seek to carry their own flag on their own airline for prestige reasons. Governments also, of course, have the power to refuse traffic rights to foreign companies or to restrict operations to the level at which their national airlines can compete. The result is often to produce too much capacity for the less efficient operator and impair the development of the stronger operator. Technical developments promise to intensify these difficulties. Aircraft have become, since the war, steadily larger, faster and more expensive to buy; and the rate of improvement tends to outstrip reasonable rates of depreciation—the new fashion is on sale before the old one is sufficiently worn out— and airlines, not daring to be less up-to-date than their rivals, have found themselves almost constantly in a state of re-equipment. For an industry which breaks even only with difficulty this has already been a serious problem; but at least hitherto the growth in traffic has more or less kept pace with the growth in capacity offered by successive increases in size and speed, while the big operators have found, in smaller operators and in their own second line or feeder services, a market for their replaced but far from worn-out aircraft. The new turbo-jet aircraft, however, are so much larger and faster than their predecessors that it is far from certain that there will be corresponding growth in traffic to fill them. Moreover, the aircraft they replace are themselves too large, too unsuitable, and too numerous to be smoothly absorbed by the second-hand market. With huge capital investments which only high loads can amortise, operators may face a period of intense competition where the stake is not profit but survival itself. The problems in prospect concern the Department as well as operators. What can be done through international co-operation? Can Governments help in stimulating the growth of traffic? What should be the fares policy? Or—since the eventual transition from the subsonic to the supersonic jet may be as bad or worse—should an attempt be made to get agreement that aircraft life should be better related to sane economics of amortisation and traffic changes?

In inland transport, problems of the future are of a different kind. Though often more prosaic than those of the air and sea, they are the problems that affect our daily lives more immediately, and people from all walks of life have experience and a viewpoint upon them which must be heeded, answered and guided. Many of these problems stem from the fact that in the decade after the war, when the amount of capital available for investment fell far short of what was needed, other claims were given preference. Little or nothing was available for new railways or new roads although during the same period the number of road vehicles increased at a staggering rate. It has been the business of the Department to present the claims of transport when capital investment programmes were being drawn up and then to see that the amount of money allotted for transport purposes is used in the most productive way within the policies that Governments have laid down. With the greater share of the available funds which the Department has now obtained, there is a new burden of responsibility for ensuring that first things are tackled first and that the right balance is struck between long-term and short-term needs. Further, both the road programme and the railway modernisation programme are based on the assumption that inland transport will at least maintain its present place in the national investment programme. The Department can, however, have no assurance that this will be so. The economic policies of the Government often require that public investment is rigidly controlled and restricted and the Department is obliged to keep the section of expenditure for which it is responsible under the closest watch. Finance must continue to dominate policy here.

A few examples of problems involving large capital expenditure may illustrate the point. In our cities great and immediate benefit to traffic could be achieved by constructing—at enormous cost—new through-ways and under-passes such as have recently transformed the face of some American cities. (But even a Ministry of Transport must recognise that traffic is not the only consideration and, even if unlimited funds were available, historic cities cannot be treated as if nothing else mattered.) Great benefits could also be secured, and without serious damage to the beauty and the monuments of our cities, by building multi-storey garages to relieve the curse of parking in the streets. The projected new tube line running from Victoria underneath the centre of London across to the north-east is urgently needed, but it could never pay its way because of the high cost of its construction and so it presents a real financial problem. All these projects must be assessed in economic terms to weigh the future gain to the community against the initial outlay and it is the duty of the Department to put forward as accurate and forceful a case as possible.

Questions of no less importance arise in connexion with the provision of transport services. The British Transport Commission have made a most promising start with their great and imaginative modernisation plan for the railways, and with decentralisation and reorganisation of management. At the same time they are taking advantage gradually of the new freedom in charging policy given them by the 1953 Transport Act, and are putting the railways in a position to play their full part in meeting the transport needs of the country. But no one supposes that a vastly improved service by rail for passengers and goods, together with better facilities for lorries and buses in the shape of better roads, will solve all the problems of inland transport, even if we were to leave out of account inland waterways and coasting shipping—with its own unique contribution in peace as in war—which obviously cannot be done. The trend of traffic continues roadwards and away from the older forms of transport. Meantime the capital obligations of the Commission grow as the modernisation plan takes effect, and the burden of deficits, until such time as modernisation redresses the balance, is a cause of great anxiety and presents the Commissioner with a serious problem of maintaining morale.

Further, there are political problems—quite apart from those which are the subject of party politics—which are inseparable from the existence of nationalised industries. These mainly turn on the question of accountability, which has been dealt with in Chapter I. The Minister's statutory powers and responsibilities mean that he must satisfy himself, and be in a position to satisfy his colleagues and Parliament, that the policies of the industries for which he is answerable are sound and that they are developing on the right lines. But that is not the whole story. It is enough to say here that it seems unlikely that the present methods of maintaining the balance between the vital importance of preserving the independence of the Boards of the industries in the commercial management of their affairs on the one hand and, on the other, the desire to assert the right of the public and their representatives in Parliament to exercise supervision over the way their trustees exercise their stewardship will always remain as they are today. There are in fact two problems here, first the degree of control exercised by the Minister whether through his statutory powers or less formally and, second, the exercise of the right of Parliament by debates on the Reports, or by such other means as setting up Select Committees, to elicit information direct. The Ministry must again be constantly on the watch and be ready with suggestions as the climate of opinion changes. As a generalisation it is perhaps legitimate to say, in the light of ten years' experience of the working of the difficult relationship between the Minister, Parliament and the industries, that too much interference is a greater danger than too little.

With all these problems constantly pressing in upon the Ministry the tasks may at times seem almost overwhelming. But it is exhilarating to work in an atmosphere where the practical job to be done is so vast and where success is very rewarding. The influence of transport on the daily lives of people and its importance to their well-being, and even their existence, is not always appreciated. In war it has been twice brought home through shortages in essential supplies due to interruption of our shipping services, and through the imminent danger of complete starvation when the enemy in each of the two World Wars almost succeeded in cutting our lifeline across the Atlantic. But in peace adequate transport facilities are generally available and, apart from particular grumbles about particular services, are taken for granted. Nevertheless, the material quality of a civilisation can be measured by the quality of its transport. Backward communities can exist with little or nothing, but vast and complex societies must have vast and complicated transport facilities. It is a stimulus to all who work in the Department to know that they have some part, however small, in the great transport developments which more and more rapidly are shaping the future of our civilisation.

Appendices

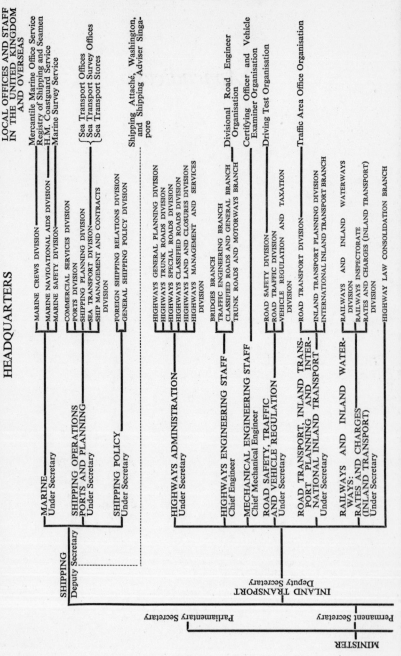

APPENDIX A

MINISTRY OF TRANSPORT AND CIVIL AVIATION ORGANISATION CHART

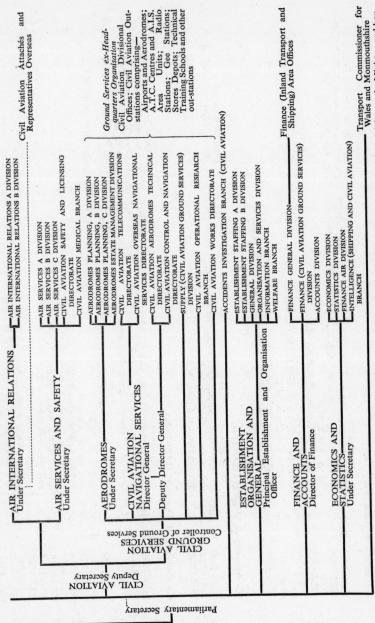

NOTE: Legal advice is provided by the Treasury Solicitor and/or the Lord Advocate. There is also a Chief Aeronautical Adviser to the Minister, and hon. advisers on scientific matters, finance, business, shipping in port, and marine insurance.

APPENDIX B.—MINISTERS AND PERMANENT HEADS OF THE VARIOUS DEPARTMENTS CONCERNED SINCE 1919–1921 WITH THE FUNCTIONS NOW BORNE IN THE MINISTRY OF TRANSPORT AND CIVIL AVIATION

A.—Board of Trade (1921–1939)

Shipping

Presidents

1921–1922	Rt. Hon.	Stanley Baldwin, M.P.
1922–1924	,,	Sir Philip Lloyd-Greame,* K.B.E., M.C., M.P.
1924	,,	Sidney Webb, M.P.
1924–1929	,,	Sir P. Lloyd-Greame,* K.B.E., M.C., M.P.
1929–1931	,,	W. Graham, M.P.
1931	,,	Sir P. Cunliffe-Lister, G.B.E., M.C., M.P.
1931–1937	,,	Walter Runciman, M.P.
1937–1940	,,	Oliver Stanley, M.C., M.P.

* later Sir P. Cunliffe-Lister, now the Earl of Swinton.

Heads of the Mercantile Marine Department

1921–1929	Sir Charles Hipwood, K.B.E., C.B.
1929–1939	Sir E. Julian Foley, C.B.

B.—Ministry of Shipping (1939–1941)

Shipping

Ministers

1939–1940	Rt. Hon.	Sir John Gilmour, Bt, G.C.V.O., D.S.O., M.P.
1940 (April)	,,	Robert Spear Hudson, M.P.
1940 (May)	,,	Ronald Hibbert Cross, M.P.

Director-General

1939–1941	Sir Cyril W. Hurcomb, K.C.B, K.B.E.

C.—Ministry of Transport (1919–1941)

Inland Transport

Ministers

1919–1921	Rt. Hon.	Sir Eric Geddes, G.C.B., G.B.E., M.P.
1921–1922	,,	Viscount Peel, G.C.S.I., G.B.E.
1922	,,	The Earl of Crawford and Balcarres, Kt., F.R.S.
1922–1924	,,	Viscount Stonehaven, G.C.M.G, D.S.O.
1924		Harry Gosling, C.H., M.P.
1924–1929	Rt. Hon.	Lord Mount Temple
1929–1931	,,	Herbert S. Morrison, M.P.
1931–1933	,,	P. J. Pybus, C.B.E. M.P.
1933–1934	,,	Oliver Stanley, M.C., M.P.
1934–1937	,,	Leslie Hore-Belisha, M.P.
1937–1939	,,	E. Leslie Burgin, M.P.
1939–1940	,,	D. Euan Wallace, M.C., M.P.
1940	,,	Lord Reith, G.C.V.O., G.B.E., C.B., T.D.
1940–1941	,,	Lord Brabazon, M.C.

Permanent Secretaries

1919–1921	Sir R. Francis Dunnell, K.C.B.
1921–1923	Sir William F. Marwood, K.C.B.
1923–1927	Sir John R. Brooke, C.B.
1927–1937	Sir Cyril W. Hurcomb, K.C.B, K.B.E.
1937–1941	Sir Leonard Browett, K.C.B.

D.—Ministry of War Transport (1941–1946) and Ministry of Transport (1946–1953)

Shipping and Inland Transport

Ministers

1941–1945 Rt. Hon. Lord Leathers, C.H.*
1945–1951 Alfred Barnes, M.P.
1951–1952 Hon. John S. Maclay, C.M.G., M.P.
           (also Minister of Civil Aviation)
1952–1953 Rt. Hon. Alan T. Lennox-Boyd, M.P.
           (also Minister of Civil Aviation)
* Secretary of State for the Co-ordination of Transport, Fuel and Power, 1951–1953.

Permanent Secretaries

1941–1947 Sir Cyril W. Hurcomb, G.C.B., K.B.E.
           (with title of Director-General from 1941 to 1946)
1947–1953 Sir Gilmour Jenkins, K.C.B., K.B.E., M.C.

E.—Air Ministry (1919–1944)

Civil Aviation

Secretaries of State

1919–1921 Rt. Hon. Winston S. Churchill, M.P.
1921–1922 Captain the Rt. Hon. F. E. Guest, G.B.E, D.S.O.
1922–1924 Rt. Hon. Sir Samuel J. G. Hoare, C.M.G., M.P.
1924   „ Lord Thomson, C.B.E., D.S.O.
1924–1929 „ Sir Samuel J. G. Hoare, Bt., G.B.E. C.M.G., M.P.
1929–1930 „ Lord Thomson, C.B.E., D.S.O.
1930–1931 „ Lord Amulree, G.B.E., K.C.
1931–1935 Most Hon. the Marquess of Londonderry, K.G., P.C., M.V.O.
1935–1938 Rt. Hon. Viscount Swinton, G.B.E., M.C.
1938–1940 „ H. Kingsley Wood, M.P.
1940   „ Sir Samuel J. G. Hoare, Bt., G.C.S.I., G.B.E, C.M.G., M.P.
1940–1945 „ Sir Archibald Sinclair, Bt., C.M.G., M.P.

Heads of Department of Civil Aviation

1919–1922 Major-General Sir Frederick H. Sykes, G.B.E., K.C.B., C.M.G.
1922–1930 Air Vice-Marshal Sir Sefton Brancker, K.C.B., A.F.C.
1931–1941 Sir Francis Shelmerdine, C.I.E., O.B.E.
1941–1945 Sir William Hildred, C.B., O.B.E.

F.—Ministry of Civil Aviation (1945–1953)

Civil Aviation

Ministers

1944–1945 Rt. Hon. Viscount Swinton, G.B.E., C.H., M.C.
1945–1946 „ Lord Winster, J.P.
1946–1948 „ Lord Nathan, T.D., D.L., J.P.
1948–1951 „ Lord Pakenham
1951   „ Lord Ogmore
1951–1952 Hon. John S. Maclay, C.M.G., M.P. (also Minister of Transport)
1952–1953 Rt. Hon. Alan T. Lennox-Boyd, M.P. (also Minister of Transport)

Director-General

1945–1946 Sir William Hildred, C.B., O.B.E.

Permanent Secretaries

1946–1947 Sir Henry Self, K.C.B., K.C.M.G., K.B.E.
1947–1953 Sir Arnold Overton, K.C.B., K.C.M.G., M.C.

G.—Ministry of Transport and Civil Aviation (1953–)

Shipping, Inland Transport & Civil Aviation

Ministers

1953–1954 Rt. Hon. Alan T. Lennox-Boyd, M.P.
1954–1956 „ J. A. Boyd-Carpenter, M.P.
1956–   „ Harold Watkinson, M.P.

Permanent Secretary

1953–   Sir Gilmour Jenkins, K.C.B., K.B.E., M.C.

APPENDIX C

BIBLIOGRAPHY

A GREAT many books and pamphlets are now written every year on transport subjects and the Library of the Ministry of Transport and Civil Aviation already contains some 30,000 publications. A selection of these, which bear upon the duties of the Department or its predecessors, is set out below; many of them have already been referred to in footnotes.

GENERAL

An Economic History of Modern Britain (Vol. 1, Chapters III and IX; Vol. 2, Chapter V; Vol. 3, Chapter VI). Sir John Clapham, Cambridge University Press (Vol. 1, 1926; Vol. 2, 1932; Vol. 3, 1938).

The Board of Trade (Chapters V and VI). Sir Hubert Llewellyn Smith, Putnam's, 1928.

British War Economy [History of the Second World War (Civil Series)]. Sir Keith Hancock and Mrs. M. M. Gowing, H.M.S.O., 1949.

Problems of Nationalized Industry. Ed. W. A. Robson, Allen and Unwin, 1952.

Nationalisation in Britain. R. Kelf-Cohen, Macmillan, 1958.

SHIPPING

Papers relating to the Commercial Marine of Great Britain, Foreign Office, 1844.

The Anatomy of the Navigation Laws. J. L. Ricardo, Charles Gilpin, 1847.

Reports of Courts of Formal Investigation into Marine Casualties, 1854 onwards.

History of Merchant Shipping (Vols. III and IV). W. S. Lindsay, Sampson Low, Marston, Low and Searle, 1876.

Report of the Royal Commission on Shipping Rings, H.M.S.O., 1909.

Allied Shipping Control. J. A. Salter, Oxford University Press, 1921.

The War and the Shipping Industry. C. E. Fayle, Oxford University Press, 1927.

Shipping Inquiries and Courts. A. R. C. McMillan, Stevens and Sons, 1929.

British Shipping. R. H. Thornton, Cambridge University Press, 1945.

Shipping Practice. E. F. Stevens, Pitman, 1947.

The Shipping Federation. L. H. Powell, 1950.

Report of the (Faulkner) Committee on the Prevention of Pollution of the Sea by Oil, H.M.S.O., 1953.

Temperley's Merchant Shipping Acts, 5th edition, Sir William McNair and J. P. Honour, Stevens and Sons, 1954.

Merchant Shipping and the Demands of War [History of the Second World War (Civil Series)]. Miss C. B. A. Behrens, H.M.S.O., 1955.

Seafarers and their Ships. Ministry of Transport and Civil Aviation and the Central Office of Information, H.M.S.O., 1955.

INLAND TRANSPORT

Reports of Inspecting Officers of Railways, 1840 onwards.

The Story of the King's Highway. Sidney and Beatrice Webb, Longmans, Green and Co., 1913.

English Railways: Their Development and their Relation to the State. E. Cleveland-Stevens, A. Routledge and Sons, 1915.

Annual Reports on the Administration of the Road Fund 1920/21– 1955/56, H.M.S.O.

Reports of the Royal Commission on Transport, 1928–31, H.M.S.O.

Socialisation and Transport. Herbert Morrison, Constable and Co., Ltd., 1933.

Public Control of Road Passenger Transport. D. N. Chester, Manchester University Press, 1936.

The Story of British Railways. Barrington Tatford, Sampson, Low, Marston and Co., 1945.

The Obligation to Carry. A. M. Milne and A. Laing, Institute of Transport, 1946.

Road and Rail. Gilbert Walker, Allen and Unwin, 2nd edition, 1947.

Reports of the Committee on Road Safety, H.M.S.O., 1947 onwards.

Reports and Accounts of the British Transport Commission, H.M.S.O., 1948 onwards.

The Transport Act, 1947. D. Karmel and R. Beddington, Butterworth and Co., 1948.

The Story of British Roads. R. Syme, British Road Federation, 1950.

British Canals. C. Hadfield, Phoenix House, 1950.

The Transport Act, 1953. D. Karmel and K. Potter, Butterworth and Co., 1953.

Report of the (Thesiger) Committee on the Licensing of Road Passenger Services, H.M.S.O., 1953.

Road Haulage Licensing. T. D. Corpe, Sweet and Maxwell, 1953.

Economics of Inland Transport. A. M. Milne, Pitman, 1955.

Report of the (Chambers) Committee of Inquiry into London Transport, H.M.S.O., 1955.

Red for Danger. L. T. C. Rolt, The Bodley Head, 1955.

The British Transport Commission: Proposals for the Railways, Cmd. 9880, H.M.S.O., 1956.

Law of Carriage by Inland Transport, 3rd edition. Kahn-Freund, Stevens and Sons, 1956.

Roads in England and Wales, H.M.S.O., 1956/57 onwards.

Inland Transport [History of the Second World War (Civil Series)]. C. I. Savage, H.M.S.O., 1957.

Report of the (Bowes) Committee of Inquiry into Inland Waterways, H.M.S.O., 1958.

CIVIL AVIATION

Civil Aircraft Accident Reports, H.M.S.O., 1922 onwards.

Report of the (Maybury) Committee on Development of Civil Aviation in the United Kingdom, Cmd. 5351, H.M.S.O., 1937.

Report of the (Cadman) Committee of Inquiry into Civil Aviation, Cmd. 5685, H.M.S.O., 1938.

British Air Transport (the Swinton Report), Cmd. 6605, H.M.S.O., 1945.

British Air Services (the Winster Report), Cmd. 6712, H.M.S.O., 1945.

London Airport: Report of the Layout Panel: Civil Aviation Publication No. 4, H.M.S.O., 1946.

Reports and Accounts of the British Overseas Airways Corporation, H.M.S.O., 1946/47 onwards.

Reports and Accounts of the British European Airways Corporation, H.M.S.O., 1946/47 onwards.

Annual Reports of the Air Transport Advisory Council, H.M.S.O., 1947/48 onwards.

Some International Aspects of Air Transport. Sir George Cribbett, Sixth British Commonwealth and Empire Lecture reprinted in the Journal of the Royal Aeronautical Society, 1950.

Shawcross and Beaumont on Air Law. C. N. Shawcross and K. M. Beaumont, Butterworth and Co., 1951.

Annual Reports of the British Independent Air Transport Association, 1951/52 onwards.

London's Airports, Cmd. 8902, H.M.S.O., 1953.

Civil Aerodromes and Ground Services: Select Committee on Estimates, H.M.S.O., 1955.

London Airport—The Official Story of the New World Air Centre. Ministry of Transport and Civil Aviation, H.M.S.O., 1956.

The Economics of European Air Transport. Stephen Wheatcroft, Manchester University Press, 1956.

Report of London Airport Development (Millbourn) Committee, Civil Aviation Publication No. 145, H.M.S.O., 1957.

Index

"A" Licences, 107–108, 112, 114, 119
Accident Inquiries:
    aircraft, 19, 193–195
    boiler explosions, 72–73
    marine casualties, 72–73
    railway, 142–144
Accountability of the nationalised industries, 21–23, 214
Admiralty:
    and merchant shipping in the nineteenth century, 27
    and sea transport of the Forces, 32, 53
    and shipbuilding, 46
    represented in Shipping Diversion Room, 87
    responsible for H.M. Coastguard, 73
    Signal and Radar Establishment, 71
Advisers to the Minister, honorary, 219
Aerial Navigation Acts, 36–37
Aerodromes:
    between the wars, 39–40
    Calvert approach lighting system, 184
    Commandants, 171, 201
    Constabulary, 171
    Consultative Committees, 172
    Control Tower, 172, 185
    development, 172–173
    finance, 173–176, 204
    fire service, 171, 185
    licensed, 176
    overseas, 176–177
Aeronautical Information Service, 171, 180
Air Corporations:
    relationship between the Minister and, 21–23, 158, 161–164, 206, 214
Air Corporations Act, 1949, 162, 163
Air France, 157
Air International Relations, 158–161
Air Ministry, 37, 167, 169, 173, 177, 186
    Secretaries of State for Air, 221
Air Navigation Regulations, 189, 192, 196
Air Registration Board, 19, 38, 190–191, 192, 196
Air Safety Board, 195

Air Traffic Control, 39, 170, 171, 179, 180–182, 183, 184, 187, 211
Air Training Corps, 167
Air Transport Advisory Council, 165, 206
Air Transport Licensing Board, 38
Aircraft, licensing of, 190–191
Aircrew, licensing of, 192
Aluminium, use of in shipbuilding, 78
Amalgamation of Ministries, 16, 32, 40, 201–202
American Bureau of Shipping, 69
Association of British Aero Clubs and Centres, 167
Automatic train control, 144

"B" Licences, 107–108, 112, 114, 119
Belisha crossings, 146
Bermuda Agreement, 160
Berne Convention on railways, 20
Bevin, Mr. Ernest, 111
Bills, preparation of, 24–25
Blackbushe Airport, 170
Board of Trade:
    and docks and canals, 35
    and merchant shipping, 16, 27–32,
    and railways, 16, 33, 35
    Presidents of, 220
    responsible for H.M. Coastguard, 73
Boiler explosion inquiries, 72–73
Bowes Committee on Inland Waterways, 94
Bridewater, Duke of, 92
Brindley, James, 92
British Airways, 37, 157
British European Airways:
    creation of, 38
    powers and duties, 157, 161–164
    relationship between the Minister and, 21–23, 158, 161–164, 206, 214
British Gliding Association, 167
British Overseas Airways Corporation:
    and African airways, 166
    and Qantas, 166
    first set up, 37–38, 157
    powers and duties, 157, 161–164
    relationship between the Minister and, 21–23, 158, 161–164, 206, 214
    subsidiaries, 166
British Railways (*see* Railways)

GEORGE ALLEN & UNWIN LTD
London: 40 Museum Street, W.C.1

Auckland: 24 Wyndham Street
Bombay: 15 Graham Road, Ballard Estate, Bombay 1
Calcutta: 17 Chittaranjan Avenue, Calcutta 13
Cape Town: 109 Long Street
Karachi: Metherson's Estate, Wood Street, Karachi 2
New Delhi: 13–14 Ajmeri Gate Extension, New Delhi 1
São Paulo: Avenida 9 de Julho 1138–Ap. 51
Singapore, South East Asia and Far East, 36c, Prinsep Street
Sydney, N.S.W.: Bradbury House, 55 York Street
Toronto: 91 Wellington Street West